THE SHAKESPEAREAN FOREST

The Shakespearean Forest, Anne Barton's final book, uncovers the pervasive presence of woodland in early modern drama, revealing its persistent imaginative power. The collection is representative of the startling breadth of Barton's scholarship: ranging across plays by Shakespeare (including *Titus Andronicus, As You Like It, Macbeth* and *Timon of Athens*) and his contemporaries (including Jonson, Dekker, Lyly, Massinger and Greene), it also considers court pageants, treatises on forestry and chronicle history. Barton's incisive literary analysis characteristically pays careful attention to the practicalities of performance, and is supplemented by numerous illustrations and a bibliographical essay examining recent scholarship in the field.

Prepared for publication by Hester Lees-Jeffries, featuring a Foreword by Adrian Poole and an Afterword by Peter Holland, the book explores the forest as a source of cultural and psychological fascination, embracing and illuminating its mysteriousness.

ANNE BARTON was the author of *Essays, Mainly Shakespearean, Byron: Don Juan, The Names of Comedy, Ben Jonson, Dramatist* and (as Anne Righter) *Shakespeare and the Idea of the Play*, as well as many essays and introductions. In 2000, she retired as Professor of English at the University of Cambridge, where she was a Fellow of Trinity College; she had previously been a Fellow of New College, Oxford, and Girton College, Cambridge, and was a Fellow of the British Academy. From the 1960s onwards, her work had a profound influence on the Royal Shakespeare Company and the performance and academic study of early modern drama more generally. Anne Barton died in 2013.

HESTER LEES-JEFFRIES is University Lecturer in English at the University of Cambridge, and a Fellow of St Catharine's College.

PETER HOLLAND is McMeel Family Professor in Shakespeare Studies at the University of Notre Dame.

ADRIAN POOLE is Emeritus Professor of English Literature at the University of Cambridge, and a Fellow of Trinity College.

THE SHAKESPEAREAN FOREST

ANNE BARTON

Emeritus Professor of English, University of Cambridge
Fellow of Trinity College

CAMBRIDGE
UNIVERSITY PRESS

CAMBRIDGE
UNIVERSITY PRESS

University Printing House, Cambridge CB2 8BS, United Kingdom

One Liberty Plaza, 20th Floor, New York, NY 10006, USA

477 Williamstown Road, Port Melbourne, VIC 3207, Australia

314-321, 3rd Floor, Plot 3, Splendor Forum, Jasola District Centre, New Delhi - 110025, India

79 Anson Road, #06-04/06, Singapore 079906

Cambridge University Press is part of the University of Cambridge.

It furthers the University's mission by disseminating knowledge in the pursuit of education, learning and research at the highest international levels of excellence.

www.cambridge.org
Information on this title: www.cambridge.org/9780521573443
DOI: 10.1017/9781139015257

First published 2017

A catalogue record for this publication is available from the British Library

ISBN 978-0-521-57344-3 Hardback

To James Carley

Contents

Figures

Foreword

by Adrian Poole

The Shakespearean Forest had its genesis in lectures, first the Northcliffe lectures at University College London in 1994, then the Trinity College Clark lectures at Cambridge University in 2003. Anne Barton gave many distinguished lectures throughout her long career and received many honours. She did not share Falstaff's scorn for honour (or honours); indeed she relished it (and them), including the Fellowship that Trinity conferred on her in 1986 after her return to Cambridge. Having retired from her University Chair in 2000, she was particularly pleased by the invitation to develop material that had gone into the earlier set of lectures, on a subject so close to her heart. It is not unprecedented for a Fellow of Trinity to take up the Clark lectureship, but it is rare. In 1953 G. M. Trevelyan, recently retired from being Master, delivered his reflections on 'A Layman's Love of Letters'.

We owe the Clark lectures to the generosity of William George Clark (1821–78), Fellow of Trinity College from 1844 until his death, serving as public orator of the University and as Vice-Master of the College. His most enduring achievement was the Cambridge Shakespeare (1863–6), co-edited with John Glover, then with W. Aldis Wright, first published in three volumes (1863–6). The subsequent one-volume Globe edition (1864) was for many years the standard edition of Shakespeare across the world.

Clark's bequest was designed for lectures 'on some aspect or period of English Literature'. They were inaugurated in 1884 when Sir Leslie Stephen spoke on 'Addison and Pope'. For the first dozen years, lecturers were appointed for three-year periods and required to deliver twelve lectures a year. In 1897, they became in principle an annual affair, though there has been the occasional gap, notably the six years from 1915 to 1921. Stephen was followed by other late-Victorian luminaries, including Edward Dowden and Edmund Gosse, whose 1885 publication *From Shakespeare to Pope* (based on lectures delivered the previous autumn) attracted notoriously hostile attention from John Churton Collins for its slipshod scholarship. (Henry James said that Gosse had 'a genius for inaccuracy', and James was a *friend*.) The interwar years boasted some speakers whose names still reverberate powerfully, such as T. S. Eliot ('The Metaphysical Poetry of the Seventeenth Century', 1926)[1] and E. M. Forster ('Aspects of the Novel', 1927), and other significant figures, including Walter de la Mare and Harley Granville-Barker. Since 1945, there has been a stream of eminent scholars and critics, including G. Wilson Knight, F. R. Leavis, I. A. Richards, Geoffrey H. Hartman, Jerome McGann, Christopher Ricks, V. A. Kolve, Helen Vendler, Frank Kermode and Mary Carruthers; and of writers, some no less distinguished for their creative than for their critical work (and vice-versa), including C. Day Lewis, Robert Graves, Louis MacNeice, L. P. Hartley, Stephen Spender, William Empson, Donald Davie, Tom Stoppard, Toni Morrison, John Hollander, Adrienne Rich, Seamus Heaney and Paul Muldoon. Many of the lectures have resulted in or contributed to subsequent publications such as Muriel Bradbrook's *Shakespeare the Craftsman* (1969), David Piper's *The Image of the Poet* (1982) and Geoffrey Hill's *The Enemy's Country* (1991).

In recent years, topics have ranged liberally beyond the confines of English literature as Clark, Stephen and Gosse and their late-Victorian audiences would have understood them to encompass 'Irony and Solidarity' (Richard Rorty, 1987), 'Grace, Necessity and Imagination': Catholic Philosophy and the Twentieth-Century Artist' (Rowan Williams, 2005), 'Imaging Colour' (Elaine Scarry, 2007) and 'Becoming Freud: the Psychoanalyst and the Biographer' (Adam Phillips, 2014). The lectureship has provided hospitality for scholars and critics with bases in disciplines other than literature and languages other than English, reflecting the permeability of boundaries and the readiness to cross them that characterizes the condition of work in the humanities in the late twentieth- and early twenty-first centuries.

Nevertheless, in the course of well over a century of Clark lectures, there has been a continuing emphasis on recognizably traditional 'aspects' of English literature, amongst which Shakespeare has recurred with unsurprising frequency. Anne Barton's lectures on 'The Shakespearean Forest' take their place in a lineage that includes her mentor Muriel Bradbrook (1968), and contemporaries and colleagues including

---

[1] In his edition of Eliot's *The Varieties of Metaphysical Poetry*, the Clark lectures at Trinity College, Cambridge, 1926, and the Turnbull lectures at the Johns Hopkins University, 1933 (London: Faber and Faber, 1993), Ronald Schuchard has a helpful Appendix (II), listing the Clark lecturers and their subjects from 1884 to 1993, pp. 319–22.

Barbara Everett ('Getting Things Wrong: Tragi-comic Shakespeare', 1989), Stephen Orgel ('Imagining Shakespeare', 1996) and Quentin Skinner ('Shakespearean Invention', 2012). Further back in time, though not necessarily thereby exempt from Anne's capacity for incisive judgment, we find lecturers turning readily to Shakespeare in the decades before World War I, and again in the quarter-century from 1925 onwards, including John Middleton Murry ('Keats and Shakespeare', 1925), W. W. Greg ('The Editorial Problem in Shakespeare', 1939), John Dover Wilson ('The Fortunes of Falstaff', 1943) and F. P. Wilson ('Marlowe and the Early Shakespeare', 1951). Other well-known Shakespeareans who chose not to speak specifically or exclusively on Shakespeare include E. M. W. Tillyard (1960), G. Wilson Knight (1960) and L. C. Knights (1971).

Anne Barton was not the first woman to give the Clark lectures. In 1932, Virginia Woolf was invited to do so, but declined, so the honour went to Helen Darbishire in 1949 when she spoke on 'The Poet Wordsworth'. Nor was Anne the first woman Fellow of Trinity (as she had been the first woman Fellow of New College Oxford). Nevertheless, as a senior figure from outside Cambridge, her admission to Trinity's Fellowship in 1986 was of historic importance. Her intellectual and personal authority helped pave the way for a significant increase in the number of women Fellows in the 1990s and beyond.

Trinity had to work quite hard to get her. In 1984, she took up the Grace 2 Chair in the Faculty of English, but it was two years later before she became a Fellow of the College. This hiatus was required by a University rule then governing the number of professors from outside its Fellowship that a College could appoint. There was a way round this quota if the College was prepared to wait for two years and lodge the immigrant in a virtual antechamber, or as Anne herself called it, in purdah. Trinity found a convenient holding station on the Hills Road for Anne and another exotic professor from outside Cambridge in the same boat, an electrical engineer named Alec Broers. Rumour had it that Anne entertained the future Vice-Chancellor by reciting Shakespearean sonnets over the breakfast counter. Rumour is probably false, but it is something of which Anne was perfectly capable.

Between 1986 and 2003, Anne was a big presence in College life. She was always a charismatic teacher and she remained so until near the end, not suffering the foolish or indolent gladly, if at all, but inspiring the eager and impressionable. Like many others, I had myself been one such youth, back in the late 1960s, sitting at her feet on the Sidgwick Site, and listening to her rapid, impassioned, beautifully cadenced lectures. After retirement from her University Chair, and more particularly after the Clark lectures three years later, Anne did not much move out of her elegant rooms in Trinity's Nevile's Court, but she continued to teach, to entertain friends and colleagues from near at hand and all over the globe, to write for the *New York Review of Books* and to work on *The Shakespearean Forest*.

It is wonderful that through the commitment of Hester Lees-Jeffries and the encouragement of Sarah Stanton, it has now been seen through to completion.

Editor's Note

by Hester Lees-Jeffries

Anne Barton had completed the bulk of her work on *The Shakespearean Forest* by 2005. Poor health, and in particular her failing sight, prevented her from finishing it. The files were passed to me in early 2014; it took some time to establish the relationship of the electronic versions and the many printouts, some annotated. It became clear that Chapters 2–6 were essentially revised and complete, albeit with some missing references, loose ends and the occasional overlap. What appears here as Chapter 1 is a composite, with some reordering, of the original introduction and a discarded additional chapter, some of which had already been incorporated elsewhere in the book. I have made very few additions, and done very little re-writing, in the main text, although I have reordered a little in places; accordingly, some traces remain of the book's origins in lectures. I have added more material in footnotes, on occasion amplifying a point there rather than in the main text, as well as glossing, or translating. All such additions and other changes have been made silently.

Although I have updated some references to works being discussed at length with a view to consistency and accessibility (all quotations from Shakespeare's plays are from the Riverside, from Jonson's works from the *Cambridge Works of Ben Jonson*, and from Lyly's plays from the Revels editions, where possible) I have not attempted to update references more generally. I have checked them where they seemed unlikely or incomplete and if necessary, found other editions. Rather than adding further critical material to footnotes, I have added a substantial bibliographical essay, which surveys at least some of the considerable literature on the forest and related subjects in early modern literature which has appeared since *c.* 2003.

Anne Barton retired from the Faculty of English in Cambridge in 2000, at the beginning of the second year of my PhD. Mine was the last cohort to attend the Faculty's Renaissance Graduate Seminar in her beautiful rooms at Trinity, where a strict hierarchy of seating operated (speaker in an armchair by the fire; senior members of the faculty on the sofa and various other chairs; graduate students on the floor, mostly behind the sofa, and sometimes in the cats' bed). They could be intimidating, but there was always a sense of occasion. Even before I had arrived, Anne had been kind: in those almost pre-email days, she was the only member of the Faculty to write back when I approached her as a possible supervisor. It may have helped that I had been taught as an undergraduate in New Zealand by one of her former doctoral students, and that my MA thesis supervisor there had, like Anne, been supervised as a doctoral student by Muriel Bradbrook. My 'registration viva', in the summer of 2000, must have been one of her last official Faculty undertakings, but she remained in touch and continued to take an interest in my work, and to lend me books. She employed me as a research assistant when she was preparing the Clark lectures, on which this book is largely based; she wrote references for me through two rounds of research fellowship competitions (no small undertaking, in the days before online application systems). When I was appointed to my first teaching post in 2006, she invited me for dinner and cooked, although she could barely see, and (typically) invited as the other guest the current chair of the English Faculty. She was my first patron in Cambridge, in the best sense. To my shame, we lost touch in her last years, through illness and the usual early career pressures. I did not know her well. The work I have done in preparing this book for the press is not a labour of love, but rather of profound gratitude – not simply for what Anne did for me, but for the work she has left us, and for her example as a scholar, critic, writer and teacher.

I am grateful to Adrian Poole for his foreword here, and for trusting me with this work (and passing on the files), to Peter Holland, for his afterword and for his encouragement and advice at many stages (including copies of the comments he had made on the manuscript in 2004), to Emily Hockley at Cambridge University Press and especially to Sarah Stanton, who has been both wise and patient in seeing *The Shakespearean Forest*, finally, through the press.

Acknowledgements

Thanks to University College, London, and Trinity College, Cambridge and to Justine Williams, Peter Cochran, Caroline Gonda, Teresa Grant, Alison Hennegan, Peter Holland, Hester Lees-Jeffries, Adrian Poole, Barbara Ravelhofer and Sarah Stanton, and to the Cambridge University Library. (AB)

These acknowledgements are based on a short, undated note among Anne Barton's papers; no doubt other names would have been added. Trinity College provided generous assistance with the costs of the illustrations and other research expenses. Robert Macfarlane gave generous and invaluable advice about further reading. Ezra Horbury prepared the index. (HL-J)

A version of Chapter 3, 'The Wild Man in the Forest', appeared in *Comparative Criticism* 18 (1996), pp. 21–54.

All quotations from Shakespeare's works are from the *Riverside Shakespeare*.

Extracts from *Black Venus* by Angela Carter, published by Vintage, are reprinted by permission of The Random House Group Limited.

Extract from 'The Most of It' by Robert Frost from *The Poetry of Robert Frost*, edited by Edward Connery Lathem and published by Jonathan Cape. Used by permission of the Estate of Robert Frost and The Random House Group Limited.

CHAPTER I

Into the Woods

In March 2002, English newspapers reported that London had been granted official 'forest' status.[1] This pronouncement did not mean what it would have meant for Shakespeare, and for people living centuries before (and after) his time: that all beasts of chase in the area, especially deer (except those kept in private parks for which a royal licence had been granted), were now the property of the Crown and under the protection of special Forest Law. It merely signalled the appointment by the Forestry Commission of an official charged with looking after existing woodland in greater London – in Hyde Park, for instance, or Epping Forest – and also with planting new woods in what the officer himself – a Mr Melville – was quoted as calling the capital's wastelands and 'urban deserts'. Those 'urban deserts' for a moment surprised. Could the newly appointed Melville be remembering *As You Like It*, whose exiled Duke talks about the deer in the forest of Arden as 'native burghers of this desert city' (2.1.23)? He wasn't, of course. He was using the word 'deserts' in its current sense: places barren of vegetation, like the arid sands of Arabia. Shakespeare's Duke Senior, speaking in an Arden full of greenwood trees, had not meant that at all – nor did any of the characters either in this or innumerable other woodland plays of the period who regularly invoke 'desert' to describe their surroundings. Arden is a 'desert' simply because, as Orlando later puts it, it is 'unpeopled' (or so he initially thinks) and remote, two things the 'urban deserts' the Forestry Commission had its eye on most certainly are not.

'Forestry', the Commission's official went on to say, 'is now about people and not necessarily about trees'. But it had not necessarily been 'about trees' in this country for hundreds of years after the Norman Conquest. A 'forest' was primarily somewhere, rich in game, that had been subjected to the particular restrictions of Forest Law. It could designate such signally treeless regions as Exmoor, although in literature this is

[1] *Independent*, 31 March 2002.

almost never the case. As for woodland being important for 'recreation and
the environment, education and health', as Mr Melville put it – that
package would have been incomprehensible in Shakespeare's time. It also
happens to be a bit problematic in our own. In April 1995, almost seven
years before London acquired its 'forest' status, one newspaper promised
readers across the country that 'the secure forest' would soon become part
of their everyday lives.[2] This bulletin was prompted by the announcement
that thirteen new forests were to be created on fringe land just outside
a number of major cities, and what it grappled with was the fact that
although city-dwellers often liked walking in woodland, they were also –
particularly the women – frightened of it. Those interviewed on a planned
outing in the remnants of Robin Hood's Sherwood near Nottingham
tended uneasily to remember a recent murder on Wimbledon Common,
certain nasty events in the very woodland where they were speaking, and to
talk about darkness, hiding places for attackers, and an indefinable sense of
being trapped among the trees. Hence 'the secure forest' – well-lit, sign-
posted and patrolled, with provision for teddy-bears' picnics, escorted
wildlife walks, 'Pooh-sticks' adventures and only a very small amount of
rigorously monitored 'wild-wood' for those few seeking 'a wilderness
experience'.

One wishes the Forestry Commission good luck. Its officials face,
however, an insurmountable difficulty. It is the nature of forests, both in
literature and life, *not* to be safe. That is not simply because they have
always been, and remain to this day, favoured locations for rape and
murder. Men and women innocently walking in them, or attempting to
journey through to the other side, have never known what they might
suddenly meet, whether animal, human or (still worse) a disconcerting
mixture of the two. (A. S. Byatt's 'The Thing in the Forest', published in
2004 in her *Little Black Book of Stories*, is yet another variant on the last.)[3]
Although woods may continue to shrink and be demolished all over the
world, the dread of encounters there with the uncanny or even (as Actaeon
discovered long ago, to his cost, when he surprised a goddess bathing) the
divine, refuses to go away. In 1999, that somewhat overblown woodland
film *The Blair Witch Project* owed much of its enormous box-office success
to the fact that large numbers of cinema-goers believed that what they were
watching was a documentary: that all of these horrifying events had really
occurred and been clumsily filmed by the young and doomed student

[2] *Independent*, 9 April 1995.
[3] A. S. Byatt, *The Thing in the Forest*, in *Little Black Book of Stories* (New York: Alfred A. Knopf, 2004).

researchers investigating supernatural manifestations in the Maryland woods.

* * *

In an essay called 'Overture and Incidental Music for *A Midsummer Night's Dream*', Angela Carter drew a distinction between the forests of Northern Europe and the English wood:

> The English wood is nothing like the dark necromantic forest in which the Northern European imagination begins and ends, where its dead and the witches live, and Baba-yaga stalks about in her house with chicken's feet looking for children in order to eat them. . . . An English wood, however marvellous, however metamorphic, cannot, by definition, be trackless, although it might well be formidably labyrinthine. . . . But to be lost in the forest is to be lost to *this* world, to be abandoned by the light, to lose yourself utterly with no guarantee you will either find yourself or else be found . . . for the forest is as infinitely boundless as the human heart.[4]

In 'Overture and Incidental Music', Titania's changeling child, the Indian boy, has little sympathy with either place. Wrenched away from his mother's warm south of mango and lemon groves, he is appalled by dripping English woodland, and by fairies afflicted (like himself) with the 'damn occidental common cold'.[5] His misery is considerable, yet he shows no signs of thinking he would be better off astray in the 'existential catastrophe'[6] of Baba Yaga's sunless forest: that vast, unmapped terrain where, as Michel Pastoureau has written, in a brilliant essay on the mediaeval forest as symbolic universe,

> les noms des lieux forestiers sont associés à la couleur noire, jamais à la couleur verte. C'est l'idée d'opacité, de ténèbres, de nuit terrifiante que prend en charge la toponymie, et non pas celle de végétation, de nourriture, de ressourcement. (forest place names are always associated with the colour black, never with the colour green. It's the idea of opacity, of shadows, of terrifying night which takes charge of the nomenclature, and not that of vegetation, nourishment, natural resources).[7]

In mocking Shakespeare's 'wood near Athens' – a place merely 'enchanted', not 'haunted', as forests are – Carter's principal targets were Victorian prettiness, Mendelssohn's music and what she saw as deplorable

---

[4] Angela Carter, *Black Venus* (London: Chatto, 1985), pp. 67, 68.   [5] Ibid., p. 67.   [6] Ibid., p. 67.
[7] Michel Pastoureau, 'La forêt médiévale: un univers symbolique', in ed. André Chastel, *Le château, la chasse, et la forêt (3ᵉ Rencontres internationales d'archéologie et d'histoire de Commarque, 1988)* (Bordeaux: Sud-Ouest, 1990), pp. 81–98 (p. 84).

nineteenth-century nostalgia for something that has never existed, except in fiction: a green and harmless sylvan world. Shakespeare, she thought, was much to blame for this, the more so because he must have been aware that actual Elizabethan woodland, even if without the resonance of the Northern European forests, was unromantic and harsh. The wood of *A Midsummer Night's Dream*, she complained, although 'the true Shakespearian wood', was 'not the wood of Shakespeare's time, which did not know itself to be Shakespearian, and therefore felt no need to keep up appearances'.[8]

The Oxford English Dictionary's entry for 'wood' occupies approximately six times as much space as that for 'forest'. (There is a similar disproportion, in the French Grand Robert, between 'bois' and 'forêt'.) The reasons for this are largely the same on both sides of the Channel, and they go considerably beyond the fact that, thanks to the axe and the saw, not to mention engrained and ancient human fears, both countries have for centuries been far less rich in forests than in relatively tamed and small-scale woods. The words 'bois' and 'wood' are unlike 'forêt' and 'forest' in that they signify not only an assemblage of living trees, but an indispensable and richly symbolic product: one which, as Pastoureau has shown, was long regarded as *materia prima*, heading the list of substances used or worked by man. Not until the fourteenth century did wood begin to be displaced in this symbolic hierarchy by cloth, the French 'etoffe', 'stuff' or 'material'.[9] Forests were often metaphoric – Thomas Wyatt's 'the heart's forest', or the 'forêt de longue attente' (forest of long waiting) of Charles d'Orléans[10] – but they have not penetrated human life and speech in the way that wood (both with and without the definite or indefinite article) for centuries has. Even today, we 'touch wood' to ward off misfortune, talk about not being 'out of the woods yet' or unable 'to see the wood for the trees'. The OED lists a vast number of such colloquialisms, many of which, such as the pun on 'wood' as 'enraged' or 'mad' – Demetrius' 'And here am I, and wode within this wood, / Because I cannot meet my Hermia' (*A Midsummer Night's Dream* 2.1.192–3) – have fallen into disuse. The French dictionary amasses its own equivalents.

---

[8] Carter, *Black Venus*, pp. 68, 69.   [9] Pastoureau, 'La forêt médiévale', pp. 87–8.

[10] The standard English translation is prosaic; a more obviously fraught forest can be found in another of Charles d'Orléans' *ballades*, which begins 'En la forest d'Ennuyeuse Tristesse' ('in the forest of Grievous Sadness'). *The Penguin Book of French Verse 1: To the Fifteenth Century*, ed. Brian Woledge (Harmondsworth: Penguin, 1961). The poet himself composed an English version: 'In the forest of noyous hevynes . . . '. See *The English Poems of Charles of Orleans: Edited from the Manuscript Brit. Mus. Harl. 682*, ed. Robert Steele (2 vols. (Early English Text Society) (Oxford: Oxford University Press, 1941–6), p. 81.

Both 'bois' and 'wood' are native words in their respective languages, 'wood' being Old English (*wudu*) in origin. 'Forestis', on the other hand, the source of 'forêt' and 'forest', is a Merovingian Latin intruder, and etymologically unclear. It may derive from *foris* ('outside'), a reference to the apartness of royal forests, which both in France and (for a much longer time) in England were subject to laws different from those in the rest of the kingdom. On the other hand, it may not. John Manwood, English author of *A Treatise and Discourse of the Lawes of the Forrest*, a comprehensive work first published in 1598, certainly knew that he was being whimsical (if imaginative) when he explained that the word *forest* was both Latinate, and compounded of the two English words, *For* and *Rest*: meaning 'a safe abyding and priuiledged place for the kings wild beastes for rest, which two woords (*For* and *Rest*) being put together and made one word, is *Forrest*, taking his name of the nature of the place'.[11] Despite such moments of whimsy, Manwood knew his forests and their laws: he had been a gamekeeper in Waltham Forest and a justice of the New Forest. His playful etymology only emphasizes the tendency of forests, not least in the drama of Shakespeare and his contemporaries, to be so volatile, to shift so cunningly between the imaginary and the real, the distant and the close at hand, as to be difficult to pin down.

The actual wood of Shakespeare's time was, of course, a severely diminished entity. Already, in 1587, William Harrison was complaining, in his *Description of England*, that although 'there is good store of great wood or timber here and there even now in some places of England, yet in our days it is far unlike to that plenty which our ancestors have seen heretofore, when stately building was less in use'.[12] When the remaining English forests speak (as they often do) in Drayton's *Poly-Olbion* (1612–22),[13] it is usually either to lament an ancient greatness now destroyed by enclosure, the axe and the plough, or to fret over a future which they recognize as desperately uncertain. The determined effort to clear woods, usually in order to produce arable land, goes back to time immemorial, and continues, with disastrous consequences, in third-world countries today. It was the Roman conquest, however, that significantly changed the landscape of Britain. After laying

---

[11] John Manwood, *A Treatise and Discourse of the Lawes of the Forrest* (London, 1598), D3. Manwood had previously published *A Brefe Collection of the Lawes of the Forest* (1592) for private circulation. An enlarged edition of the *Treatise*, printed posthumously in 1615, incorporated material from the earlier work.

[12] William Harrison, *The Description of England*, ed. Georges Edelen (Ithaca, NY: Cornell University Press, 1968), p. 276.

[13] See p. 8, and Chapter 5, pp. 112–15.

waste much of the original woodland of the Mediterranean (a catastrophe that turned out to be irreversible), the Romans briskly set about de-foresting southern England too, cutting down trees in vast numbers as fuel for their iron works. The woods began to revive after their departure, but really took on a new lease of life only when William the Conqueror – a dedicated hunter said to love the stags as though he were their father – greatly extended the royal game preserves, often taking in whole counties and, as in the case of the so-called 'New Forest', obliterating entire villages in the process. For centuries, the forests of England would be a battleground between the nobles and the Crown, as forests were relinquished or their bounds curtailed, and then clawed back again, under successive monarchs. It was one of the things Magna Carta was about. Meanwhile, both Crown and nobles were storing up trouble for themselves in terms of ordinary people: subjects who lived within or on the outskirts of royal forests, or chases in private hands, and claimed traditional (but often unwritten) rights to pasture their cattle, sheep and pigs there at certain times of the year, to collect firewood, or even hunt on land that they owned within these larger domains.

England was still sufficiently well wooded during the reign of Henry VIII to be able to export large timber for building ships and houses, as well as considerable quantities of firewood, to Holland, Flanders and northern France. Then, under Elizabeth, the situation changed. In what many economic historians now regard as the real industrial revolution, furnaces for producing iron (largely used for arms production), copper smelting, glass and salt works all began quite literally to burn up the woods. The pace accelerated greatly under the Stuarts. It was a destruction compounded by an increasing use of oak, as opposed to cheaper materials, in the construction of private dwellings;[14] the requirements of Elizabeth's burgeoning navy, and a shift away from wood-pasture in rural areas in favour of arable fields, the latter increasingly created by grubbing up woodland in ways that did not allow it to re-establish itself.

The royal forests were to some extent protected, at least for a time. Elizabeth, every bit as keen a hunter as her father, was still personally slaughtering deer well into the last years of her reign and, although parsimoniously inclined to do so on land belonging to her subjects,[15] she was scrupulous in the management of her own reserves. Her Stuart successor's

---

[14] Commented on by Harrison, *Description of England*: he laments that 'when our houses were builded of willow, then had we oaken men; but now that our houses are come to be made of oak, are men are not only become willow but a great many, through Persian delicacy crept in among us, altogether of straw', p. 276.

[15] See p. 18.

passion for the chase verged on the pathological, arousing a good deal of criticism on the grounds that, meanwhile, his kingly duties were neglected. Charles I, although more fastidious than James – he did not, for instance, insist upon being lowered into the gaping bellies of dead stags, on the grounds that the blood would strengthen his weak ankles – nevertheless attracted criticism too for the amount of time he wasted chasing deer. The Crown, however, was suffering acutely in the sixteenth and seventeenth centuries from Falstaff's complaint, 'an incurable consumption of the purse' (*2 Henry IV*, 1.2.236–7). Towards the end of her life, Elizabeth was forced to sell off part of the royal forests in order to raise money for her Irish wars. Both James and Charles followed her example. Almost invariably, the purchasers enclosed the land they had acquired, and then exploited it commercially, greatly to the detriment of the woods and, in most cases, that of common people in the area, whose way of life had depended on them for hundreds of years.

Under James, it became increasingly apparent that the country's woods and forests, and the game they sheltered, were no longer the envy of foreign visitors, as they had been during the reign of Henry VIII. Belated attempts were made to do something about this, including reviving the old forest laws, which in many parts of England had fallen into decay. Charles I has been severely criticized for trying to reinstate these laws, together with the special courts – the forest 'eyres' – which tried offenders against the 'vert' of the venison, but it seems likely, as Kevin Sharpe argued, that although the king certainly needed the revenue arising from fines, he was also genuinely concerned to halt the destruction of the forests.[16] John Evelyn's *Sylva* of 1664 is sometimes cited as the first real plea for the value and importance of woodland in England. Even, however, under James, landowners had been urged, with varying degrees of success, to cherish or at least replace slow-growing timber trees, with the interests of the royal navy in mind, if nothing else. Arthur Standish's *The Commons Complaint*, the first recorded book of English forestry, went through a series of editions after 1611, all of them dedicated to King James. But it is also significant that, from roughly 1600 onwards, poachers of any consequence were increasingly prosecuted by the Privy Council sitting as the court of Star Chamber.[17]

There are no royal forests, in the legal sense, in Shakespeare. But he is remarkably alert to woodland facts and terminology, even if he often

---

[16] Kevin Sharpe, *The Personal Rule of Charles I* (New Haven and London: Yale University Press, 1992), pp. 13, 243–5.

[17] Poaching is further discussed on pp. 16–18, 76, 78, 82.

employs them not to clarify but confuse. The forest in *Titus Andronicus*, scene of the emperor's 'solemn hunting', Lavinia's rape and the murder of Bassianus, is a place continually changing its character and identity.[18] Sylvan nomenclature in *A Midsummer Night's Dream* and *As You Like It* is more consistent. The word 'forest' makes only three appearances in the *Dream* – two of them referring to places elsewhere – against twenty for 'wood'. *As You Like It* reverses these figures: thirty-one mentions of forest, a mere three of 'woods' or 'wood'. And, indeed, these two locales are very different. The 'palace wood' of the *Dream*, a mere 'mile without the town' (1.2.101–2),[19] is subject (as Egeus knows when the lovers are found there) to the same 'sharp Athenian law' that only a few leagues away Hermia and Lysander could escape. It stands, presumably, in the sort of proximity to the residence of Theseus and Hippolyta that Windsor Forest did to its castle in Shakespeare's time. This wood is by no means as cosy as Carter makes out, although it seems to have required Peter Brook, in his revolutionary production for the RSC in 1970, to persuade the proscenium-arch theatre of this fact. It is certainly large enough to get lost in, as Lysander and Hermia discover.

The wood near Athens has two radically different aspects: the daylight wood and the wood at night, the latter occupying most of the play. In this, as in almost every other regard, it is unlike the Forest of Arden, which certainly has its discomforts and dangers, but where it never seems to get dark. Shakespeare inherited *As You Like It*'s forest from Thomas Lodge's *Rosalynde*, which is set in France's 'Ardennes',[20] but, as is well known, 'Arden' was also the maiden name of Shakespeare's mother Mary, a surname derived from the ancient Warwickshire forest within which her family had lived. Once so great, it was said, that a squirrel could travel the entire length of the county without once needing to touch the ground, Arden in Shakespeare's day was only a shadow of its former self. Michael Drayton makes it – or rather, her – lament in *Poly-Olbion* the rapacity of 'those gripple wretch[es]' who spoiled 'my tall and goodly woods, and did my grounds enclose'.[21] By 1599, Arden was largely confined to the north side of the Avon, where patches of dense woodland were interspersed not only with the occasional village, but (as Camden reports) included pastures, and even a few cornfields and iron mines. Because it had never been

---

[18] See Chapter 6, pp. 124–5.
[19] On the 'palace wood' and its distance from the town, see also Chapter 6, p. 125.
[20] See the longer discussion in Chapter 6, pp. 128–30.
[21] Michael Drayton, *Poly-Olbion*, in ed. J. William Hebel, *The Works of Michael Drayton* (Oxford: Basil Blackwell, 1933), vol. IV, p. 276.

a royal forest, enclosure, tree felling and clearing had proceeded there virtually unchecked, with the result that isolated clumps of woodland remained in the sixteenth century (Anne Hathaway's cottage in Shottery abutted on one of these), but only place names – Henley-in-Arden, or Arden's Grafton – to indicate that such villages had once been wholly encompassed by trees. Local memories, however, of the past greatness of Arden had been handed down over generations, and remained potent. Villages *in* a forest, frequently encountered in early modern drama, were a very English phenomenon. Actual French forests, not just those of romance, sometimes concealed a chateau in their depths. But French villages tended to stay outside; they marked forest limits, as opposed to being incorporated.[22]

Reaction, beginning in the second half of the twentieth century, against what might be called the Quiller-Couch view of Shakespeare's Arden ('he who knows Arden has looked into the heart of England and heard the birds sing in the green midmost of a moated island' etc.)[23] was inevitable. But it may have gone too far: readers and audiences are now likely to be told that the play consistently dispraises the country, that in Arden, the local women are vain and foul, the clergyman illiterate, the backwoods dialect lacking in grace and beauty, and that Duke Senior and his entourage, passively enduring what they know, despite the songs and the stoic rhetoric, to be a very nasty place, just can't wait to leave it behind. Richard Wilson's new historicist approach, in his book *Will Power* (1993), is more intelligent. But perhaps he is so concerned to politicize Arden, seeing it only as a nexus of Elizabethan social disorder and discontent – all of this radicalism, of course, ultimately defused and contained in the usual Foucauldian manner – as to lose touch with the play, and with the meaning in context of the individual lines he so ingeniously wrests to a narrow purpose.

Shakespeare's Arden is certainly memorable, but neither as nostalgic rural England, anti-pastoral, nor Wilson's complex of dark allusions to contemporary food and enclosure riots. At once imaginary, remembered, and a real, contemporary place, the forest of *As You Like It* presents many different faces, depending to some extent (as woodland always does) on the time of year, but also on the way different characters experience and come

---

[22] On chateaux in forests and villages on their borders, see Gabriel Fournier, 'Forêts et châteaux aux XIIIe et XIVe siècles', in ed. Chastel, *Le château, la chasse, et la forêt*, pp. 39–66, and Philippe Ménard, 'Le château en forêt dans le roman médiéval', ibid., pp. 189–214. See Chapter 5, pp. 95–7.

[23] 'Introduction' to *As You Like It*, ed. Sir Arthur Quiller-Couch (Cambridge: Cambridge University Press, 1926), p. xi.

to know it. It refuses, in fact, to stay still. When first mentioned in Act 1, by
Charles the wrestler, Arden looks ostentatiously fictional: the home of
a peculiarly English legend that has met up with a classical myth. Here, we
are assured, the banished Duke lives 'like the old Robin Hood of England',
many young gentlemen flocking to him every day to 'fleet the time
carelessly, as they did in the golden world' (1.1.116–18). But the place itself,
when we ultimately get there in Act 2, isn't like that.[24]

Although Duke Senior's exile in *As You Like It* appears to be
a comparatively recent event – he is '*already* in the forest of Arden'
(1.1.114), Charles informs Oliver – it is clear in Act 2 that these banished
men have actually experienced 'the icy fang / And churlish chiding of the
winter's wind' (2.1.6–7) in the open air. Orlando and Adam come close to
starving after they arrive in Arden, and the first impressions voiced by
Rosalind, Celia and Touchstone are anything but ecstatic: 'Ay, now am
I in Arden, the more fool I. When I was at home, I was in a better place'
(2.4.16–17). Considering what Duke Frederick's court was like, that says
a lot. An 'uncouth forest', 'desert place' or 'desert inaccessible / Under the
shade of melancholy boughs' (2.5.6; 2.4.72; 2.7.110–11), Arden initially
strikes all the strangers who enter it as uninhabited and desolate. Even
Duke Senior, despite the daily increase of his retinue (he seems to be
equipped with pages too by the end) is still talking about 'this desert city'
(2.1.23) in Act 2 as though Arden were some early monastic *desertum-civitas*:
a loosely organized settlement in the wilderness formed by disciples imitating
the original – and essentially solitary – desert saints. Only gradually does it
become apparent, to such characters and to the theatre audience, that this is
not the way things really are.

Editors of *As You Like It* tend to be much exercised by the fact that Duke
Senior's 'banquet' is set out, in full view of the audience, during the fifth
scene of Act 2, even though no one actually eats it until 2.7. Why don't
Orlando and Adam, those lost and famished travellers, notice the food
sitting there unattended in scene six and help themselves? The New Arden
editor's suggestion, that this *al fresco* meal should be removed almost as
soon as it appears, then re-introduced after an intervening scene only
eighteen lines long, seems theatrically impractical, and unlikely.
The whole point, surely, is that this bounty spread out on the stage, plainly
visible to the theatre audience, is something that the newcomers to Arden
cannot yet see. For Orlando and Adam, this is still a primitive and trackless
forest, like Brocéliande: a 'desert', Orlando tells Adam, in which he is not

---

[24] See the discussion of Robin Hood in Chapter 4, *passim*, and in Chapter 6, pp. 131–2.

even sure that savage beasts can survive (2.6.6–7), let alone a banished duke. We, on the other hand, are being silently reminded how easy it is for Arden to seem less civilized than it is. Yet we too still have a good deal to learn about this place.

It is a common feature of Elizabethan and Stuart plays with forest settings that all sorts of unlikely people are drawn to the woods in the final act. This is true of Arden, with its sudden incursion of Duke Frederick, and the second son of Sir Rowland de Boys – as it was, for that matter, of the woods in *The Two Gentlemen of Verona* and *A Midsummer Night's Dream*.[25] What is special about *As You Like It* is its gradual revelation, to the strangers and to the audience, of a forest society that was there long before the arrival of the various exiles from farmland and court: one that will go on in something approximating to the old way after the aristocratic visitors have left. When Orlando nervously asks Duke Senior and his fellow foresters in Act 2 if they have 'ever been where bells have knoll'd to church' (2.7.114), the Duke assures him that indeed, once upon a time, they have. What he doesn't point out – presumably because he doesn't yet know it – is that there is in fact a chapel in the forest, 'in the next village', of the kind often supplied to remote, sylvan parishes, even if its vicar, Sir Oliver Martext, a man happy to join together singularly ill-sorted couples under a tree and without any calling of banns, leaves much to be desired. William, Audrey's disappointed suitor, thanks God that he was 'born i'th' forest here' (5.1.22–4), and so presumably was the tellingly named Silvius. Phebe, Audrey, Corin, and his master the 'old carlot' (3.5.108), gravitate between its 'purlieus' (4.3.76) – Shakespeare introduces the legal term for a cleared area on the edge of a forest retaining certain privileges within – and Arden itself.

As the play unfolds, this forest becomes increasingly populous – and not just because of all the immigrants. Pastoral since Theocritus and Virgil had usually combined fields with woods, a tradition carried over into Renaissance drama: in Italy generally *drammi dei boschi* ('woodland dramas') appears to have been a term used interchangeably with *commedia pastorale*. Rather like winter and rough weather, foresters and shepherds are 'sure together', and indeed rivalry between them informs a number of sixteenth- and seventeenth-century English plays, in some of which (Sidney's *The Lady of May*, for instance, or the anonymous *Maid's Metamorphosis* of 1600)[26] a woman must declare her preference for one occupation or the other, after she has heard the arguments of suitors on

---

[25] See Chapter 6, pp. 122–4.   [26] See Chapter 5, pp. 97–101.

both sides. An antagonism mirroring, at several removes, the real-life conflict in rural areas between the requirements of deer and of sheep (or, less prettily, pigs and cattle) it also harbours an acknowledgement that shepherds and foresters exploit, and are obliged to share, what is basically the same environment.

In *As You Like It*, Shakespeare conjoined a timeless, essentially literary tradition with something nearer to home: memories of the largely disafforested Warwickshire parish in which he grew up, merged with a recreation of the vanished sylvan community that Arden had enfolded hundreds of years before. Rosalind, Celia and Touchstone have been in the forest for only a few minutes before they stumble upon shepherds – Corin and Silvius – and immediately feel much better. 'I like this place', Celia is saying a few moments later, 'and willingly could waste my time in it' (2.4.94–5). At no time, of course, were palm trees and olives, serpents and lionesses, features of Warwickshire Arden. Especially towards the end of *As You Like It*, Shakespeare seems to be trying to cut his play historically and socially adrift, deliberately fictionalizing a place that before Act 5 had also been shadowing a joint fifteenth- and late sixteenth-century reality. Then, all at once, we are given love at first sight between Celia and Oliver, the latter a wild as well as bad man abruptly reformed; an improbable spate of marriages, presided over by a god, Hymen himself; and finally, Jaques de Boys' revelation that wicked Duke Frederick, coming to Arden with the intention of doing everybody in, has suddenly been converted by an 'old religious man' (5.4.160). Who would have suspected that so persuasive a hermit was living quietly all this while on the outskirts of the forest? It all seems calculatedly unreal. But you have to watch Shakespeare like a hawk.[27]

* * *

On Midsummer Day 1509 in what Edward Hall described as a 'triumphaunt Coronacio*n*',[28] Henry VIII became king of England and Katherine of Aragon, his brother's former wife, England's queen. A state banquet and then jousts followed at Westminster Palace. On the next day, six mounted knights calling themselves the scholars of Pallas, who had issued a challenge to all comers, were answered by eight servants of Diana, who explained that

---

[27] Hermits and Arden are further discussed in Chapter 6, pp. 132–5.
[28] Edward Hall, *The Union of the Two Noble and Illustre Families of Lancastre and York* (London, 1550), 'The firste yere of Kyng Henry the viij', fol. 4ᵛ (a4ᵛ). In this and subsequent quotations, contractions have been silently expanded.

beeyng in their pastyme of huntyng, newes were [sic] brought unto theim, that Dame Pallas knightes, were come into these partes, to doo deedes of armes: wherefore, they had lefte their huntyng and chase, and repaired also thether, to encounter with the knightes of Pallas, and so to fight with them, for the love of ladies to thutterance.[29]

These knights of Diana, clad in green, ornamented with 'Bramble branches of fine Golde, curiously wroughte', rode into the lists to the sound of many horns, accompanied by foresters, and by

[a] Pagente made lyke a Parke, paled with pales of White and Grene, wherein wer certain Fallowe Dere, and in the same Parke curious Trees made by crafte, with Busshes, Fernes, and other thynges in lykewise wroughte, goodly to beholde. The whiche Parke or diuyse, beyng brought before the Quene had certayn gates thereof opened, the Dere ranne out thereof into the Palaice, the greye houndes were lette slippe and killed the Dere: the whiche Dere so killed, were presented to the Quene and the Ladies, by the foresayd knightes.[30]

Diana's servants then stipulated that the scholars of Pallas, if victorious in the ensuing combat, should have 'the dere killed, and the grey houndes that slewe them'.[31] They themselves, should they conquer, would be content to take only their opponents' swords. Something about this proposal disturbed Queen Katherine and she sent to the king for advice. Henry too proved less than happy. 'Conceyvyng', Hall records, 'that there was some grudge and displeasure between theim, thynkyng if suche request wer to theim graunted, some inconuenience might ensue', he not only ruled it out of order, but commanded the two parties should now tourney together only briefly, 'geuyng but a certayn strokes', after which the jousts were to be broken up and ended.[32] It is possible that Henry and his consort were aware of some smouldering personal animosity between two or more of the contenders that might render this mimic battle unacceptably violent. There had been no sign of this, however, on the first day's tilts, when exactly the same knights confronted each other (until darkness interrupted them), a golden spear and a crystal shield being the prizes to be won. On that occasion, the adversaries of the scholars of Pallas gave themselves no collective name or identity. The more elaborate scenario of the next day, on the other hand, was fraught with tensions unusual in courtly tournaments of this kind.

As 'scholars of Pallas', goddess of wisdom and learning, the challenging knights were linked with a long humanist tradition, its roots in classical

---

[29] Ibid., fol. 5ᵛ (a5ᵛ).   [30] Ibid., fol. 5ᵛ (a5ᵛ).   [31] Ibid., fol. 5ᵛ (a5ᵛ).   [32] Ibid., fol. 6 (a6).

antiquity, that deplored hunting not only as a waste of time, but an activity harmfully inuring men to bloodshed and cruelty. Thomas More's was only one voice among many when he made his Utopians despise blood sports:

> How can you possibly enjoy listening to anything so disagreeable as the barking and howling of dogs? And why is it more amusing to watch a dog chasing a hare than to watch one dog chasing another? In each case the essential activity is running – if running is what amuses you. But if it's really the thought of being in at the death, and seeing an animal torn to pieces before your eyes, wouldn't pity be a more appropriate reaction to the sight of a weak, timid, harmless little creature like a hare being devoured by something so much stronger and fiercer?
>
> So the Utopians consider hunting below the dignity of free men, and leave it entirely to butchers, who are, as I told you, slaves. In their view hunting is the vilest department of butchery, compared with which all the others are relatively useful and honourable.[33]

It was not for expressing sentiments like these that Henry, twenty-six years later, had More's head cut off. Yet the king was himself a passionate hunter, certainly not inclined to be squeamish about watching terrified, captive deer run down and slaughtered by hounds within an enclosed tiltyard, or to sympathize with anyone who chose to avert his eyes from the spectacle. Others felt differently.

Hunting (of deer, above all) anywhere in England was supposed to be the prerogative of the aristocracy or at least, after 1430, of gentlemen possessed of an annual income of forty shillings or more from freehold land. (The Game Act of 1603 would raise it to ten pounds.) One defence commonly invoked against humanist objections was that hunting provided young men of the right social class with invaluable training in the management of horse and weapons, cultivating endurance and battle skills of potential value in the nation's defence. This idea went back to the *Cyropaedia* of Xenophon, and its continuing strength can be seen in the knightly display of the 1509 coronation tilt. By enclosing their animal victims within a pageant made like a paled deer park, rather than an unenclosed forest like that of a later pageant in 1511,[34] the servants of Diana the huntress (scarcely associated with parks herself) made a statement about their own social status and that of hunters like them. Not only were private deer parks very costly to create and maintain, they required an expensive licence from the Crown. Wealth, rank and martial

---

[33] Thomas More, *Utopia*, trans. Paul Turner (Harmondsworth: Penguin, 1965), Book 2, p. 95.
[34] See Chapter 2, pp. 21–4, 28.

prowess: all three were being advertised by Diana's knights. Their opponents, the scholars of Pallas, although also gorgeously attired, made lesser claims. An insult, moreover, was implied by the announcement of the hunting party that, if victorious, they would strip the scholars of swords they were (by implication) unworthy to wear. If themselves defeated, they would simply hand over their hounds and slaughtered deer. That was potentially awkward, not only because the kill had already been formally presented to Queen Katherine and her ladies, but because venison in England, officially a commodity that would neither be bought nor sold, was a highly charged gift, usually underlining the superiority of the donor, whether it was the king distributing bucks and does at his pleasure from the various royal forests, or landowners using presents of venison from their estates to cement local alliances and loyalties.

Given such history, precedents, and complex and enduring tensions, it is unsurprising that hunting scenes, often involving real dogs, are ubiquitous in Elizabethan and Stuart drama. They were attractive for symbolic reasons, as well as for the spectacle and sound effects they could provide. Although deer are sometimes imagined, in non-dramatic works of the period, as complaining about their persecution by man – as in Gascoigne's *Noble Arte of Venerie*, or 'wyl bucke his Testament'[35] – it is rare, on the whole, for human characters in plays to express any sympathy for the hunt's victims. Sir Ralph's lady in Henry Porter's *The Two Angry Women of Abington* does point out that 'Life is as deere in Deare as tis in men': it is 'bad play, / When they are made to sport their liues away / . . . The stoutest of you all thats here, / Would runne from death and nimbly scud for feare'.[36] Her plea, however, has no effect on the hunters. She is left to take herself home in disgust, while her husband pots away (quite illegally, in the gathering dark) at some roe deer he saw earlier, 'downe by the groves'. Shakespeare is quite unusual in the kind of compunction he makes many of his characters express, nor is it (as Jaques and Duke Senior attest) by any means an exclusively feminine reaction. Arden's weeping stag, the doe in *Titus* that has 'receiv'd some unrecuring wound', poor Wat the hunted hare in *Venus and Adonis* or the reluctance of the Princess of France in *Love's Labour's Lost* to do what is expected of her and

---

[35] John Lacy, *Wyl Bucke His Testament* (London, ?1560), STC 15118.5; see also Oxford Rawlinson MS C.813 and British Library Cotton Julius A V. The attribution to Lacy is conjectural; he signs the last page, but could be the scribe or the author of the recipes for venison which follow the 'testament'. See Edward Wilson, '*The Testament of the Buck* and the Sociology of the Text', *Review of English Studies*, 45 (1994), 157–84.

[36] Henry Porter, *The Pleasant History of the Two Angry Women of Abington* (London, 1599), E4-E4ᵛ.

'spill / The poor deer's blood, that my heart means no ill':[37] it all makes one wonder about that Stratford legend according to which Shakespeare in his youth, 'having fallen into ill Company ... made a frequent practice of Deer-stealing'.[38]

Rowe, who got it from the actor Betterton, who presumably had been listening to local Stratford gossip, first publicized this story in 1709. But, as Samuel Schoenbaum points out in his *Documentary Life* of Shakespeare,[39] it had already been jotted down by Richard Davies, in the late seventeenth century, in notes neither Betterton nor Rowe could possibly have seen. Seized on with delight by the Baconians (there's the man of Stratford for you, a common poacher sneaking around with other local louts in Sir Thomas Lucy's Charlecote Park), it's been something of an embarrassment, ever since the nineteenth century, to Bardolators. Not because of the slaughter, but because of its illegality, and the apparently low company young Will kept. Shakespeareans, for their part, eager to discredit the tale, have been quick to point out that, in the late sixteenth century, Sir Thomas did not as yet have a licence to empark, though he did possess rights of free warren: meaning rabbits. But, of course, there were plenty of Warwickshire deer running free in the neighbourhood, and no reason to believe that the Lucys didn't encourage them to take up residence near the house, where they could easily be got at by themselves – and others.

Roger Manning's *Hunters and Poachers: A Cultural and Social History of Unlawful Hunting in England 1485–1640* (1993) sheds considerable light not only upon the young Shakespeare's rumoured escapades, but upon many plays in the period, including his own. Manning, drawing on a great deal of previously unpublished material in the Public Records Office, makes a number of important points. In the first place, it is clear that, however illegal, poaching was not regarded as socially disreputable. In England, especially during the late sixteenth and early seventeenth centuries, it was an activity cheerfully engaged in by an overwhelming number of the gentry and even nobility, including (on at least one occasion) Queen Elizabeth herself. For such people, venison for dinner, or the black market, tended to be a secondary consideration, if indeed it figured at all. Heavily armed, in

---

[37] *As You Like It*, 2.1.36f.; *Love's Labour's Lost*, 4.1.34–5; *Titus Andronicus*, 3.1.90; *Venus and Adonis*, 679ff. Unless otherwise stated, all Shakespeare quotations are taken from *The Riverside Shakespeare*, ed. G. Blakemore Evans (Boston: Houghton Mifflin, 1974).

[38] Nicholas Rowe, 'Some Account of the Life, &c. of Mr. William Shakespear', in Shakespeare, *Works*, ed. Rowe (1709), vol. I, p. v, quoted in Samuel Schoenbaum, *William Shakespeare: A Compact Documentary Life* (rev. ed.) (New York and Oxford: Oxford University Press, 1987), pp. 97–8.

[39] Schoenbaum, *William Shakespeare*, p. 98.

many cases, as though going into battle, accompanied by a remarkably democratic mixture of friends, eager household servants, and people from the local village (sometimes including the vicar), men who often possessed well-stocked deer parks of their own, regularly broke into those of their neighbours, viciously assaulting keepers and killing more game than they could carry away. They did it for fun, although (as Manning demonstrates) family vendettas – some of them extending over half a century and more – might also be involved. Poaching, then as now, encouraged male bonding and machismo conduct. It had also become, in the late sixteenth and early seventeenth centuries, a substitute for military activity, something denied many of these people by Elizabeth and the pacific James. There is evidence to suggest that it was subtly encouraged by the queen.[40]

Poaching, of course, apparently a deeply atavistic male urge, still goes on. The classic account of why men who need neither the food nor the money, and often have shooting rights of their own, nevertheless cannot resist the temptation of unlawful hunting, is Richard Jefferies' book *The Amateur Poacher*, first published anonymously in 1879. Jefferies, how-ever, was talking about something relatively thoughtful and restrained, and requiring considerable skill. He would have been appalled by the sixteenth- and seventeenth-century practice of 'havocking'. Deer were said to have been 'havocked' when poachers with greyhounds – not the sort that run around the track at White City, but something more formidable, like the modern Scottish deerhound – broke into someone's park or chase and systematically slaughtered everything in sight: stags, does, fawns, indiscri-minately and in such number that the carcasses could not be collected and were simply left to rot. The OED at present has no entry for the verb 'to havock' in this sense, recognizing it only as a military command to give the enemy no quarter. But, as Manning has discovered, from at least 1572 onwards, 'havocking' appears both in Star Chamber complaints and else-where to describe another kind of warfare: the wholesale and wanton annihilation of somebody else's deer.[41]

Forests and deer parks had always been particularly vulnerable in England during periods of popular unrest. They were attacked in 1381 as part of the peasant revolt against Richard II, and again in 1549 and 1569, when pales and fences were torn down and game destroyed. In the next century, the outbreak of the Civil War was heralded by riotous poaching,

---

[40] Roger B. Manning, *Hunters and Poachers: A Cultural and Social History of Unlawful Hunting in England 1485–1640* (Oxford: Clarendon Press, 1993), pp. 55–6, and see Chapter 2, 'Poaching as a symbolic substitute for war', pp. 35–56, *passim*.

[41] Ibid., pp. 47–8.

first in Suffolk and then, by April 1642, in Windsor Great Park and Windsor Forest. Although some of this venison was eaten, that was by no means the only statement being made. The commons, however, were neither the only nor the worst offenders. In 1572, the havocker was Queen Elizabeth herself. Accompanied by the Earl of Leicester, she rode unannounced into Lord Henry's park near Berkeley Castle during the owner's absence and killed twenty-seven red deer stags on the first day alone. After that, the keepers lost count. When Lord Henry, who was proud of his harts and hinds, returned to confront the carnage, he impetuously disparked – returning the land to open country. Elizabeth wasn't going to find anything to kill when she next came that way on a progress. He thought better of it, however, after receiving an anonymous letter reminding him that his family was under a cloud (his brother-in-law had recently been executed for treason), and that Leicester, who had taken quite a fancy to Berkeley Castle, would be glad of any excuse to have it added to his own domain.

It is, of course, impossible to know whether the young Shakespeare had seen, or even perhaps become involved with, a havocking. Even in an age far less squeamish than our own, it cannot have presented a pretty sight. What *is* clear is that on a number of occasions in the plays, he uses the word in this special sense only recently recovered, and that we can now restore to the passages in question a precision and resonance long obscured. Philip Brockbank was characteristically acute when he remarked, in a note to his New Arden edition of *Coriolanus*, that Menenius' plea to the tribunes in Act 3 – 'Do not cry havoc where you should but hunt / With modest warrant' (3.1.273–4) – has echoes in *King John*, *Julius Caesar* and *Hamlet*, in all of which 'havoc' is associated with hunting. 'But there is', he puzzled, 'no independent evidence of its use in sport'.[42] We now know that there is. Nor was Shakespeare the only poet to exploit it. 'See with what heat these dogs of hell advance / To waste and havoc yonder world'. That, for instance, is Milton's God in Book 10 of *Paradise Lost*. The whole passage suddenly comes into focus when you realize that Milton is thinking of the world as a once paradisal deer park, broken into by 'hell-hounds' who now are 'crammed and gorged, nigh burst / With sucked and glutted offal'.[43]

Brockbank's list of Shakespearean examples can be extended. In *Coriolanus*, Menenius is trying to prevent the tribunes from whipping the Roman crowd into a murderous anti-patrician frenzy, when they might

---

[42] *Coriolanus*, ed. Philip Brockbank (Arden Second Series) (London: Methuen, 1976), 3.1.272n.

[43] John Milton, *Paradise Lost*, ed. Alastair Fowler (revised second edition) (Harlow: Pearson Education, 2007), 10.616–7, pp. 630–3. Fowler notes only the more familiar military sense of 'havoc', citing *Julius Caesar*.

proceed against Caius Martius legally and with restraint. A smashing of deer-park pales by the populace, and resulting mayhem may or may not be what Henry IV has in mind when he talks, just before the battle of Shrewsbury, about 'moody beggars, starving for a time / Of pell-mell havoc and confusion' (5.1.81–2) – the hunting image here is less distinct. But there can be no mistaking it in *Julius Caesar* – 'Cry "Havoc!" and let slip the dogs of war' (3.1.273) – in *Henry V*, where the 'weasel' Scot is accused of creeping into England to 'havoc more than she can eat' (1.2.170, 173), or in the last scene of *Hamlet*:

> This quarry cries on havoc. O proud death,
> What feast is toward in thine eternal cell,
> That thou so many princes at a shot
> So bloodily hast strook?   (5.2.364–7)

'Quarry' was the technical term in the period for a heap of slaughtered deer. Even without it, it seems obvious that Fortinbras is revolted by a spectacle that, however inevitable as a consequence of military action, 'shows much amiss' in the palace of Elsinore. That was probably what Lord Henry felt too, as he surveyed what was left of his red deer at Berkeley Castle. Hunting may have been a quintessentially aristocratic, even royal pursuit, with its own laws, tropes and language, but (as Fortinbras' response to the 'havoc' of *Hamlet*'s denouement demonstrates, as much as Queen Katherine's in the tiltyard in 1509) it was not necessarily a civilized one, not least etymologically. As such, it reflected the ambiguities, as much as the attractions, of its own forest, or woodland, setting. The way in which the hunt could, at a word, transform from a courtly ritual (however cruel and macabre it might seem to modern eyes) to a scene of apparently indiscriminate slaughter reflects the properly liminal status of the forest itself, its symbolic and mythic density, its allusive thickness and uneasy mysteries.

* * *

All over the world, forests themselves have since time immemorial been destroyed, felled, and then grubbed up to prevent regrowth, not just for economic reasons, to obtain timber and create arable land, as with the rainforests of Borneo and the Amazon today, but out of fear. Yet fear is one major source of their attraction, their grip on the human imagination; they can occasion deep-seated anxiety, which the rational mind cannot dismiss out of hand. The giants, wild men and outlaws that lie in wait there can claim a very extensive English and European mythology as mysterious woodland inhabitants and hazards. The 'safe' and predictable forest of twenty-first-century London, even (or especially) one carefully pro-grammed in small areas to deliver the 'wilderness experience', is not a forest at all, but a contradiction in terms.

This book is about much earlier and variously amenable forests and how they were regarded and used in English drama of the sixteenth and early seventeenth centuries, including, but by no means limited to, that of Shakespeare. It deals with forest symbolism, with ideas of the forest as a sentient being, capable of listening and even responding to some of the things humans do and say in it, and with the relationship, sometimes harmonious, more often troubled, between the forest and its neighbour and opposite, the city. As has already been seen, hunters and poachers, as well as people who for one reason or another make their home in the woods – wild men, outlaws, exiles and solitaries – populate a surprising number of plays. So do more ordinary people, those charcoal burners, smiths, woodmen and game wardens for whom sylvan residence was a professional necessity. Some among all these woodland dwellers moved freely between the woods and the town. Others could not, or else chose to stay hidden among the trees. Forests themselves, whether native or foreign, imaginary or real, seem to have fascinated Elizabethan, Jacobean and Caroline audiences and haunted the imaginations of dramatists who wrote for them. The latter were doubtless prompted in many cases by their source material: a body of literature extending over many countries and ages which frequently suggested or demanded forest settings. The predilection of the sixteenth- and seventeenth-century English theatre for woodland scenes is nonetheless striking, given the problems attendant upon staging them. Were public and even private theatre audiences expected merely to 'think, when we talk of [forests], that you see them' – as with the invisible horses conjured up by the opening Chorus of *Henry V* (Prologue line 26)? How realistically and to what extent were trees – whether single or grouped – physically represented on stage? It is with an exploration of this still fiercely debated issue that the present study begins.

CHAPTER 2

Staging the Forest

On New Year's Day 1511, amid general rejoicing, Katherine of Aragon gave birth, at Richmond, to a son. The infant Prince of Wales was to die less than two months later, but initially he seemed robust, and Henry VIII lost no time in commissioning two days of spectacular royal entertainments in honour of Katherine and his new male heir. On 12 February, the king himself jousted at Westminster Palace (he had been a mere spectator at the tilts accompanying his coronation in 1509), before an audience that included the queen and her ladies, members of the court, London's civic dignitaries and a probable ten thousand onlookers of humbler social status. Henry's challenge 'against all comers' was supported, on this occasion, by three 'aydes': the Earl of Devon, Sir Thomas Knyvet and Sir Edward Nevile. Identified individually as 'Cure loial', 'Bon voloire', 'Bon espoir' and 'Valiaunt desire',[1] they announced themselves collectively as 'Les quater Chivalers de la forrest salvigne', designations situating them firmly within a French romance tradition. *The Great Tournament Roll of Westminster*, commissioned by Henry himself as a record of the occasion, shows Knyvet as 'Valiaunt desyre', and also the king himself, as 'Cure loial', going into action before the queen and her ladies, who sit to admire his prowess in the stands above. The extraordinary artificial forest, however, from which they issued, mounted and fully armed, into the lists that had been set up before the north front of Westminster Palace, was scrupulously, and rather surprisingly, English.[2]

'La Forrest Salvigne' was a meticulous and very expensive work of art, intended for re-use. Edward Hall (who probably never saw the device, or the single performance in which it figured) lingers over it in his chronicle.[3]

---

[1] 'Loyal Heart', 'Good Will', 'Good Hope', 'Valiant Desire'.
[2] Peter T. Hadorn, 'The Westminster Tournament of 1511: A Study in Tudor Propaganda', *Research Opportunities in Renaissance Drama*, 31 (1992), 25–45 (25, 35).
[3] Edward Hall, *The Union of the Two Noble and Illustre Families of Lancastre and York* (London, 1550), 'The ij yere of Kyng Henry the Viij', fol. 9ff. (b3ff.).

But it is only from the detailed, and dispassionate, account book kept by Richard Gibson, Yeoman of Henry VIII's Revels until his death in 1534, that the pageant can really be visualized, and the enormity of its savage, and almost immediate, destruction understood.[4] This rolling stage (requiring forty men to propel it) was on a grand scale: 26 feet long, 16 feet across and 9 feet high. The king and his companions, wherever on (or conceivably under) the pageant car they may have been concealed, rode, until its 'dores' opened at the 'tyem apoynted'[5] to release them, in the depths of a forest. Around them waved (according to Gibson) 12 hawthorns, 12 oaks, 12 hazels, 10 maples, 10 birches, 16 dozen fern roots and branches, 60 broom stalks and 16 furze (gorse) bushes. Also present, apart from rocks, were 6 fir trees, holly, ivy, fennel stalks and 2,400 'turnd' (i.e. artificially manufactured)[6] acorns and hazelnuts for which the office of the Revels had paid 8 pence a hundred. The forest also contained two dozen 'in bosyd' ('embossed') birds, red deer, conies and (according to Hall) six foresters, 'garnished in cotes and hodes of grene Ueluet'.[7] A golden castle gleamed at its centre, in front of which sat a maiden, weaving a garland of roses for the queen. Conducted into the tiltyard by 'certayne men appareiled like wildemen, or woodhouses [i.e. wodewoses]',[8] the pageant appeared to be drawn by two great heraldic beasts, a Tudor lion of gold damask, and an 'antelope' of silver. The latter had gilded tusks as well as horns, and although Gibson absent-mindedly calls it an 'olyvaunt' [elephant] at times,[9] it was probably a yale, the mythical beast, part of Margaret Beaufort's coat of arms, still rampant over the gates of Christ's College and St John's College in Cambridge.

Some features of this show were conventional. Wild men had been frequent participants in English court entertainments at least since the time of Edward III.[10] Equally familiar, from mediaeval French romances such as *Perceforest*, *Le Chevalier au Lion* or Chrétien de Troyes' *Conte du Graal*, was the castle hidden in the heart of the woods, a place usually (whether for good or ill) enchanted, visible sometimes only to the knight for whom its particular adventure was intended, and often vanishing with

---

[4] Appendix 3 of 'Revels Account of Richard Gibson for the Westminster Tournament', in ed. Sydney Anglo, *The Great Tournament Roll of Westminster: A Collotype Reproduction of the Manuscript* (Oxford: Clarendon Press, 1968), pp. 116–33. PRO E. 36/217.

[5] Ibid., p. 116.   [6] Ibid., p. 124.

[7] Hall, *Lancastre and York*, 'The ij yere of Kyng Henry the Viij', fol. 9ᵛ (b3ᵛ).

[8] Ibid., fol. 9ᵛ (b3ᵛ).

[9] Anglo, *Great Tournament Roll*, pp. 119, 122, 123, 126, 127, 130, 132; sometimes Gibson deletes 'oliphaunt' and writes 'antelope' instead.

[10] See Chapter 3.

the first light of day. The romance forest, however, whether Brocéliande, Ardennes or the Morois – dark, almost impenetrable, thorny and traced by the faintest of paths – was arboreally vague.[11] Certainly, the meticulously enumerated tree species of the 'Forrest Salvigne' are alien to it. Henry's pageant forest of 1511 was all the more remarkable since, although real wood was used in its framework, and a few winter evergreens (such as holly) gathered, it was otherwise, at great expense, entirely man-made. The individual shapes and sizes of its myriad leaves, for instance, were delicately cut out of green sarsenet, a fine silk material, and then backed with stiffened paper. By February, a combination of humans and the pigs turned loose into royal and other forests during autumn months to be fattened for slaughter must have devoured the annual crop of acorns and hazelnuts. Undeterred, Gibson arranged for his late summer trees to be laden with wooden replicas painstakingly turned by hand.

There was, of course, a different mediaeval tradition, classical in origin, in which tree species were particularized. When Orpheus, in Book 10 of Ovid's *Metamorphoses*, begins to play his lyre on a 'wide-extending plain ... devoid of shade',[12] twenty-six kinds of trees, natives of many different regions, are drawn by the music. They walk, some from great distances, to assemble around him, becoming a strangely improbable forest as he sings. Later writers – Seneca, Lucan, Statius and Claudian in the ancient world, then Boccaccio and Chaucer – reproduced Ovid's catalogue with greater or less variation, commonly omitting any explanation of how so many incompatible species could suddenly be found in one place. Spenser is unusual, in Book 1 of *The Faerie Queene*, in suggesting that Una and the Red Crosse Knight, had they been sufficiently alert to the suspect nature of a wood containing not only poplar, oak and aspen, but cedars, olive trees and myrrh, might prudently have turned back before reaching Errour's den.[13] No anomalous species, however, are present in Henry VIII's 'Forrest Salvigne'. This wood, moreover, despite its French name, was unmistakably native, a typical English mixture. Beech, for instance, along with oak, the dominant tree of the great French forests, but flourishing only in the south-east of England and Wales, was not included.

[11] Brocéliande is the forest of Arthurian romance, usually located in Brittany and sometimes identified with Paimpont forest; the Morois is the wood in which Tristan and Isolde wander in their romance. Ardennes (the vast forested region mostly in modern Belgium) is the setting for Thomas Lodge's romance *Rosalynde*, discussed pp. 128–30.

[12] Ovid, *Metamorphoses*, trans. Frank Justus Miller, 2 vols. (London: Heinemann Ltd., 1916), 10.86–8; vol. II, p. 71.

[13] Edmund Spenser, *The Faerie Queene*, ed. Thomas P. Roche (London: Yale University Press, 1978), Book I, Canto i, stanzas 7–9, p. 43.

The spectacular particularity of the 'Forrest Salvigne' probably contributed to its undoing. Dragged into Westminster Hall after the tournament began, and placed under guard, the pageant was enthusiastically pillaged by a mob that included some of the king's own officers.[14] (Two of its keepers had their heads broken when they tried to resist.) The colossal labour of many days and nights, it did not even survive long enough for its image to be reproduced in *The Great Tournament Roll of Westminster*. 'FYNEM', Gibson wrote sadly against his last entry explaining why 'noon therof byt the baar tymbyr cvm near to the kynges ews nor stoor'[15] ('none thereof but the bare timber came near to the king's use nor store'), a marginal comment reflecting more than just the end of this protracted section of his accounts. For a number of reasons, nothing quite like the 'Forrest Salvigne' was ever created again. A disastrous fire at Westminster in the following year meant that the royal tournaments were transferred to Greenwich, too far to transport pageants of such size and elaboration from the workshops in Blackfriars. Although in March 1515, work was begun on a 'pallys marchallyn'[16] even larger than the 'Forrest Salvigne' (it measured 36' x 28' x 10'), assemblable in four separate sections, it was never finished, but abandoned incomplete. A warning note may have been struck by a pageant smaller than either of these, the 'Golldyn Arber' in a garden of pleasure, described by Hall as made 'accordingly as the natural trees, herbes, or floures ought to be',[17] but mingling apples, pears, roses and gillyflowers with Mediterranean olive and orange trees. It actually broke through the floor while it was being constructed. Even at the Field of the Cloth of Gold in 1520, a byword for extravagance, it was on banquets, pavilions, apparel and jewels – and on a single great 'Tree of Chivalry' for which Gibson had to procure several cart-loads of timber, not to mention thousands of red satin cherries and white satin flowers – that the money was spent, rather than on complicated and mobile scenic devices.

As a sylvan spectacle excusing its audience from any imaginative effort, the 'Forrest Salvigne' remained unrivalled for almost a century. Then, the painted cloths, flats and shutters designed by Inigo Jones for court masques, or for special performances of plays at Oxford, or Somerset House, once again (although by very different means) bodied forth entire

---

[14] Hall, *Lancastre and York*, fol. 11 (b5).   [15] Anglo, *Great Tournament Roll*, p. 133.
[16] The sense is obscure. It might be 'martial', or 'marshal' (OF mareschal), specifically pertaining to horses or (more likely) to heraldry, as in 'Earl Marshal' or 'Knight Marshal', or else relate to 'march' meaning 'border', as in the Welsh Marches.
[17] Hall, *Lancastre and York*, fol. 10ᵛ (b4ᵛ).

woodland scenes. Between *The Masque of Blackness* in 1605, the first Ben Jonson/Inigo Jones collaboration, and William Davenant and Jones' *Salmacida Spolia* of 1640, the depiction of trees became increasingly sophisticated. *Blackness* had been content with an initial curtain (removed as soon as the masque began) on which, as on many a woven arras, 'was drawn a landscape, consisting of small woods, and here and there a void place filled with huntings',[18] but Thomas Campion's *The Lord Hay's Masque* of 1607, probably also designed by Jones, gradually unveiled a complex woodland set ascending by degrees to the Bower of Flora, the House of Night and Diana's Tree of Chastity on the midmost and highest hill, the whole complete not only with 'shrubbes and trees' but 'artificial Battes and Owles, continually moving' on wires.[19] Nearer to the audience, nine golden trees, 15 feet in height, danced at the command of Night, and then opened three by three to reveal the noble masquers disguised as very aristocratic wild men, or wodewoses, clad in cloth of silver overlaid with green taffeta leaves.[20] Charles I's masque *Britannia Triumphans*, in 1637, reproduced the familiar romance castle in 'a vast forest', allowing its knight and squire, giant and damsel to move about it freely, thanks to painted side wings and a back shutter. In *Salmacida Spolia*, performed in 1640, Envy's anti-masque tableau of a storm-wrecked forest was displaced by a grove of Spenserian 'vine-prop' elms, abundantly wreathed with grapes, heralds of Concord and the descent to earth of the Good Genius of Great Britain. In sketch after sketch, some for masques now unidentifiable, Jones presents illusionist forests, woods and groves combining (in ways unimaginable by the creators of the 'Forrest Salvigne') the emblematic and artificial with the recognizably real. The elaborate, beautifully drawn tree wings in Figure 3, although now impossible to pin down to any particular masque, are typical of Jones in the realism and care with which they delineate woodland.

Scenic resources of this kind would not be available for some time in the commercial theatres, nor for professional performances, by royal command, at court. Yet dramatists persisted, throughout the reigns of Elizabeth and her immediate successors, in writing innumerable plays set wholly, or in part, within a wood or forest. To what extent were their audiences expected to conjure up these woodland settings purely in their

---

[18] Ben Jonson, *The Masque of Blackness*, in ed. David Lindley, *The Cambridge Edition of the Works of Ben Jonson* (Cambridge: Cambridge University Press, 2012), vol. II, p. 512.

[19] Thomas Campion, *The Lord Hay's Masque*, in ed. Walter R. Davis, *The Works of Thomas Campion* (London: Faber & Faber, 1969), p. 212.

[20] Ibid., pp. 211, 220, 221–2.

Figure 1. Inigo Jones, design for *Britannia Triumphans* (1637)

Figure 2. Inigo Jones, design for *Salmacida Spolia* (1640)

Figure 3. Inigo Jones, two designs for stage wings, with trees

own imaginations? Or did staging the forest frequently involve some literal realization, even if it was only in the form of a few bushes, or a single, substantial property tree? In the public playhouses, stage pillars supporting the so-called 'heavens' might conveniently stand in for trees required by the plot to be climbed, hidden behind, or have love-poems inflicted on them. Were they inclined to handle the issue differently from such indoor, private theatres as the Blackfriars, or the court?

* * *

Apart from the moment when all the foresters blew their horns as the doors opened to release the knights, Henry VIII's sylvan pageant had been purely visual. Queen Katherine was expected to receive the maiden's garland, and graciously permit the tournament to begin, but there was no accompanying text, not even of the rudimentary kind attached to the deer-park pageant *The Scholars of Pallas and Knights of Diana* at the coronation tilts of 1509,[21] let alone anything resembling the 'book' of a Jacobean or Caroline masque. An 'interlude', however, was performed in the Hall at Westminster on the second evening of the 1511 festivities, by gentlemen of the Chapel Royal. What this play was, and just how they staged it, remains unknown. The actors may simply have accommodated themselves to the space (according to Edward Hall 'hanged rychely ... scafolded and rayled on al partes')[22] as set up for the night's other, more grandiose entertainments. Alternatively, small canvas houses, remaining fixed throughout, might have represented distinct stage locales, as they would continue to do throughout the reign of Elizabeth in some court and private theatre plays, and probably, on rare occasions, in the public theatres as well. The Revels accounts testify not only to the construction of palaces, cities, castles and senate houses for this purpose, but to occasional expenditure on a wood, a 'wilderness' or a single, important tree.[23]

Thus, between 1572 and 1574, money was disbursed for 'armes of oke for the hollow tree', 'Tymber for the forest, ij shillings vj d', 'Pap*er* for patternes *and* for leaves of trees', 'fflagbroches for the knobbes of the tree',[24] and 'for provision *and* cariage of trees and other things to the Coorte for a wildernesse in a playe viiij sh. vj d'. There was also a need for ivy, holly 'for a forest', and (significantly) for 'great hollow trees'.[25] Fairly clearly, as with the pageant of the 'Forrest Salvigne', although fresh holly and ivy were obtainable all year round, at little or no expense, most of

---

[21] See Chapter 1 pp. 12–15.   [22] Hall, *Lancastre and York*, fol. 10ᵛ (b4ᵛ).
[23] Glynne Wickham, *Early English Stages: 1300–1660*, 3 vols. (London: Routledge & Kegan Paul Ltd., 1963), vol. II, part 1, p. 296.
[24] 'fflagbroches' is obscure; from the sense, and possible cognates in OED, it might be brushwood.
[25] See Peter Cunningham, *Extracts from the Accounts of the Revels at Court in the Reigns of Queen Elizabeth I and King James I from the Original Office Books of the Masters and Yeomen* (London: F. Shoberl, 1842), pp. 1–99 and George F. Reynolds, '"Trees" on the Stage of Shakespeare', *Modern Philology* 5 (1907), 153–68.

this foliage was artificial. Presumably, these tree properties could be re-used, then (perhaps) sold off to the professional companies when they began to look tired, or predictably familiar. They might even (as certainly seems to have been the case with costumes originally commissioned by the Revels Office) be handed over to the actors as part payment for a court performance. Surviving texts from the 1570s are in short supply, but the anonymous *Sir Clyomon and Sir Clamydes* (1576), a play associated with the Queen's Men which may have been seen at court, is exactly the kind of work for which such items might be envisaged. Based on the French *Perceforest*, it specifies a 'Forest of Marvels' and an 'Isle of Strange Marshes', in addition to various other locales. Versions, moreover, of one of its stage directions, '*Enter* Neronis *in the Forrest*',²⁶ recur in some later printed plays: '*Enter Albert in the woods*',²⁷ in a comedy called *The Hog Hath Lost His Pearl* (1613), for instance, or '*Enter Timon in the woods*', in Shakespeare.²⁸ Are such formulae – not to be confused with the more ambiguous stage direction 'as from the woods' – merely a nudge to the reader's imagination (or to the playhouse bookkeeper), or do they point to some kind of arboreal effect realizable not only at court, but in the private theatres and at public playhouses such as the Globe?

Although no Revels accounts relating to it survive, the text of George Peele's pastoral, *The Arraignment of Paris*, performed at court by the Children of the Chapel in 1584, testifies to the persistent appearance there for three-dimensional tree properties. The entire play takes place in the 'woods of Ida', a sylvan landscape in a vale on Mount Olympus, surrounded by unseen 'plains' where shepherds tend their flocks, but characterized itself by a multitude of references throughout to 'groves' and 'thickets'.²⁹ There is now no way of ascertaining how much actual greenery may have been imported in order to realize this setting as a whole. A stage direction in Act 1, however, specifies that Paris and the nymph Oenone 'sit under a tree together'.³⁰ An artificial tree must have been present, freestanding and of reasonable size. Diana's leafy 'bower', large enough to

---

²⁶ Betty J. Littleton, *Clyomon and Clamydes: A Critical Edition* (The Hague: Mouton & Co, 1968), l. 1254, p. 118.
²⁷ Robert Taylor, *The Hog Hath Lost His Pearl*, ed. D. F. MacKenzie, The Malone Society Reprints (Oxford: Oxford University Press, 1972), 4.1177.
²⁸ See Alan C. Dessen, *Recovering Shakespeare's Theatrical Vocabulary* (Cambridge: Cambridge University Press, 1995), p. 59.
²⁹ George Peele, *The Arraignment of Paris*, in eds. C. F. Tucker Brooke and Nathaniel Burton Paradise, *English Drama 1580–1642* (Boston: D. C. Heath and Company, 1933), 1.4.23, 2.1.4, 3.4.51, 4.3.7, pp. 6–15.
³⁰ Ibid., 1.5.17.

contain seven seated deities, also seems to have been a tangible object. At one point in Act 2, moreover, 'a Tree of Gold laden with crowns and diadems of gold'[31] rises up from beneath the stage at the goddess Juno's command, before sinking down again after Paris rejects the wealth and power it offered.

Thomas Dekker's comedy, *Old Fortunatus*, seen at court in 1599, is especially interesting in its arboreal effects.[32] At the beginning, Fortunatus himself is hopelessly lost in a wood. Footsore and weary, he lies down beneath a 'tree', having first courteously asked its permission 'to sleepe under your leaues',[33] and has a remarkable dream, one from which he awakes to find it truth. This clearly substantial tree, which remains throughout, must have been placed on stage before the play began, unlike the two trees of Vice and Vertue carried on near the end of the first act by a number of characters who, according to the stage direction, then 'set the trees into the earth'.[34] These also seem to have been sizable, not to mention stable. Other stage directions, this time in Act 4, not only indicate that Fortunatus' son Andelocia 'climes up' the tree of Vice, but that he actually 'stands fishing with his girdle' on one of its branches for a particularly tempting crimson 'Apple that growes highest'.[35] The only text of this play, the 1599 quarto, apparently reflects a court performance in the presence of the queen. What happened when the Admiral's Men offered it, as they demonstrably did, to the general public at the Rose Theatre? Was Dekker's text substantially altered from the one that survives, in ways that went beyond simply replacing the Prologue and Epilogue at court, and omitting the final compliment to Elizabeth as a member of the audience? How were the wood and the three trees necessary to the plot handled in a very different acting space?

Any answer, in this case as in so many others, must be conjectural. What evidence there is for the presence of stage trees in the public (and indeed the private) playhouses is complicated, and continues to be variously interpreted by theatre historians. The trend in recent years has been to argue that the pillars supporting the stage 'heavens' in some theatres, notably the Globe, would not only have been arboreally sufficient, but in most cases preferred, because theatrically simpler and more economical, given agile actors and audiences content to accept architectural columns as oaks. But there are a great many problems with this kind of minimalist insistence on

[31] Ibid., 2.2.40.   [32] See also the discussion in Chapter 6, p. 119.
[33] Thomas Dekker, *Old Fortunatus*, in ed. Fredson Bowers, *The Dramatic Works of Thomas Dekker* (Cambridge: Cambridge University Press, 1953), 1.1.60, p. 116.
[34] Ibid., 1.3.19.   [35] Ibid., 4.1.75–85.

the bare stage. Even Alan C. Dessen, its most considerable current proponent, cannot ignore the famous 'j rocke', 'ij mose banckes', and 'the cittie of Rome', in Philip Henslowe's inventory of stage properties possessed by the Admiral's Men for the Rose Theatre in 1598, as well as his 'baye tree', 'Tantelouse tre', and 'tree of gowlden apelles'.[36] This last may well have been devised for Robert Greene's *Friar Bacon and Friar Bungay*, a comedy written in the late 1580s or early 1590s and seen, like *Old Fortunatus*, both at the Rose and, on more than one occasion, at court. Conjured up by Friar Bungay and purporting to be the famous tree of golden apples in the Hesperides, it must have surfaced 'miraculously' from the space below stage, complete not only with golden apples, but with its legendary dragon guardian entangled in the foliage and 'shooting fire' – surely a somewhat risky if spectacular effect.[37] Threatened with having its branches wrenched off by the spirit of Hercules, at the command of a rival foreign magician, it narrowly escapes mutilation (doubtless to Henslowe's relief) thanks to the superior wizardry of Friar Bacon, and is quietly carried off stage at his command, still more or less intact, by a combination of Hercules and the discomfited foreign necromancer himself. It must have been at least shoulder-high.

Also clearly substantial was that 'great tree', according to the stage direction, which 'suddenly riseth up' from the stage trap in the anonymous *A Warning for Fair Women*,[38] a domestic tragedy belonging to the Lord Chamberlain's Men which may have been performed at the Globe in 1599. Large enough not only to startle, but physically separate the would-be adulterers Anne Sanders and Captain Browne, who had been advancing with amorous intent from opposite sides of the stage in the play's second dumb show, it is rashly cut down by Browne, after which the two lovers are able to 'run togither and embrace'.[39] This tree, as the personification of Chastity soon makes plain, represents Anne Sanders' husband, now doomed to be felled himself by the murderous hand of Browne. Two questions occur here, and they are by no means unique to this play.

[36] Dessen, *Recovering Shakespeare's Theatrical Vocabulary*, pp. 59–63. The full list can be found in Andrew Gurr, *The Shakespearean Stage 1574–1642*, 4th edition (Cambridge: Cambridge University Press, 2009), pp. 229–30, as well as in *Henslowe's Diary*, ed. R. A. Foakes and R. T. Rickert (Cambridge: Cambridge University Press, 1961, 2002), pp. 319–21.

[37] Robert Greene, *The History of Friar Bacon and Friar Bungay*, in eds. C. F. Tucker Brooke and Nathaniel Burton Paradise, *English Drama 1580–1642* (Boston: D. C. Heath and Company, 1933), 9.84, p. 85.

[38] Charles Dale Cannon, *A Warning for Fair Women: A Critical Edition* (Paris: Mouton, 1975), l. 1266, p. 134.

[39] Ibid., l. 1273.

The below-stage space at the Globe, and presumably at the Rose (let alone at court) cannot have been much more than four feet in depth. How was it possible to accommodate there, and release vertically, a tree of the height seemingly required? An actor (the god Pluto, for instance, in *The Arraignment of Paris*) could kneel down to facilitate his imminent discovery. A large stage tree, even if hinged, must have been far more intractable to handle. Equally perplexing, how could such a tree be hewn down on stage, in full view of the audience, and then reappear intact for the next performance? Theatrical budgets, and craftsmen, were after all limited.

Somewhat less problematic is the phenomenon of those three-dimensional hollow trees recorded in the Revels accounts for the 1570s, but surviving as hardy perennials in much later plays performed in many different kinds of theatre. These must always have had one specific purpose, and it was not just to look picturesque. Their dramatic function was to enclose and release an actor, something no stage column could very effectively pretend to do. The majority of characters confined in this way are female. A few, dryads and hamadryads, for instance, seem entirely comfortable inside their tree, its trunk the living body encompassing their souls; they are free to make brief expeditions outside it, but their lives are symbiotic and co-extensive with that of the tree itself. In a second, quite different and more popular scenario, the tree conceals a being forcibly imprisoned; one remembers Ariel, the victim of that nasty colonialist Sycorax, in the vividly recalled past of *The Tempest*, or, more pertinently, Earine, the witch Maudlin's victim in the staged present of *The Sad Shepherd*, the pastoral Jonson left unfinished when he died in 1637.[40] Inhabitants such as these, shoved inside a tree by sorcery, are understandably not happy about their situation at all.

John Lyly exploited both alternatives. His eight comedies (with one exception) were all written for the child actors and performed, during the 1580s and early 1590s, for private, paying audiences in an indoor theatre, and then (usually) at court. G. K. Hunter observed that Lyly 'seems to have acquired a trick tree at some point in his career, which he became rather devoted to'.[41] It would appear to have sported varying artificial foliage according to the particular arboreal species required. *Endimion* (1588) featured an aspen, in which the sorceress Bagoa is reported to have been imprisoned. She is magically released, on stage, in Act 5 through the power

---

[40] See the discussion of *The Sad Shepherd* in Chapters 4 and 5.
[41] G. K. Hunter, *John Lyly: The Humanist as Courtier* (London: Routledge & Kegan Paul, 1962), p. 110.

of Cynthia: 'I will try whether I can turn this tree again to thy true love'.[42] It must have been hollow, present throughout, and capacious enough to enclose a child actor.

Described on its title page as 'A Witty and Courtly Pastoral', *Love's Metamorphosis* (c. 1590) is what the Italians called a *favola boscherrecia*, a woodland play. It also contains an inhabited tree, its species unidentified, but probably represented, as in Lyly's source, Book 8 of Ovid's *Metamorphoses*, as an oak. It is chopped down by the mean-minded character Erisicthon at the end of Act 1, killing its resident hamadryad Fidelia, after which the 'tree, hacked in pieces' lies there, a reminder of his barbarity, for the rest of the play.[43] As with *A Warning for Fair Women*, the question of just how such a versatile (and doubtless costly) stage tree was not only convincingly cut down but later re-assembled in order to feature in subsequent performances remains unclear. Although it also requires a three-dimensional Siren's 'Rocke', and a temple of Cupid, all the action takes place in a forest sacred to Ceres, bounded on one side by those arable fields from whose crops Erisicthon derives most of his prosperity, and on the other by the sea. Erisicthon regards the forest, and the game it shelters, as his personal property too which, legally, it might well be. (Lyly was by no means just a mythological dramatist.) The three aptly named 'amorous foresters', Ramis, Montanus and Silvestris, driven by ungovernable passion – as foresters usually are in imaginative literature of the period – are (by implication) in his employ, but Erisicthon is foolish enough to resent sharing 'his' woods with Ceres and her chaste nymphs, the objects of the woodmen's frustrated desire. He knows better by the end of the play, after the outraged goddess has sent Famine to gnaw his vitals. A strained accord finally prevails in the forest. Although Lyly at one moment punctures the modest illusion of his simultaneous staging (Protea rescues her lover Petulius from the Siren by directing him to 'follow me at this door, and out at the other')[44] the comedy otherwise is consistent (unlike *Endimion*) in its presentation of a single, sea-girt wood, into which characters freely come, but out of which no one is required by the plot (or the audience's imagination) to stray.

Hollow trees, like the one in *Love's Metamorphosis*, reappear over a considerable span of time, and under very different theatrical circumstances.

[42] John Lyly, *Endymion*, ed. David Bevington (The Revels Plays) (Manchester: Manchester University Press, 1996), 5.4.291–2.
[43] John Lyly, *Love's Metamorphosis*, ed. Leah Scragg (The Revels Plays) (Manchester: Manchester University Press, 2008), 2.1.5–6.
[44] Ibid., 4.2.112.

In 1603, William Percy completed (at a country abode he identified, rather endearingly, as 'Wolves Hill, my Parnassus')[45] a play entitled *The Faery Pastorall, or Forrest of Elves*. Although there is no record of any performance, Percy, who had spent some time in London, certainly designed his work for the stage, quite specifically in fact (as a note in the manuscript indicates) for the children of St Paul's. It is easy to see why the Master of Paul's Boys, if he ever received a copy, might have been less than enthusiastic. *The Forrest of Elves* is a dreadful play. Still, incoherence and atrocious verse scarcely diminish the interest of Percy's carefully itemized stage properties. These include a fairy chapel, a mysterious 'Musick tree', a magic well with rope and pulley, a 'fourme of turves', a 'hollow oak with a vice of wood to shutt to' and a 'greene Bank being pillowe to the hed'.[46] This sounds like a more complicated, pastoral version of the old stage 'howses' recorded in Tudor interludes such as *Thersites* (1537) ('Mulciber must have a shop made in the place and Thersites cometh before it')[47] as well as some of the items listed in the Elizabethan Revels accounts. Percy was clearly aware that he was asking for a good deal, and that even in an indoor theatre, there were likely to be difficulties, not least those posed by the encroachment of spectators who had paid to sit on stools in the acting area itself. If the properties enumerated, he conceded sadly, 'will not serve the turne by reason of the Concourse of the People on the Stage, then you may omitt the sayd Properties which be outward and supplye their Places with their Nuncupations only in Text Letters',[48] that is, with written labels.

Before dismissing Percy's preferred staging as the un-professional lunacy of the bard of Wolves' Hill, it would be as well to remember the pseudo-history, *John a Kent and John a Cumber*, by that very professional dramatist Anthony Munday, performed probably by Strange's Men at the Curtain theatre shortly before 1590. The playbook, written in Munday's own hand, with a few marginal additions by the theatre's book-keeper, survives. In his third act, Munday signals the entrance, in succession, of four 'antique[s] queintly disguysde': the first appearing 'ffrom one end of the Stage',

---

[45] William Percy, *The Faery Pastorall, or Forrest of Elves* (London: The Shakespeare Press, 1824), p. 190. Percy (1574–1648), the third son of Henry Percy, eighth earl of Northumberland, wrote six extant plays, all apparently intended for the children's companies. He studied in Oxford, moved in Catholic literary circles and published a sonnet sequence, *Sonnets to the Fairest Coelia*, in 1594. He was periodically in dire financial straits, spent some time in prison, and died in some obscurity in Oxford.

[46] Ibid., p. 94.

[47] Thersites in Marie Axton (ed.), *Three Classical Interludes*, Tudor Interludes (Cambridge: D. S. Brewer, 1982), p. 38.

[48] Percy, *The Faery Pastorall*, p. 94.

the second 'ffrom the other end of the Stage', the third 'ffrom under the stage' (i.e. the trap) and the last (climactically) 'out of a tree, if possible it may be'.[49] Like Percy's acknowledgement that, in a private theatre, performance circumstances might dictate the replacement of his three-dimensional stage properties with 'their Nuncupations only in Text Letters', Munday's 'if possible it may be' points to flexible staging, in this case by professional troupes frequently called upon to transfer plays (and properties) from one kind of theatre space to another. As it happens, *John a Kent* also contains references to a 'castell', apparently three-dimensional, to and from which exits and entrances were made, and whose door *John a Cumber* at one moment 'makes fast'.[50] Munday seems, however, not to have worried about its availability. Nor, judging from his text, was he concerned about bringing on stage a considerable property tree, even if it proved unable to contain an 'antique' issuing from what sounds like a hinged door like the one Percy later proposed for *The Forrest of Elves*. Identified at one point by John as 'the Chestnut tree hard by'[51] (and probably recognizable as such, like those hawthorns, oaks and maples whose leaves were so artfully imitated in the 'Forrest Salvigne'), Munday's tree may have been carried on specially for Act 3. Or it might have done duty throughout, serving as discovery space, the site of a meeting and stage ornament, before being enchanted by Shrimp, the magician's attendant, and becoming 'this accursed tree'[52] around which Marion and Sydanen's unwelcome suitors are forced to dance, in full view of the audience, 'still circkling it and never getting thence'.[53]

Many stage directions, as well as instructions to the actor, are implicit in the dialogue of sixteenth- and early seventeenth-century plays. Trees, however, present special problems of interpretation, as stage beds and thrones do not. It is often difficult to know when the dramatist intended them to be physically present and when he would have been content either with a stage post or something supplied purely by the audience's imagination. Yet the evidence presented in many texts does seem strong. 'Do you *see* that tree' (my emphasis), Dulcimel asks her father in Act 4 of Marston's *The Fawne* (1604) 'that leans just on my chamber window'? 'A well-grown plane tree', she continues, offering easy access to her bedroom.[54] It is, of

---

[49] Anthony Munday, *John a Kent and John a Cumber*, ed. Muriel St Clare Byrne, The Malone Society Reprints (Oxford: Oxford University Press, 1923), l. 780–836, pp. 25–6.
[50] Ibid., line 848, p. 27.   [51] Ibid., line 1028, p. 32.   [52] Ibid., line 1420, p. 43.
[53] Ibid., line 1395, p. 43.
[54] John Marston, *The Fawne*, ed. Gerald A. Smith (London: Edward Arnold Ltd., 1965), 4.1.586 and 599, pp. 93–4.

course, a covert message to her lover, and her foolish father promptly delivers it: 'Sir, sir, this plane tree was not planted here / To get into my daughter's chamber, and so she pray'd me tell you. / What though the main arms spread into her window, / And easy labor climbs it?'[55] This tree certainly sounds quite as much like a stage property as those in Percy and Munday, or in Dekker and *A Warning for Fair Women*. There is no need for it to be hollow; it merely needs to be pointed out and then scaled, as it duly is in Act 5: 'Tiberio climbs the tree', the stage direction says, 'and is received above by Dulcimel, Philocalia and a Priest' (5.1).

The Fawne was a children's play, designed for and performed in the private theatre at Blackfriars. Although he concedes that 'a property tree would certainly enhance the effect here', Alan Dessen still concludes that 'theatrical efficiency would warrant use of the stage posts'.[56] But there don't seem to have been any stage posts at Blackfriars. Even if there were, perhaps, pilasters ornamenting the tiring house wall (and there is no evidence for their existence), it is difficult to see how even the most acrobatic child performer could negotiate one and manage, with any dignity, to get into a gallery window above. In *Romeo and Juliet*, a public theatre play, Romeo ascends to and leaves Juliet's chamber window in Act 3 explicitly by way of a ladder of 'cords' (2.4.189; 3.2.132–6) she lowers to him, certainly not a stage post. There were many debates during and after the construction of Shakespeare's Globe, on the Bankside in London, about the original placing and size of such structural posts, but they can never have been jammed up so closely to the back or side walls of the stage as to facilitate ascents and descents of this kind.

There is also no possibility that they can have been central, in the middle of the stage. While a modern, minimalist theatre may prefer audiences simply to imagine Herne's Oak,[57] around which Parson Evans instructs a good part of the Windsor community to circle in the last act of *The Merry Wives of Windsor* ('guide our measure round about the tree', 5.5.79), it is difficult to believe that Shakespeare's did, wedded as it was to visual spectacle, and the emblematic embodiment of ideas, whether at a court performance, at Blackfriars, or (even) the Theatre or the Globe. Herne's Oak, the already venerable originals of which must have been familiar to many members of the audience, cannot have been either non-existent, or a painted backdrop, let alone (like Henslowe's 'tree of gowlden apelles') relatively small. Nor does an inconveniently off-centre stage post make

---

[55] Ibid., 4.1.647–50.   [56] Dessen, *Recovering Shakespeare's Theatrical Vocabulary*, p. 62.
[57] See the discussion of *The Merry Wives of Windsor* in Chapter 6, pp. 125–8.

Figure 4. Adriaen van der Venne, Interior of a circus, from *Tafereel van de Belacchende Werelt* (The Hague, 1635); a tree property is visible backstage

sense as focus for the play's long and crowded final section. A substantial property tree seems indicated, probably carried on specially for Act 5.

* * *

There is, unfortunately, only one piece of visual evidence so far for the use of tree properties in the period. In 1953, Richard Southern discovered a 1635 engraving by Adriaen van der Venne, depicting a complicated indoor stage at a fair. The Netherlands are not England, and the engraving is relatively late, yet as Southern pointed out, the picture as a whole throws considerable light both on a typical Elizabethan 'private house' theatre and on the details of common travelling theatre presentation of the time.[58] And one of its most striking features is the presence, just behind the back curtain, of two sizeable trees waiting to be carried on for the next scene. Southern was reluctant to suggest that the der Venne

---

[58] See Richard Southern, *The Seven Ages of the Theatre*, 2nd edition (London: Faber & Faber, 1964), pp. 184–6.

engraving necessarily bears on practice at the Rose, the Globe, or any other public theatre equipped with stage posts. (Not all of the public amphitheatres were; the Hope playhouse, built by Philip Henslowe and Edward Alleyn in 1613, was constructed without such posts because it was intended for alternative use as a bear-baiting arena.) Yet the image is suggestive, especially when taken together with a specific criticism of what an anonymous Italian critic, writing in the 1630s, felt to be an inappropriate theatrical reliance upon three-dimensional and literal tree properties of this kind:

> As the perfection of dramatic poetry does not lie in representing the naked truth of human actions but in imitating them by means of a plot invented in somebody's mind – in the same way the more the art of performing poetic action on the stage decorates and expresses the truth with fake ways, the more it should be esteemed as praiseworthy and admirable; . . . thus we see that while we could make a sylvan scene with real trees and bushes, nonetheless the most skilled in this art have chosen to use paintings of trees and shrubs, of valleys and hills, as it seems to them that using a tree to represent a tree is an imitation lacking in artifice and invention.[59]

The property tree, in other words, is both too real and not real enough.

The preference of the anonymous Italian author here is clearly for complex illusionist stage sets like those Inigo Jones created in the 1630s for Charles I's *Britannia Triumphans* and *Salmacida Spolia*.[60] Painted flats and shutters of this kind were not necessarily incompatible in the period with stage trees introduced among them as occasional two-dimensional 'relieves', as Jonson's *The Sad Shepherd* attests. Still, trees in the early modern theatre presented aesthetic problems in a way chairs, tables, thrones or torches meant to persuade an audience that it was dark even in a playhouse flooded with afternoon light, did not. Those things, after all, were man-made objects, manufactured perhaps for the theatre, but capable of being transferred without much difficulty to the world outside, a principle which largely applies to costumes too. In Shakespeare's time they were, as is well known, sometimes smuggled temporarily out of the playhouse by the actors and (in defiance of the sumptuary laws) flaunted in the London streets. Henslowe felt it necessary to forbid the members of his

---

[59] Kristine Hecker, *The Concept of Theatre Production in Leone de' Sommi's* Quattro Dialoghi *in the Context of his Time*, p. 203, in ed. Ahuva Belkin, *Leone de' Sommi and the Performing Arts* (Tel Aviv: Tel Aviv University, 1997), pp. 189–209. Translated from P. Fabbri and A. Pompilio (eds.) *Il Corago o vero alcune osservazioni per metter bene in scena le composizioni drammatiche* (Firenze: Olschki, 1983), p. 30.
[60] Discussed pp. 24–5.

theatrical company to do this, not because he cared about the sumptuary laws, but quite clearly out of anxiety about the resultant wear and tear on his rich and valuable costumes.

This kind of interchangeability persists in the modern theatre, and not only with respect to stage garments. When a particular production has come to an end, things like chairs and tables, unless put into store with an eye to some later theatrical use, are likely (if not destroyed) to be randomly distributed and find themselves pressed into service in the 'real' world. That must always have been true. Carefully fabricated property trees, equipped with artificial foliage and (in some cases) hinged doors to admit or release a prisoner are a different matter. Obvious imitations of natural living things that were familiar enough, but themselves impossible actually to uproot and bring on stage, let alone keep verdantly in leaf, artificial trees (unlike beds and thrones, costumes and torches) could not really exist outside the theatre. The destructive plundering of Henry VIII's 'Forrest Salvigne' (and, later, of the sets for some Inigo Jones masques) after the performance ended suggests a temporary desire for some souvenir or trophy. But no one was likely to bear off a stage tree and try to plant it in a garden. However solid and beautifully crafted, these were palpable frauds, sterile imitations of a thing human beings had not created. (As one rather bad twentieth-century poet put it: 'Only God can make a tree'.)[61]

That almost certainly is why, in *Staged Properties in Early Modern English Drama*, a collection of essays published in 2002,[62] all sixteen of the contributors, although referring frequently to Henslowe's inventory of 1598 (which is printed in the back of the book as an appendix) unanimously shy away from the tree of Tantalus and tree of golden apples that confront them there. This is an avowedly cultural materialist volume, concerned (as its Introduction states) to correct what it sees as the old hierarchy privileging 'the aesthetic over the economic, the textual over the theatrical, the ineffable over the material, the human over the mechanical, the subject over the object'.[63] It is primarily interested in what the Introduction calls 'alternate social dramas of economic exchange, production and ownership',[64] which is why the essays concentrate on furniture, including beds, chairs and tables, on rings and other jewellery, goblets and cups,

---

[61] Joyce Kilmer, *Trees*, as quoted in ed. Bernard Darwin, *The Oxford Dictionary of Quotations*, 2nd edition (London: Oxford University Press, 1953), p. 292.
[62] Jonathan Gil Harris and Natasha Korda (eds.), *Staged Properties in Early Modern English Drama*, (Cambridge: Cambridge University Press, 2002).
[63] Ibid., p. 7.   [64] Ibid., p. 15.

household plate and (of course) items of clothing, an interest extending to handkerchiefs and even the false stage beards required (especially, but not invariably, given the obsession in the period with facial hair as a guarantee of masculinity) by the children's companies.[65] All were commodities which could and did circulate, sometimes dizzyingly, between the tiring house (or Henslowe's pawn-broker's shop) and the world outside. Artificial trees did not; they were theatre properties of a different and less adaptable kind. And they were likely to demand from audiences a greater and more exacting imaginative effort.

Clearly there is a difference here between one sizable property tree (or two, as in the van der Venne engraving) and the idea of encumbering the stage (and the actors) with a dense forest. An entire woodland region could, however, be suggested by way of a single, large tree. One has only to look at Lyly's *Galatea* of 1585. Probably Lyly's best comedy (certainly the one that most influenced Shakespeare and, later, Ben Jonson), it requires what is described as a 'fair oak', obviously situated at the back of the playing space.[66] This tree acts as a liminal object, and as the fixed centre of a diverse panorama of woods, fields, village houses and the sea, all invisibly orientated around it. In some scenes, the tree defines the entrance to woods in which the goddess Diana habitually hunts and fairies live. In others, it marks their outer limits as perceived from within. Large, leafy and present throughout, it guides the imagination of the audience in realizing the topography of the comedy as a whole, a topography known first-hand by the dramatist himself. Lyly may have had in the back of his mind the traditional layout of Roman comedy – a visible street of houses leading on one side towards an implied marketplace, or else the country, and on the other, to the sea. If so, he transformed it imaginatively, relying upon his stage tree to organize a pastoral setting considerably more complicated, and also unmistakably English. While the vast preponderance of woodland scenes in plays of the period are located vaguely in Arcadia or Thessaly, Sicily, Flanders, Italy or Spain, specific references in the text of *Galatea* establish this place as the edge of a wood on the Lincolnshire side of the Humber estuary. A landscape radically changed in the seventeenth century, when Cornelius Vermuyden drained it, it can be reconstituted now from early maps – and Lyly's play.

[65] Hunter, *John Lyly: The Humanist as Courtier*, p. 111; see also the essay by Will Fisher, 'Staging the Beard: Masculinity in Early Modern English Culture', in eds. Harris and Korda, *Staged Properties*, pp. 230–57.

[66] John Lyly, *Galatea*, ed. George K. Hunter; *Midas*, ed. David Bevington (The Revels Plays) (Manchester: Manchester University Press, 2000), 1.1.2.

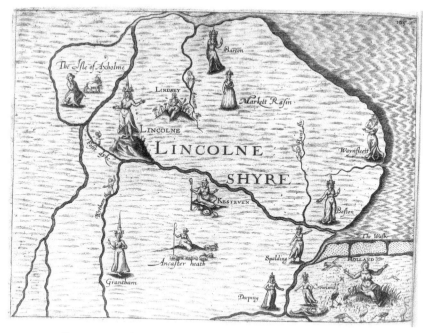

Figure 5. Lincolnshire, from Michael Drayton, *Poly-Olbion* (1612)

In 1583, Lyly had married Beatrice Browne, an heiress from Mexborough, a small town in the region. In his setting for *Galatea*, he was thinking, probably, of the isle of Axholme, ringed by the Humber and the rivers Idle, Trent and Don, and of Hatfield Chase, a royal demesne adjacent to it which could still in 1609 provide Prince Henry, who hunted there during his progress to York, with both vert and red deer stags in abundance. Until Vermuyden (to the outrage of the inhabitants) forcibly converted what had been a prospering pastoral economy into an arable one, Axholme and Hatfield retained vestiges of their ancient woods, with villages scattered through them, where the play's shipwrecked servants Rafe and Robin manage to find employment with a seedy rural alchemist, an astrologer and a fortune teller. Lyly was clearly acquainted with this landscape: not only its groves and game, villages, and grazing for sheep, but with the tidal bore in the Humber estuary (the *oegre*) that he transformed into a devouring sea-monster, the Agar of the comedy. 'In times past', Tityrus tells his daughter Galatea, 'where thou seest a heap of small pebble stood a stately temple of white marble which was dedicated to the God of the Sea'.[67] Danish invaders destroyed it, arousing Neptune's wrath. Fragments of a Roman temple, or at least the memory of one, were conceivably still present for Lyly; certainly there had been considerable Roman settlements here, subsequently overrun by the Danes. Rafe's sly allusion ('Come, let us to the woods and see what fortune we may have before they be made ships') points shrewdly as well to the general felling of timber in Lyly's time, in the interests of Elizabeth's burgeoning navy.[68]

The influence of *Galatea* upon Shakespeare's *A Midsummer Night's Dream* and *As You Like It* has long been recognized.[69] But Ben Jonson's *The Sad Shepherd*, the pastoral left unfinished at the time of his death in 1637, bears an even stronger impress of Lyly's wood-pasture play, although here again it was extensively re-thought. Like *Galatea*, Jonson's comedy is rooted in a particular English locale, in this case part of that Nottingham/ Leicestershire area through which the dramatist had walked in 1618 on his way to Scotland. Jonson's initial, and unusually elaborate, scene heading spells out the setting as a whole: '*The scene is Sherwood: consisting of a landscape of forest, hills, valleys, cottages, a castle, a river, pastures, herds, flocks, all full of country simplicity. Robin Hood's bower, his well; the witch's dimble, the swineherd's oak, the hermit's cell*'.[70] The 'castle' here must be Nottingham's; the 'river' is established in the play as the Trent, and the pastures, with their herds and flocks, are those through which Trent and its tributaries flow. References within the text itself to the nearby Vale of Belvoir, and to the village of Papplewick (seven miles north of Nottingham), home of the witch Maudlin and her brood, and to 'the drownèd lands of Lincolnshire' (2.8.26) in the distance, further define the region. Robin Hood's 'well', near Nottingham, was frequently shown in the sixteenth and seventeenth centuries to travellers such as Jonson. As for 'the ruins of a shaken abbey', said to be close by the witch's 'gloomy dimble ... o'ergrown with brakes and briars' (2.8.15–17), these must

---

[67] Ibid., 1.1.15–7.   [68] Ibid., 1.4.73–5, 74-5n.

[69] On *Midsummer Night's Dream*, see Leah Scragg, 'Shakespeare, Lyly and Ovid: the Influence of *Gallathea* on *A Midsummer Night's Dream*', *Shakespeare Survey*, 30 (Cambridge, 1977), 125–34. In addition, see the Introduction to *Midsummer Night's Dream*, ed. Peter Holland (Oxford: Oxford University Press, 1994), pp. 30, 100–1; the influence of others of Lyly's works is noted throughout the Introduction. Holland points out the close parallel between the Fairy's speech to Puck (2.1.1–58) and Cupid's in *Galatea* 1.2. For *As You Like It*, see the introductions to the play by Michael Hattaway (Cambridge: Cambridge University Press, 2000), pp. 8, 13–4 and Juliet Dusinberre (Arden Third Series) (London: Thomson Learning, 2006), pp. 10–11, 42, 346. Both editors point out that the Epilogue to *Galatea* is the only other such (perhaps) spoken by a 'girl'.

[70] Ben Jonson, *The Sad Shepherd*, ed. Anne Barton and Eugene Giddens, *The Cambridge Edition of the Works of Ben Jonson* (Cambridge: Cambridge University Press, 2012), vol. VII, p. 426. A 'dimble' is a deep, shady hollow.

be those of Byron's Newstead, which is near Papplewick and its 'glen', and indeed suffered from earthquakes, as well as from the attentions of Henry VIII.[71]

The forest 'landscape' with 'huntings' which introduced *The Masque of Blackness*,[72] early in James' reign, had been painted on a front curtain immediately dropped to discover tritons, sea-nymphs and finally the noble masquers moving forward in their great concave shell across a billowing, artificial sea. The far more various 'landscape' of *The Sad Shepherd* must have been intended for either a back-shutter, or (more likely) the fixed back-cloth, of a proscenium stage, presumably at court. Jonson would almost certainly at this date have expected side wings to represent the trees of Sherwood Forest, within whose wooded bounds all of the play unfolds, wings conducting the eye towards that distant 'landscape' of the whole region. But the staging suggested has further ramifications. When the swineherd Lorel, Maudlin's oafish son, boasts that an

agèd oak, the king of all the field,
With a broad beech there grows afore my dur [door],
That mickle mast [many beech nuts] unto the ferm [farm] doth yield.
A chestnut, whilk hath larded [fattened] mony a swine,
Whose skins I wear, to fend me fra the cold;
A poplar green, and with a kervèd [carved] seat,
Under whose shade I solace in the heat,
And thence can see gaing out and in my neat   (2.2.20–7)

there is no reason to suppose that Jonson meant his audience to pick out Lorel's chestnut, beech and poplar on the stage wings, or anywhere else in this perspective set. They could be imagined. The aged oak, specifically mentioned in the heading, was another matter. Like Lyly's aspen in *Endymion*, or the trees in *Love's Metamorphosis* and Percy's *Forrest of Elves*, this oak must have been three-dimensional and free-standing. In Act 2, Lorel opens it on stage, temporarily freeing the lost shepherdess Earine, then returns her, when she continues to spurn his love-suit, to her arboreal prison. The Argument for the unfinished third act makes it plain that Jonson intended Earine later to sing and to extend an imploring hand

---

[71] Newstead Abbey is 12 miles north of Nottingham, near Mansfield. Originally founded by Henry II as an Augustinian Priory c. 1170, it was never, in fact, an abbey, being an institution of canons rather than monks. It was suppressed as part of the Dissolution of the Monasteries by Henry VIII in 1539 and granted to Sir John Byron in 1540. Byron the poet was his (indirect) descendant. Jonson might be alluding to the earthquake of 26 February 1575, which seems to have been centred on the Derby/Staffordshire area, but there were other notable earthquakes in 1580, 1597, 1601, 1602, 1608 and 1622, the latter two mostly affecting Scotland.

[72] See Chapter 2, p. 25.

from inside the tree.[73] This, on such a Caroline set, would probably be managed by way of a 'relieve': a three-dimensional cut-out disclosed when required between the shutter and the back-cloth. An expedient marrying the old structural 'mansions' of the late mediaeval and early Tudor stage (and of *Lord Hay's Masque*) with advanced Serlian perspectivism, it was presumably also used to realize Robin Hood's 'bower', his 'well', the 'witch's dimble' and the 'hermit's cell', all of which Jonson is unlikely to have wanted on stage simultaneously.

The text and implied staging of *The Sad Shepherd*, interesting in themselves, also spell out with unusual clarity certain preconceptions about 'forest' settings, now almost forgotten, that were current in the period as a whole. They bear upon many other sixteenth- and early seventeenth-century plays. English forests of the wooded kind (the term 'forest' was, of course, also applied to stretches of open heath or moorland, although almost never in drama) tended far more than their equivalents on the continent to contain villages (such as Papplewick) or even towns within their limits.[74] They also embraced 'launds', 'assarts', glades and other open spaces in which not only sheep but Lorel's dairy cows (his 'neat') might profitably be pastured.[75] Pigs too were turned loose among the trees to rootle for acorns or beech mast. Such woods are, superficially at least, 'domesticated', far different from the trackless black wilderness of America, or of the great European forests. Sherwood, even in the thirteenth century, could easily have been mapped, and human settlements were never far away. Jonson's Robin Hood strolls casually out into the Vale of Belvoir to invite shepherd guests to a woodland feast; even his archetype in the ballads and old plays seems to have been as familiar with Nottingham and Mansfield as the greenwood that sheltered him. Not only justifiably nervous travellers, but local millers, potters and friars frequently come his way. Yet, as Elizabethan, Jacobean and Caroline dramatists recognized (long before Thoreau), it is always dangerous to underestimate the numinous power, and the wildness, of even a small and apparently tractable expanse of woods. That can be true even if you know, or think you know, them well.

* * *

[73] Jonson, *The Sad Shepherd*, p. 473.
[74] On villages in the forest of Arden, see Chapter 1, p. 8, and on villages in other early modern plays, see Chapter 5 *passim*, especially pp. 102–5.
[75] 'Laund' tended to refer to untilled open spaces used for pasture within woodland; 'assarts' were cleared for arable use.

Even without any apparent impetus from a single tree property of the kind demanded by *Galatea*, spectators in the period seem to have been inclined to raise up stage forests in their minds whenever they seemed appropriate. In the spring of 1611, the astrologer Simon Forman jotted down in his notebook what he chose to remember from performances of *Macbeth*, *Cymbeline* and *The Winter's Tale* he had attended at the Globe, recording the narrative sequence of events in these plays with what Andrew Gurr has described as 'nearly complete accuracy'.[76] Yet Forman apparently thought he saw 'Mackbeth & Bancko 2 noble men of Scotland Riding thorowe a wod' at the beginning of the tragedy, in which place they were accosted by '3 women feiries or Nimphes'.[77] Apart from the fact that the two actors cannot actually have been on horses, it seems odd initially that Forman's imagination should insist on turning Shakespeare's specific 'heath' (1.2.6) or 'blasted heath' (1.3.77) into a wood, a place of trees, and his witches into 'women feiries or Nimphes', creatures usually associated with woodland. He does something like this again when reporting *Cymbeline* and *The Winter's Tale*. Although Shakespeare never says that Belarius' cave near Milford Haven is in a wood, that is how Forman twice records it: 'a Cave in the wodes', near which the supposedly dead Fidele is later 'laid ... in the wodes'.[78] Again, with no explicit guidance from what he had heard spoken, he believed he witnessed Perdita, in *The Winter's Tale*, 'carried into bohemia & ther laid in a forrest & brought up by a sheppard'.[79]

These woodland or forest suggestions, particularly striking because Forman's memoranda are otherwise so stripped and laconic, have led some scholars to argue that stage trees must have been introduced at the Globe for the scenes in question. This seems unlikely. Unlike Herne's Oak in *The Merry Wives of Windsor*, or the plane tree in *The Fawne*, or the trees in *Endymion*, *Galatea* and *Love's Metamorphosis*, they could serve no useful theatrical function and would indeed have been an encumbrance. Forman's trees, like his horses, seem to have been generated by a complex of associations and pre-suppositions. In the case of *Macbeth*, it seems likely that he unconsciously superimposed upon what he actually saw at the Globe his memory of Holinshed's *Chronicle*. There, Macbeth and Banquo

---

[76] Andrew Gurr, *Playgoing in Shakespeare's London*, 3rd edition (Cambridge: Cambridge University Press, 1987), p. 134.

[77] Ashmolean MS 208, as quoted in Kenneth Muir (ed.), *Macbeth* (London: Methuen & Co. Ltd., 1962), p. xiii.

[78] Ashmolean MS 208 as quoted in J. M. Nosworthy (ed.), *Cymbeline* (London: Methuen & Co. Ltd., 1955), p. xv.

[79] Ashmolean MS 208 as quoted in F. W. Moorman (ed.), *The Winter's Tale* (London: Methuen & Co. Ltd., 1922), p. x.

do ride 'thorough the woods', and 'in the middest of a laund' (a clearing or glade among trees) encounter 'three women in strange and wild apparell' whom they take to be either 'the weird sisters . . . or else some nymphs or feiries, indued with knowledge of prophecy'.[80] Although both Boccaccio in *The Decameron* and the anonymous author of *Frederyke of Jennen* (who between them provided Shakespeare with most of his source material for *Cymbeline*) mention, in the first instance, 'a deepe solitary valey, very thickly beset with high and huge spreading Trees'[81] and, in the second, a 'wod' outside the town as 'a convenient place' for the heroine's murder,[82] there is no real need to assume the influence on Forman of either text. The conviction that woods are just the place to entrain and rape or murder an unsuspecting young woman is, as a convention in English literature, at least as old as Malory's story about the sylvan misadventure of Brangwayne, 'mayden and lady unto La Beale Isode'.[83] It persists, moreover, in real life, television announcements nowadays that police are searching 'nearby woodland' in relation to the unexplained disappearance of some unfortunate being virtually formulaic. Edna O'Brien's novel *In the Forest* (2002), about the murder of a woman and her child in a thick wood inhabited by a man who liked to call himself 'the fox', is based on events that actually (and appallingly) occurred in Ireland in 1994.[84]

An appropriately wooded Welsh landscape somewhere on the way to Milford Haven had already been suggested to Forman by way of reference to Belarius' 'cave', the princes' pursuit of venison in the mountains above, the sound of hunting horns, and the strong likelihood that all three men were attired, like the foresters of the 'Forrest Salvigne', in traditional (and camouflaging) green. Imogen's tell-tale surrender of herself to Pisanio in the very next scene as 'th'elected deer before thee' (3.4.109), and her shuddering reaction to what she calls 'this place' (3.4.103) to which he has decoyed her, could only have confirmed Forman's woodland impression. As for *The Winter's Tale*, Forman's imagination would have received no prompting from Greene's *Pandosto*, Shakespeare's source, even if he knew that prose romance. There is no savage and hunted bear in Greene, and no Antigonus figure to bring the abandoned infant to shores he identifies as 'the deserts of Bohemia' (3.3.2). A combination of

---

[80] Geoffrey Bullough, *Narrative and Dramatic Sources of Shakespeare*, 8 vols. (London: Routledge & Kegan Paul, 1975), vol. VII, pp. 494–5.
[81] Ibid., vol. VIII, p. 56.   [82] Ibid., pp. 70–1.
[83] Eugène Vinaver (ed.), *The Works of Sir Thomas Malory*, 3rd edition, 3 vols. (Oxford: Clarendon Press, 1990), vol. I, p. 419.
[84] Edna O'Brien, *In the Forest*, 2nd edition (London: Phoenix, 2003).

Shakespeare's bear-hunt and that very significant word 'deserts', places remote, sparsely inhabited and almost by definition wooded, must for Forman have created it all.

* * *

In 1808, Samuel Taylor Coleridge jotted down what he called 'Desultory Remarks on the Stage, and the present state of the higher drama'. He was writing about a nineteenth-century theatre far more illusionist and better equipped than Shakespeare's, but the distinctions he was concerned to make bear nevertheless upon Forman's experience, and what must have been that of many of his contemporaries. A painter such as Claude Lorraine, Coleridge suggested, imitates a wooded landscape at sunset,

> (only) as a Picture . . . while [in the theatre] a Forest-scene is not presented to the Audience as a Picture, but as a Forest: and tho' in the *full* sense of the word we are no more *deceived* by the one than by the other, yet are our feelings very differently affected, and the Pleasure derived from the one is not composed of the same Elements, as that afforded by the other – even on the supposition, that the *quantum* of Both were equal. In the former [that is, the Claude painting], it is a *condition* of all genuine delight that we should *not* be deluded . . . In the latter, (inasmuch as its principal End is not in or for itself, as <is the case> in a Picture, but to be an assistance and means of an End out of itself), its very purpose is to produce as much Illusion as its nature permits. These and all other Stage Presentations, are to produce a Sort of temporary Half-Faith, which the Spectator encourages in himself & supports by a voluntary contribution on his own part, because he knows that it is at all times in his power to see the thing as it really is.[85]

It is with that 'voluntary contribution', the subtly varied nature, in the early modern theatre, of Coleridge's 'Half-Faith' – something subtly different from the more famous willing 'suspension of disbelief' – that this book is largely concerned.

---

[85] Samuel Taylor Coleridge, *1808 Lectures on Principles of Poetry*, in ed. R. A. Foakes, *The Collected Works of Samuel Taylor Coleridge: Lectures 1808–1819 on Literature*, 2 vols. (London: Routledge & Kegan Paul Ltd., 1987), vol. I, pp. 133–4.

CHAPTER 3

The Wild Man in the Forest

The seventh square on the chessboard, the Red Queen tells Alice, 'is all forest. When Alice arrives on the outskirts of this forest in the looking glass world, she feels a little apprehensive; it seemed 'much darker than the last wood':

> 'Well, at any rate it's a great comfort', she said as she stepped under the trees, 'after being so hot, to get into the – into the – into *what?*' she went on, rather surprised at not being able to think of the word. 'I mean to get under the – under the – under *this*, you know!' putting her hand on the trunk of the tree. 'What *does* it call itself, I wonder? I do believe it's got no name – why, to be sure it hasn't!' ... And now, who am I? I *will* remember, if I can! I'm determined to do it!'[1]

She can't, however, because she has entered what the Gnat had already warned her was 'the wood ... where things have no names'.[2]

In Martin Gardner's *The Annotated Alice*, a marginal gloss identifies this wood as 'the universe itself, as it is apart from symbol-manipulating creatures who label portions of it because ... "it's useful to the people that name them" ... the world by itself contains no signs'.[3] But Lewis Carroll, whose own idiom was less semiotic, must also have been thinking of *nemus*, one of the classical Latin terms for a wood. *Nemus* is a word with complex associations: with *nemesis*, obviously, but also with *nemo* (no one) which is what individuals are all too likely to become when astray in a forest. It forms part of ancient woodland designations such as *locus neminis* (the place of no one), or *res nullius* (belonging to no one), the last being (in a sense) *res publica's* dark twin.[4] In Book 6 of the *Aeneid*,

---

[1] Lewis Carroll, *Through the Looking-Glass and What Alice Found There*, in ed. Martin Gardner, *The Annotated Alice* (Harmondsworth: Penguin, 1965), pp. 225–6.
[2] Ibid., p. 225.   [3] Ibid., p. 227.
[4] Robert Pogue Harrison, *Forests: The Shadow of Civilisation* (Chicago: University of Chicago Press, 1992), p. 49.

Virgil twice uses the generic noun *nemus* to describe the wood in which Aeneas plucks the Golden Bough, a wood flowing, almost without interruption, into the terrible forests around the Acheron, in the underworld, the place of non-being.[5]

There is, of course, another more common classical Latin word for 'forest': *silva*, a term far less negative than *nemus*. A feeling of human rapport with woodland underlies the given names 'Silvius' and 'Silvia', both of which had appeared in Virgil long before Shakespeare pressed them into service in *As You Like It* and *The Two Gentlemen of Verona*. *Sylvanus*, the ancient woodland god, is a benevolent deity, or he was before his reincarnation, thinly disguised as the vengeful Selver, in *The Word for World Is Forest*, Ursula le Guin's angry novel about the Vietnam War.[6] *Sylvan*, the adjective English derives from *silva*, has characteristically been associated, ever since it appeared (together with classical fauns and satyrs) in the sixteenth century, with a pastoral tradition more soft than hard. Nothing, however, is ever simple about forests, or about the names people choose to call them by.

There is one other woodland designation from the ancient world that deserves attention. *Hyle*, the classical Greek word for 'forest', could also mean Chaos: primordial matter, shapeless, and with only the potential of forms. Aristotle, among others, uses it in this way. And, in the fourth century AD, *hyle* behaved rather as forest fires do; it leaped, by way of Chalcidius and Servius' influential commentary on Virgil, across an intervening empty space to merge with *silva*. 'That which the Greeks call *hyle*', Servius wrote, glossing a passage from Book 1 of the *Aeneid*, 'the poets name *silva*, that is the chaos of the elements, whence all things are created'.[7] Once made, the connection was there to stay, informing Renaissance allegories like the one Marsilio Ficino offered of the Judgement of Paris in the woods of Mt Ida: 'Paris, the son of an eastern king, pastures his flock in a wood: that is, the soul created by God delights with the senses in the material confusion of the elements'.[8] It is a way of thinking not unrelated to the way forests appear in Elizabethan and Stuart literature, and more particularly in drama.

[5] Virgil, *Aeneid*, in ed. and trans. H. R. Fairclough, *Virgil* (London: Heinemann, 1935), 4.238, p. 386.

[6] Ursula le Guin, *The Word for World is Forest*, 2nd edition (London: Gollancz, 1977).

[7] Quoted by Corinne J. Saunders, *The Forest of Medieval Romance* (Cambridge: D. S. Brewer, 1993), p. 21.

[8] From Ficino's second commentary on Plato's *Philebus*, quoted (and translated) by Richard Cody in *The Landscape of the Mind: Pastoralism and Platonic Theory in Tasso's 'Aminta' and Shakespeare's Early Comedies* (Oxford: Clarendon Press, 1969), p. 7.

Nulli penetrabilis. 182

A SHADIE Wood, pourtraicted to the sight,
With vncouth pathes, and hidden waies vnknowne:
Resembling *CHAOS*, or the hideous night,
Or those sad Groues, by banke of *ACHERON*
With banefull *Ewe*, and *Ebon* overgrowne:
  Whose thickest boughes, and inmost entries are
  Not peirceable, to power of any starre.

Thy Imprese *SILVIVS*, late I did devise,
To warne the what (if not) thou oughtst to be,
Thus inward close, vnsearch'd with outward eies,
With thousand angles, light should never see:
For fooles that most are open-hearted free,
  Vnto the world, their weakenes doe bewray,
  And to the net, the first themselues betray.

Cc1· Vnum

Figure 6. Henry Peacham, 'Silvius', from *Minerva Britanna* (1612)

Henry Peacham's emblem book *Minerva Britanna, or A Garden of Heroicall Devises*, was published in 1612. In devising an impresa for the appropriately named 'Silvius', Peacham counselled him, in effect, to realize the implications of his name. Under the Latin heading *Nulli penetrabilis* ('penetrable by no one'), a wood lies beneath stars and a crescent moon:

> A shadie Wood, pourtraicted to the sight,
> With uncouth pathes, and hidden waies unknowne:
> Resembling CHAOS, or the hideous night,
> Of those sad Groves, by banke of ACHERON
> With banefull *Ewe*, and *Ebon* overgrowne:
> Whose thickest boughes, and inmost entries are
> Not peirceable, to power of any starre.

> Thy Imprese SILVIUS, late I did devise,
> To warne the what (if not) thou oughtst to be,
> Thus inward close, unsearch'd with outward eies,
> With thousand angles, light should never see:
> For fooles that most are open-hearted free,
> Unto the world, their weakenes doe bewray,
> And to the net, the first themselves betray.[9]

Peacham's forest is Chaos, a classical region of hellish gloom, but it is also something more specifically Renaissance: a psychological place, the emblem of a mind that prudently hides its thoughts in darkness, allowing access to none. The forest image here is really double; it epitomizes what Silvius ought to be, but it also suggests that a world which makes such secretiveness necessary must itself be chaotic, a wood full of predators and entangling nets. Not by accident has one line of Peacham's poem – 'Not peirceable, to power of any starre' – been lifted directly from Book 1 of Spenser's *Faerie Queene*,[10] a poem whose entire world seems at times to consist of one vast, dangerous and complexly allegorized forest, a forest harbouring isolated great houses and the odd hermitage or hovel in its depths, occasional cleared spaces or a glimpse of the sea, but no sign of a village, let alone any earthly city or even town. In Dürer's famous, and very Spenserian, engraving of 1513, 'The Knight, Death and the Devil', the knight, riding fully armed through a waste forest, with a fortified castle in

[9] Henry Peacham, *Minerva Britanna or a Garden of Heroicall Devices, Furnished, and Adorned with Emblemes and Impresa's of Sundry Natures, Newly Devised, Moralised, and Published* (1612), facs. reprint (Amsterdam, 1971), p. 182.
[10] Edmund Spenser, *The Faerie Queene*, ed. Thomas P. Roche (London: Yale University Press, 1978), Book I, Canto i, stanza 7, line 6, p. 42.

Figure 7. Albrecht Dürer, *The Knight, Death, and the Devil* (1513)

the distance, pays no attention whatever to the two unwanted and hideous companions at his side – any more than Spenser's Guyon in Book 2 turns to look at the fiend following at his heels.[11] The inspiration behind Dürer's

---

[11] Ibid., Book II Canto vii, stanzas 26–7, 64, and *passim*, pp. 286, 296.

grim but steadfast hero was probably Erasmus' little book on the 'Christian Soldier'.[12] Certainly there is no mistaking just who and what his adversaries are.

* * *

There are leaf-masks of various kinds – if none quite so powerful and disturbing – scattered over most of Europe and also England.[13] Although by no means unknown in the classical world, it was as a somewhat dubious decorative motif in mediaeval churches and cathedrals that they really came into their own. Some register as lively imaginings about the sentient life of windblown leaves; others are haunted and sombre spirits, or even suggest vegetation springing from a face almost dead: the endless cycle of regeneration and decay. They may even be outrageously mocking. All, however, are reminders that forests are places of transformation, where the boundary between human life and that of animals, plants or trees is likely to become confused, and may even be obliterated. A large number of the metamorphoses recounted by Ovid – people turning into springs, rivers, flowers, beasts or trees – take place in forests. Significantly, in the wood where things have no names, Alice and the Fawn she encounters there converse as though they belonged to the same species; only when they reach the other side does the Fawn recognize that 'I'm a Fawn!' and then, with alarm, just before it flees, 'And dear me! you're a human child!'[14]

Leaf-masks are as haunting as they are because of their indeterminacy. They have a kind of dramatic embodiment. The specifically English 'Jack-in-the-Green', who processed inside a wickerwork frame smothered in leaves, is now thought to be urban and eighteenth century in origin. The phenomenon of the green man, however, was far older, and widespread: someone who came out of the forest on May morning wreathed around with leaves and branches through which human eyes and a mouth remained visible. (Shakespeare's audience may well have understood the walking wood in *Macbeth*, each of Malcolm's soldiers obscured behind a 'leafy screen' hewed from Birnam Wood, as we do not: the ritual bringing in of spring to a Scotland unnaturally arrested in winter by the usurper.)[15] It was not, however, the green man, but his more recognizably human

[12] Desiderius Erasmus, *Enchiridion militis christiani* (1515), translated into English as *The Manuell of the Christen Knight* and first printed by Wynkyn de Worde in 1533.
[13] See Kathleen Basford, *The Green Man* (Ipswich: Brewer, 1978), *passim*, and William Anderson, *Green Man: The Archetype of Our Oneness with the Earth* (London: Harper Collins, 1990).
[14] Carroll, *Through the Looking-Glass*, p. 227.
[15] See the discussion of *Macbeth* in Chapter 2, p. 45, and Chapter 6, pp. 136–7.

Figure 8. Hans Burgmair, *The Fight in the Forest* (c. 1503)

cousin, the wodewose, or wild man, who had a real future in drama. The literature on wild men is enormous, and very tangled. As Robert Withington writes, in his book *English Pageantry*, 'The relation between wild-men, green men, foresters, Robin Hood, the Moors and the devil is very difficult to clear up.'[16] To which list, one might add hairy anchorites, fauns and satyrs, Silenus, Faunus, Pan, cannibals and outlaws in general.

A few generalizations, however, can be risked. Although the wild man occasionally has a wild woman as companion, he is more often solitary. He lives in the forest (in the Eastern tradition, the desert) and his characteristic weapon is a club, sometimes in the crude form of an uprooted tree. He is hairy almost all over, sometimes naked, but often covered with moss, ivy or animal skins, less frequently with feathers or scales. He can be enormous, like the one engaged in distinctly unequal combat with a knight. (The latter's outlook, judging from the number of previous victims littering the forest floor, is not good, despite his two-handed sword.) Or he may be of

---

[16] Robert Withington, *English Pageantry: An Historical Outline*, 2 vols. (Cambridge, MA: Harvard University Press, 1918), vol. I, p. 74.

Figure 9. Alexander the Great burning a wild man, from *Le livre et la vraye histoire du bon roy Alixandre*. (The attempted rape (left) and its punishment (right) are depicted simultaneously.)

ordinary size. Some of his kind, like the Salvage Man in Spenser,[17] despite having no language but grunts and growls, display a courteous respect for women they encounter that even Robin Hood might admire. Others, like Shakespeare's Caliban, or like the wild man in Figure 9, are uncontrollably lecherous. (He is summarily being burned alive, on the right, by Alexander the Great after trying to rape the naked lady in the foreground.) But with all of them, the most important question, not that it can always be answered, is: why and how did they come to live as they do, and is the condition permanent, or merely temporary?

Temporary, certainly, in the case of Nebuchadnezzar, punished by God for pride in the Book of Daniel, by being driven from men to 'eat grass as oxen', his body 'wet with the dew of heaven, till his hairs were grown like eagles' feathers, and his nails like birds' claws'.[18] But there grew up in both East and West a tradition of holy wild men, saints and anchorites who withdrew permanently to the desert or the forest to live a solitary life of contemplation and prayer. It isn't always easy to tell these apart from their unregenerate secular counterparts, not least when they are covered with hair, like St Mary of Egypt (sometimes conflated with the penitent St Mary

[17] Spenser, *Faerie Queene*, Book VI Canto iv, stanza 2f., p. 916f.
[18] Daniel 4.25, 32–3 (Authorised Version).

Magdalene).[19] In *Landscape and Memory*, Simon Schama (building on the work of Larry Silver) has argued that it was only at the end of the fifteenth century, after the re-discovery of Tacitus' *Germania*, that 'wild men were made over into exemplars of the virtuous and natural life', sometimes depicted 'diligently tending to flocks', or 'tilling fields'.[20]

Sexual jealousy, or at least a serious misunderstanding between lovers, was responsible for a number of mediaeval and Renaissance wild men: Lancelot, Chrétien de Troyes' Yvain or Ariosto's Orlando. This kind of wild man usually recovers his equilibrium after a brief spell of savagery, abandons the forest and re-enters society. It is harder for those born wild, whether it happened by accident, or because the wilderness mysteriously spawns such creatures. In the latter category, Lust personified, Spenser's cannibalistic wild man in Book 4 of *The Faerie Queene*,[21] clearly can never be civilized, nor can the monstrous herdsman of wild animals who haunts the forest of Brocéliande, in *Yvain*.[22] Accident, on the other hand, was responsible for the predicament of Spenser's Salvage Man, as it was for that of Orson in the mediaeval romance *Valentine and Orson* – when Orson's mother gave birth to twins in a forest, Orson got lost and was brought up by a bear – as it is of Caliban, the 'salvage and deformed slave'[23] of *The Tempest*. Left alone, at an early age, on a deserted island after the death of his mother Sycorax, Caliban (like Orson and Spenser's Salvage Man) grew up with no opportunity to learn human speech. The Salvage Man is clearly marked out for eventual reunion with aristocratic parents; Orson fortuitously meets and is civilized by his twin. The future of Caliban, taught language by later colonists, and not liking it much, is anyone's guess.

There is also the case of Merlin Silvestris. This Merlin, a prince crazed with grief after witnessing the fearful carnage of the historical battle of Arderydd, re-treats into the woods. There, he lives as a wild man, accepted by wolves and other non-human denizens of the forest, contented enough in summer, but suffering pitiably in the winter cold. Music eventually cures his madness, and he returns to court, only to find life there intolerable. Once again he flees into the Forest of Calidon, this time for good, although under somewhat more comfortable circumstances: not as a wild

[19] See Marina Warner, *Alone of All Her Sex: The Myth and Cult of the Virgin Mary* (London: Vintage, 2000), pp. 232–4.
[20] Simon Schama, *Landscape and Memory* (London: Harper Collins, 1995), p. 97.
[21] Spenser, *Faerie Queene*, Book IV, Canto vii, stanzas 5f, p. 645.
[22] Chrétien de Troyes, *Arthurian Romances*, trans. William W. Kibler (London: Penguin, 1991), pp. 298, 303, 304. For Yvain's madness in the forest, see p. 330.
[23] As in the 'Names of the Actors', included in the 1623 Folio.

man, but a pious hermit, with a house and visitors. Merlin Silvestris, the subject of Geoffrey of Monmouth's twelfth-century *Vita Merlini*, was still very much alive in Shakespeare's time, but long before then, his story had become curiously entangled with that of a related but different Merlin, the son of an incubus, who went on to become prophet and counsellor to King Arthur and was also celebrated by Geoffrey of Monmouth in his *Historia Regum Britanniae*.[24] *The Birth of Merlin*, a Jacobean play attributed to Shakespeare and William Rowley when it was first published in 1662, is largely about this second Merlin, but it not only locates his demonic birth in a forest, but insists on calling him (rather confusingly) 'Merlin Silvestris'.[25]

* * *

Wild man plays and shows, of various kinds, date back at least to the early thirteenth century. Some, like the one depicted here in a sixteenth-century print derived from Brueghel's painting, 'The Combat of Carnival and Lent', are part of a rich popular tradition. Like his original, this Wild Man, a peculiarly scaly example of the type, is in deep trouble. His club, although fearsomely spiked, will clearly be useless against the crossbow about to be fired at him. The emperor himself, moreover, who stands with crown and sceptre on the left, is sanctioning the execution. Especially problematic is the figure of the woman at the right, who holds out to the Wild Man a ring that in this version he doesn't see. (In the painting, where the wodewose is mossy rather than scaly, the victim does see it, and the woman seems to be acting as a lure.) Here, the situation is more ambiguous. Does the ring symbolize marriage, one of those social bonds the wild man must be punished for ignoring? And is he to die as a personification of Carnival, as it gives way to Lent? Or, in a neat inversion of the green man play, of winter vanquished by spring? What is clear is that, whether performed by amateur or, as here, by semi-professional actors (in the background, money is being collected from the audience), the hunting and death of the wild man was for centuries a subject of folk drama across most of Europe.

But the wild man also came to court. In England, he had arrived there at least as early as 1348, when twelve 'wodewose' heads were required for an

---

[24] Geoffrey of Monmouth, *Historia Regum Britanniae*, ed. Lewis Thorpe (Harmondsworth: Penguin, 1976).
[25] John Matthews, *Merlin: Shaman, Prophet Magician* (London: Mitchell Beazley, 2004), pp. 32–4. *The Birth of Merlin* is discussed in Chapter 6, pp. 136–7.

Figure 10. 'The Masquerade of Valentine and Orson' (1566), after Pieter Brueghel, *The Combat between Carnival and Lent*

entertainment to amuse Edward III.[26] In 1392, Charles VI of France and five of his courtiers got themselves up as wild men in close-fitting garments, rubbed with pitch, to which flax had been applied in tufts, like shaggy hair, with fatal results. The Duke of Orleans, eager to discover the identity of the masquers, and ignorant of the king's order that no one should come near with a torch, inadvertently set them ablaze. Charles himself escaped, partly because he was not chained together with the others, and so did one masquer who managed to immerse himself in a butt of dishwater, but the other four were burned alive. The disaster gave rise to a good deal of murmuring among the common people of Paris, to the effect that it was God's judgement, and that Charles ought 'to withdrawe hym selfe fro suche yonge ydell wantonnesse, whiche he had used overmoche beynge a kyng'.[27]

Royalty, however, was too fond of such 'wantonesse' to heed advice of the sort, or to allow the tragedy (news of which rapidly reached England) to

---

[26] See Robert Hillis Goldsmith, 'The Wildman on the English Stage', *Modern Language Review* 53 (1958), 481–91.

[27] Jean Froissart, *Of the Chronycles of Englande Fraunce Spayne Portyngale Scotland Bretayne Flaunders and Other Places Adjoynyge*, trans. Sir John Bourchier Lord Berners, 2 vols. (Oxford: Basil Blackwell, 1928), vol. II, part 3, p. 991.

blight or discourage other wodewose entertainments. Henry VIII spent Twelfth Night in 1515 watching 'eight wyldemen, all appareiled in grene mosse ... with Uggly weapons and terrible vysages' fight with eight knights, who at last drove them out of the hall.[28] In 1522, he entertained the emperor Charles V with a masque of foresters and 'woodwos'. With its three-dimensional representation, in little, of the castle in the depths of the forest common in mediaeval romance, Henry's pageant 'Forrest Salvigne' of 1511,[29] also anticipates both the landscapes of *The Faerie Queene* at the end of the century, and those that the authors of Elizabethan romance plays like the anonymous *Sir Clyomon and Sir Clamydes* of 1570, or *Common Conditions* (1576) were shortly going to be asking audiences to visualize on a predominantly bare stage. Those particular Westminster festivities also ended in disaster, though scarcely on the scale of the one in Paris eighteen years before. On the second day, King Henry, Queen Katherine, and the other noble participants all wore costumes on which their names had been embroidered in letters of massy gold. After the dancing ended, the king ordered these letters to be detached and given to the foreign Ambassadors and gentlewomen present,

> whiche thing the common people perceyuyng, ranne to the kyng, and striped hym into his hosen and doublet, and all his compaignions in likewise. Sir Thomas Kneuet stode on a stage, and for all his defence he lost his apparell. The ladies likewyse were spoyled, wherefore the kynges garde came sodenly, and put the people backe, or els as it was supposed more in conuenience had ensued.[30]

Amazingly, there appear to have been no casualties, and no reprisals. The King and Queen, with her ladies, retired to a banquet in a private chamber and decided to laugh off 'these hurtes', all that was taken away being 'but for honoure and larges'.[31] London goldsmiths fearlessly bought up the snatched letters. An entertainment that began with elaborately contrived mock wildness had ended, nevertheless, with something very like the real thing.

* * *

Wodewoses impressed into service at court, or in civic pageantry – they appear quite frequently from 1533 onwards in London Lord Mayors' shows,

---

[28] Edward Hall, *The Union of the Two Noble and Illustre Families of Lancastre and York* (London, 1550), 'The vj yere of Kyng Henry the Viij', fol. 55ᵛ (kɪᵛ).
[29] See pp. 21–4.   [30] Hall, *Lancastre and York*, 'The ii Yere of Kyng Henry the Viij', fol. 11 (b5).
[31] Ibid.

usually to frighten onlookers away from the path of the procession with their clubs – tend to be stalwart supporters of the establishment, an establishment whose merits their subservience both supports and confirms. In his classic study, *Wild Men in the Middle Ages*, Richard Bernheimer points out that by the fifteenth century, wild men often figured in family coats of arms, or as their heraldic guardians.[32]

Even royalty was pleased to accept wodewose servants, not only to support coats of arms, but when unexpectedly confronted by them in the flesh, in masques and shows. Robert Langham's enraptured description of the Earl of Leicester's estate at Kenilworth, as prepared for Queen Elizabeth's famous visit in July 1575, makes it sound like one of Henry VIII's more elaborate and costly pageants, except that here, the forest and the castle, the garden, rocks and animals were both real, and on an enormous scale. Predictably, there was a wild man. He emerged from the woods, covered in moss and ivy, to confront the Queen's party by torch-light as she returned late from hunting on the second day. Although perplexed as to why God should have condemned him 'in savage wise, / for evermore to be', he was able (with the help of a friendly Echo) to identify Elizabeth with little difficulty, shower her with praise, and tender humble service. Unfortunately, when he then (as Langham reports) 'for the more submission, brake hiz tree a sunder', the top of it narrowly missed the Queen's horse, which was probably used to wild men by now, but not to being assaulted by them. It shied, and nearly unseated her – an unscripted incident that George Gascoigne, who wrote the wild man's speeches, and also played the part – carefully left out of his printed version. According to Langham, Her Majesty graciously indicated that no damage had been done: 'No hurt, no hurt'.[33] That, however, may not have been all, or even the first thing, she said.

There is something oddly disingenuous about Gascoigne's explanation in *The Princely Pleasures at Kenelworth* as to why a later 'shew to have bene presented before hyr majestie in the Forest' was not, in fact, performed: 'the cause whereof I cannot attribute to any other thing, then to lack of opportunitie and seasonable weather'.[34] In this show, which Gascoigne

---

[32] Richard Bernheimer, *Wild Men in the Middle Ages: A Study in Art, Sentiment, and Demonology* (Cambridge: Harvard University Press, 1952), pp. 177–85.

[33] *Robert Langham: A Letter*, in ed. R. J. Kuin, *Medieval and Renaissance Texts* (Leiden: E. J. Brill, 1983), p. 46.

[34] George Gascoigne, *The Princely Pleasures at Kenelworth Castle*, in ed. John W. Cunliffe, *The Complete Works of George Gascoigne*, Cambridge English Classics, 2 vols. (Cambridge: Cambridge University Press, 1910), vol. II, pp. 96, 106–7, 120.

insisted on printing, the goddess Diana and her train come to Kenilworth in quest of a lost fellow-huntress, inevitably named 'Zabeta'. But it also includes an interlude, 'To Entertayne *Intervallum Temporis*', featuring Audax, the earlier wild man's mossy son, which looks very like a hastily introduced apology for the accident with the club. Audax was to have implored Elizabeth to cure his father of the blindness which suddenly overtook him 'uppon such wordes as hyr highnesse dyd then use unto hym'[35]: words which must have been considerably more irate than the regal recovery – 'No hurt, no hurt!' – which was all that Langham tactfully chose to remember. Elizabeth, however, had had enough.

In all the outdoor shows for Elizabeth in which a wild man appears, not only Kenilworth but in the entertainments, possibly by John Lyly, at Cowdray in 1591, and Rycote in 1592, the mere sight of the Queen and her party suffices to civilize the wodewose. To complain that wild men ought not to be masters of stanzaic verse, or elegant Ciceronian prose, is to miss the point; the piquancy of the situation – and the compliment to the Queen – depends upon her presence suddenly enabling them to speak like this. Civil herself, Elizabeth is also the cause that civility is in others. Although visually still savage, smothered in ivy, moss or hair, inwardly her wild subjects have been tamed. In the public theatres, however, where there could be no recourse to the transforming presence of the Queen, reintegrating the wild man into society was likely to be more complicated. (When Ben Jonson instructed an actor to impersonate Elizabeth, in the final moments of *Every Man out of His Humour* in 1599, in order to humanize Macilente, there was an outcry, and the ending had to be dropped.)[36]

* * *

The last decade of Elizabeth's reign seems to have been the period of the wild man's greatest popularity on the public stage. Certainly, the Admiral's Men performed a *Nebuchadnezzar* in 1596, and there was at least one play – possibly two – at roughly the same time about Valentine, and Orson, his shaggy twin. These are lost, together with an indeterminate number of others for which not even titles have been preserved. What we do have (apart from the dumb show of wild men at the beginning of *Gorboduc* in

---

[35] Ibid., p. 107.
[36] Ben Jonson, *Every Man Out of His Humour*, ed. Randall Martin, *The Cambridge Edition of the Works of Ben Jonson* (Cambridge: Cambridge University Press, 2012), vol. I, pp. 235, 239–40, 243–4; 5.6.77SD, 78–117, 421–2.

1562) are *Mucedorus*, an anonymous comedy destined to be reprinted again and again by popular demand after its revival in 1610, and two romance plays by Robert Greene, *Orlando Furioso* and *James IV*, all of them from the early 1590s. Interesting in themselves, the last three also bear upon Shakespeare's *Timon of Athens*, a later and more important play.

Bremo, in *Mucedorus*, is a wild man who, 'like a king', in his own view of the situation, 'commandes within these woods': woods through which he wanders alone 'with restlesse rage', seeking for prey.[37] When first introduced, midway through Act 2, he is complaining because there are 'no passengers this morning' through the forest, 'a chance that seldom doth befall'.[38] The complaint parodies one familiar from mediaeval romance, and (more importantly) from the Robin Hood ballads. In the fifteenth-century *Gest of Robyn Hode*, Robin tells his men: 'To dyne have I no lust, / Till that I have som bolde baron, / Or some unketh [unknown] guest'.[39] Bremo, however, is a cannibal. Later, when he comes upon the princess Amadine, straying in search of Mucedorus, her shepherd lover, he proposes to have her for dinner in a sense considerably less sociable than Robin Hood's. Amadine's beauty, however, arouses other instincts, and soon he is promising, 'Thou shalt bee fed with quailes and partridges, / With blacke birds, larkes, thrushes and nightingales / . . . And all the dainties that the woods affords'.[40] He hopes to transform her into a wild woman mate. Amadine will have none of it, and yet Bremo (unlike Spenser's cannibal, Lust) never thinks of raping her. In the end, he is killed by a hermit, Mucedorus in disguise. Adding insult, moreover, to mortal injury, Mucedorus informs Bremo, before doing him in with his own club, that he is an anachronism. It was only 'in time of yore' that 'men like brutish beasts / Did lead their lives in loathsome celles and woodes'.[41] They don't do it now.

Bremo appears to belong to the category of those born wild. (We are not told how he learned human speech.) Greene's Orlando, on the other hand, like his original in Ariosto, extends the mediaeval tradition of knights such as Lancelot and Yvain, who tear off their clothes and rush into the forest because they have been crossed in love. In this play, however, the treachery

[37] *The Comedy of Mucedorus*, in ed. C. F. Tucker Brooke, *The Shakespeare Apocrypha: Being a Collection of Fourteen Plays Which Have Been Ascribed to Shakespeare* (Oxford: Clarendon Press, 1967), 2.3.7, p. 112.

[38] Ibid., 2.3.2, p. 112.

[39] R. B. Dobson and J. Taylor, *The Gest of Robyn Hode*, in *Rymes of Robyn Hood: An Introduction to the English Outlaw*, 2nd edition (Gloucester: Heinemann Ltd., 1989), First Fitte, stanza 6, p. 79.

[40] *Mucedorus*, 4.3.32–36, p. 120.   [41] Ibid., 4.3.72–3, p. 120.

of Angelica (real enough in Ariosto) is only apparent, permitting a reunion of the lovers in Act 5. What really interests Greene along the way are the savage pranks of Orlando as wild man. Muttering 'Woods, trees, leaves; leaves, trees, woods',[42] he maims or kills virtually everyone who crosses his path. ('Enter Orlando with a leg', one stage direction reads.) These atrocities are perpetrated, as they were not in Ariosto, almost entirely in a forest setting. In the Italian epic, the madman was finally cured by the knight Astolfo, who goes to Paradise and retrieves Orlando's wits, which he finds there, corked and neatly labelled, in a jar.[43] Greene's resolution is far more traditional. Like virtually all wild men, from Homer's Polyphemus to Shakespeare's Caliban, Orlando is easily overpowered by wine. The enchantress Melissa uses it to put him to sleep, after which music (as in the case of Merlin Silvestris), accompanied in Greene by a dance of woodland satyrs, restores his sanity.

Shakespeare must have known this play, probably in a version less corrupt than the one which has survived. But it was Greene's Scottish history of *James IV* that truly left its mark on him, and not just because of its cross-dressed heroine Dorothea, and the presence of Oberon, the fairy king. The play is in fact a major source for *Timon of Athens*, a work which seems to tap the wild man tradition in ways that have previously gone unrecognized. Bohan, in *James IV*, like Merlin Silvestris, has abandoned the world out of disgust. He once lived, as he tells Oberon, in the court, then exchanged it for the country, and subsequently for the city, only to find 'the court ill, the country worse, and the city worst of all'. In the last, he 'kept a great house', but 'in seeking friends, I found table guests to eate me and my meat'[44] (Shakespeare was surely remembering that line when he had Apemantus at the banquet in Act I observe 'what a number of men eats Timon, and he sees 'em not', 1.2.39–40). Now Bohan lives in his own tomb in the forest, 'where if I die I am sure I am safe from wild beasts; but whilst I live, cannot be free from ill company'.[45]

In none of the sources Bullough lists for Shakespeare's play – Plutarch's lives of Alcibiades and Marcus Antonius, and Lucian's *Dialogue of Timon* – nor in any of the possible analogues he mentions, does Timon go to live in

[42] Robert Greene, *The Historie of Orlando Furioso*, in ed. W. W. Greg, *Two Elizabethan Stage Abridgements: The Battle of Alcazar and Orlando Furioso*, The Malone Society (Oxford: Oxford University Press, 1922), lines 121–2, p. 154.

[43] John Harington, *Orlando Furioso in English Heroical Verse* (London, 1591), Canto 34, stanza 82, Bb3.

[44] Robert Greene, *The Scottish History of James the Fourth*, ed. Norman Sanders (London: Methuen, 1970), Induction, pp. 61, 64–5, 67–8.

[45] Ibid., pp. 71–2.

the woods after his ruin.[46] Plutarch's Timon never leaves Athens at all until he is about to die, when he goes to the city of Hales, in order to be buried by the sea. Lucian's tills the soil underneath Mt Hymettus, earning four *soldi* a day as a farm labourer. When Jove showers him with riches, he buys the land from his master and builds a tower above the treasure in which to live: a tower ultimately intended as his tomb. Painter, in *The Palace of Pleasure*, puts him 'alone in a little cabane in the fields not farre from Athens'.[47] Only Shakespeare makes Timon seek out the forest, and do so moreover quite specifically as a wild man:

> Nothing I'll bear from thee
> But nakedness, thou detestable town!
> Take thou that too, with multiplying bans!
> Timon will to the woods, where he shall find
> Th' unkindest beast more kinder than mankind.
> The gods confound (hear me, you good gods all)
> Th' Athenians both within and out that wall!   (4.1.32–8)

'Take thou that too' clearly accompanies the tearing off of yet another garment: badges of the civilization Timon now spurns. Lear also tries to do this, impelled by the sight of 'unaccommodated man', that 'poor, bare, fork'd animal' (3.4.106–8), in the person of the Bedlam beggar. But Lear, prevented from stripping himself by people who love him and accompany him in his madness, is not a wild man, nor is he drawn to the darkness of the woods as Shakespeare's Timon, Greene's Orlando and Bohan, or the older Merlin Silvestris, all are.

As he goes into exile, Timon looks back and implores the city wall 'That girdles in those wolves' to 'dive in the earth, / And fence not Athens' (4.1.2–3). The image is of an enclosed park whose pales have been removed, permitting the feral animals inside to range at large, and also ceasing to offer them protection. The city will become, in effect, a forest: by definition in the period, a hunting area that was not physically enclosed. Apemantus, a little later, makes this idea explicit, claiming that 'the commonwealth of Athens is become a forest of beasts' (4.3.347–8), but Timon as he leaves it forever has already in his prayers reduced the city to that primal chaos long associated with the words *hyle* and *silva*:

---

[46] Geoffrey Bullough (ed.), *Narrative and Dramatic Sources of Shakespeare*, 8 vols. (London: Routledge and Kegan Paul, 1973), vol. VI, pp. 251–345.

[47] William Painter, *The Palace of Pleasure: Elizabethan Versions of Italian and French Novels from Boccaccio, Bandello, Cinthio, Straparola, Queen Margaret of Navarre, and Others*, ed. Joseph Jacobs, 4th edition, 3 vols. (London: David Nutt, 1890), vol. I, p. 112.

Piety, and fear,
Religion to the gods, peace, justice, truth,
Domestic awe, night-rest, and neighborhood,
Instruction, manners, mysteries, and trades,
Degrees, observances, customs, and laws,
Decline to your confounding contraries;
And yet confusion live!   (4.1.32–8)

Timon never relinquishes this wish. In the woods, he does allow himself a spade with which to dig up the edible roots on which his existence depends, but it is now the entire world, not simply Athens, that he wants to afforest: a world in which 'marrows, vines, and plough-torn leas' (4.3.193) – all cultivated land – would dry up and disappear, leaving 'tigers, dragons, wolves, and bears' to inherit an earth innocent of human beings and their settlements (5.3.189). Apemantus is grotesquely out of touch when he suggests that the Timon he addresses in his retreat might expect 'the bleak air, thy boisterous chamberlain, / Will put thy shirt on warm', these 'moist trees / That have outliv'd the eagle, page thy heels', or 'the cold brook, / Candied with ice, caudle thy morning taste' (4.3.222–6). Not only are the allegations untrue, for Timon, it is unendurable that the natural world should be anthropomorphized in this way.

And yet there are respects in which Timon has not only adjusted to the forest, but can identify with it. He never sentimentalizes the non-human creation. Not only do the sun, the moon and earth, even the sea, all function at the expense of something else, every four-legged species has a natural enemy and lives in fear. He indignantly spurns Apemantus' proposal to relinquish his humanity and become an animal ('a beastly ambition', 4.3.327), but he enters easily into the plight of a tree: an oak whose leaves 'have with one winter's brush / Fell from their boughs, and left me open, bare, / For every storm that blows' (4.3.264–6). He can also celebrate his wild environs:

Behold, the earth hath roots;
Within this mile break forth a hundred springs;
The oaks bear mast [acorns], the briars scarlet heps [hips];
The bounteous huswife Nature on each bush
Lays her full mess before you. Want? why want?   (4.3.417–21)

Timon's reply to Apemantus' query, 'Where liest a' nights, Timon?' (4.3. 292–3) – 'Under that's above me' – is not strictly true. He doesn't, in fact, dwell 'under the canopy', as the exiled Coriolanus does, 'i' th' city of kites and crows' (4.5.38, 41). He has found a cave to live in, some rude clothing, even that primitive tool the axe in addition to his spade. When the senators of Athens come to implore his help, he makes a territorial, almost a domestic, claim upon the place he lives in: 'I have a tree, which grows here in my close' (5.1.205). In his later scenes, Timon seems to be passing through a transition like that of Merlin Silvestris, from wild man to sylvan recluse. Unfortunately, other human beings refuse to leave him alone, especially after rumour spreads about his gold. The very same hypocrites and flatterers who flocked to him in Athens persist in seeking him out in the woods. And this Timon finds intolerable. Like Greene's Bohan, he constructs a tomb for himself, then (rather more radically) climbs into it to die. But there is something tantalizingly ambiguous about his asseveration near the end: 'And nothing brings me all things' (5.1.188). When Thomas Shadwell adapted Shakespeare's play in 1678, replacing the faithful steward with a girlfriend who actually shares Timon's life in the cave, and commits suicide after his death, this line struck him as requiring a change of tense. 'And nothing *will* bring me all things', Shadwell wrote, making it clear that 'nothing' could only signify 'oblivion'.[48] That is its primary meaning in Shakespeare too. But in the original, the present as opposed to future tense had carried with it a significant undertone obliterated by Shadwell: *nemus*, the ancient word for forest, and for that different kind of nothingness which for a while did give Timon all things, or at least everything the former spendthrift of Athens had come to require.

Although probably his most extended investigation of the subject, Timon was neither Shakespeare's first nor his last wild man. The oddly emblematic nature of the description in Act 4 of *As You Like It* – another and saner Orlando stumbling upon his banished brother, the wicked Oliver, menaced by a serpent and a famished lioness as he sleeps beneath the palm tree – has often been remarked. The lion and the snake are familiar from Chrétien's *Yvain*. But so is Oliver: 'a wretched ragged man, o'ergrown with hair' (4.3.106). The only reason for Rosalind not fainting away at the sight of the wild man himself as opposed to the 'bloody napkin' is that he has been given 'fresh array' by Duke Senior (5.1.93, 143; and presumably a shave and haircut) before he presents himself to her. Bernheimer is surely right that the twelve carters, shepherds, neat-herds and swine-herds who 'have made themselves all men of hair' (4.4.326) and dance in the sheep-shearing scene of *The Winter's Tale* were actually got up as wild men.[49] They are called 'Saltiers' in the text (4.4.327), 'Satyrs' in

---

[48] Thomas Shadwell, *Timon, the Man-hater*, in *The Dramatic Works of Thomas Shadwell Esq.*, 4 vols. (London: J. Knapton, 1720), 5.1, vol. 3, p. 368.
[49] Bernheimer, *Wild Men in the Middle Ages*, p. 201, n. 55.

a stage direction. The first term was often used of wodewoses. With the second, wodewoses were often confused – as in the 1592 entertainment at Rycote, where 'a wilde man' is instructed to 'come forth' but by line 22 of his speech, is talking about 'wee Satyres'.[50] Whatever else happened in the lost *Cardenio*, a Shakespeare/Fletcher collaboration performed at court in 1613, it must – given the hero's love madness and subsequent life as a wild man, as told in Cervantes' *Don Quixote* – have included substantial wodewose scenes.

* * *

Shakespeare's interest in wild men seems to have extended throughout his writing career, taking in Oliver, Timon, the dancers in Bohemia, Caliban, Cardenio and (in a sense) Herne the Hunter, in *The Merry Wives of Windsor*.[51] For other dramatists, it was a vogue that peaked in the 1590s and then gradually faded away. Thomas Campion's entertainment of 1613 at Caversham, for James I's queen Anne, does begin with a wodewose who appears 'out of a Bower, drest in a skin-coate, with Bases of greene Calico, set thicke with leaves and boughes; on his head he wore a false haire, blacke and disordered, stucke carelessly with flowers'.[52] What this wild man actually says – he is identified as 'a Cynick' – suggests that he may have seen a performance of Shakespeare's *Timon*:

> Cities and Courts fit tumultuous multitudes: this is a place of silence; here a kingdome I enjoy without people; my selfe commands, my selfe obeys; Host, Cooke, and Guest myselfe; I reape without sowing, owe all to Nature, to none other beholding; my skinne is my coate … this Bower my house, the earth my bed, herbes my food, water my drinke; I want no sleepe, nor health; I envie none, nor am envied, neither feare I, nor hope, nor joy, nor grieve. If this be happinesse, I have it.[53]

But in Campion's view, such happiness is false. Anne of Denmark lacked the charisma of Elizabeth. When he came to the point of civilizing his wild man, Campion relied upon the reasoned dissuasions of a richly dressed 'traveller' concealed among the royal entourage, not the transforming power of the queen. Conquered by 'reason', the reformed misanthrope obediently joined the procession as it moved through ascending stages of

[50] John Lyly, *The Entertainment at Bisham*, in ed. R. Warwick Bond, *The Complete Works of John Lyly*, 3 vols. (Oxford: Clarendon Press, 1902), vol. I, p. 472.

[51] See also Chapter 6, pp. 125–8.

[52] Thomas Campion, *The Caversham Entertainment*, in ed. Walter R. Davis, *The Works of Thomas Campion* (London: Faber and Faber, 1969), pp. 235–6, 240.

[53] Ibid., p. 236.

civility: from the fields to the enclosed park, with its Keeper and 'Robin Hood' men, then to the garden (where a gardener begged the queen to forgive 'the late wooden entertainment of the Wood-men; for Woods are more full of weeds than wits, but gardens are weeded, and Gardners witty, as may appear by me')[54] and finally into the house.

In Campion, there is already a sense that the wild man verges on being comic. In two plays by Thomas Randolph, *Aristippus* of 1626 and *Amyntas, or the Impossible Dowry* of 1630, this has become unequivocally the case. *Aristippus* was a university play, performed at Trinity College, Cambridge, where Randolph was a fellow. Its Wild-Man, who sells strong beer, has been driven mad by the increasing scholarly preference for wine: 'I am the Wild-Man', he announces, 'and I will be wild. Is this an age to be in a man's right wits, when the lawful use of the throat is so much neglected, and strong drink lies on his death-bed?'[55] Eventually, like so many wild men before him, although in rather a different spirit, he is overcome by a copious draft of wine and returns to civilization.

Aristippus is not a play that was ever intended to be taken seriously. *Amyntas*, a pastoral acted by the Children of the Revels before Charles I and Henrietta Maria at Whitehall, on the whole, was. Claius, its wild man, has lived

> Pelted with angry curses in a place
> As horrid as my griefs, the Lylibean mountain.
> These sixteen frozen winters there have I
> Been with rude outlaws, living by such sins
> As run o'th' score with justice . . .[56]

Claius, a 'rude, ill-favoured Sylvan' with 'unkempt shackled locks', clearly was attired as a conventional wild man. His past history is tragic, and yet other characters simply cannot help laughing at his appearance. They persist in referring to him as a 'walking ivy-bush', 'a withered tree o'er-grown with moss', a 'goblin' or 'this fellow with the beard all over'.[57] The play can be seen as the end of a tradition, one extending back through the Middle Ages to the time of Homer, and the *Cyclops* of Euripides. When the theatres re-opened after the Restoration, many plays would feature noble savages: Dryden's *The Indian Queen* (1665) and *The Indian Emperor*

[54] Ibid., p. 240.
[55] Thomas Randolph, *Aristippus*, in ed. W. Carew Hazlitt, *Poetical and Dramatic Works of Thomas Randolph*, 2 vols. (London: Reeves and Turner, 1875), vol. I, pp. 9–10.
[56] Thomas Randolph, *Amyntas, or the Impossible Dowry*, in ed. W. Carew Hazlitt, *Poetical and Dramatic Works of Thomas Randolph*, 2 vols. (London: Reeves and Turner, 1875), vol. I, p. 318.
[57] Randolph, *Amyntas*, 1.5, p. 287; 3.2, pp. 317–318; 4.2, pp. 332–3.

(perf. 1665, publ. 1667), for instance, Thomas Southerne's *Oroonoko* (1696) or *The Widdow Ranter* (1690) by Aphra Behn. All these characters, however, inhabit the New World, not the forests of Europe, and neither in appearance or behaviour did they ask to be identified as wild men.

In 1804, Thomas Dibdin did stage the Valentine and Orson story, to rapturous applause, in the form of 'A Grand Serio-Comic Romantick Melo-Drama in Two Acts', at the Theatre Royal, Covent Garden.[58] His 'Wild Man', in a 'close dress, as if overgrown with hair', rampages through the royal palace to which he has been brought, eating the horses' provender and forcing them to drink wine, hurling the cook into the dripping-pan and basting him with his own ladle. Even more ludicrous than Randolph's wild men, Dibdin's Orson (until magically 'endowed with reason' at the end) retains the traditional club, shaggy appearance, lecherous instincts and weak head for wine, while being almost entirely a figure of fun. However they handled the old romance, the lost Valentine and Orson plays of 1595 and 1598 cannot have been like this.

In Bavaria, and elsewhere on the continent, some rudimentary village plays involving the genuine wild man were still being performed well into the twentieth century. And there is, of course, Tarzan. Isolated instances in real life of so-called 'wild children' continue to turn up, from the early nineteenth-century 'wild boy of Aveyron' about whom Truffaut made a film,[59] to the pathetic case of Genie, the languageless and uncivilized girl who was discovered in 1970, after ten years of solitary confinement, in a suburb of Hollywood called, with excruciating irony, 'Arcadia'.[60] The French wild boy had emerged from a forest. Genie's wilderness, predictably for our age, was indoors: a totally empty room. It was no less of a *locus neminis* for that. In England, however, where, by 1642, the forests were vanishing with alarming speed, the year that the playhouses closed effectively spelled the end of the long theatrical career of the wodewose.

---

[58] The description on the Playbill for Covent Garden, 2 April 1804, quoted in Joseph W. Donohue, *Theatre in the Age of Kean* (Oxford: Blackwell, 1975), p. 114. The edition of T. J. Dibdin's *Valentine and Orson* cited here is the second, published in London in 1813.

[59] *L'Enfant Sauvage* (*The Wild Boy*), dir. François Truffaut (1970).

[60] See Russ Rymer, *Genie: A Scientific Tragedy* (New York: Harper Perennial, 1993) and Michael Newton, *Savage Girls and Wild Boys: A History of Feral Children* (London: Faber, 2002).

CHAPTER 4

'Like the Old Robin Hood of England'

On 16 April 1473, John Paston, waiting to embark for Calais, complained to his younger brother (another John Paston) about three household retainers who had recently deserted him. They were called John Myryll, Thryston and William Wood, and he seems to forget that he had already written to John about their defection, only a few days before. This time, however, he provided more details:

> I have ben *and* ame troblyd wyth myn overe large *and* curteys delyng wyth my servantys *and* now wyth ther onkyndnesse. Platyng, yowre man, wolde thys daye byd me fare-well to to-morrow at Dover, not wythstondyng Thryston, yowre other man, is from me *and* John Myryell *and* W. Woode, whyche promysed yow ... at Castre þat iff ye wolde take hym in to be ageyn wyth me þat than he wold never goo fro me; *and* ther-uppon I have kepyd hym thys iij yere to pleye Seynt Jorge *and* Robynhod *and* the shryff off Notyngham, *and* now when I wolde have good horse he is goon in-to Bernysdale, *and* I wyth-owt a kepere.[1]

This is, in many ways, an extraordinary passage. Other letters suggest that the elder Paston really had treated these yeoman who served him with comparative informality and respect. The younger John remembered them by name in personal greetings he sent his brother and even on one occasion promised them an excellent dinner at Norwich if only they would nag Paston about getting him a goshawk, a 'sowyr hawke' or a tiercel 'provyd'.[2]

William Wood's promises may have been unreliable, but he was certainly versatile. As a seasoned soldier, present at the siege of Castre, he would have been invaluable to his master during the new French campaign. He could manage horses and (apparently) a longbow. On 3 June,

---

[1] Norman Davis (ed.), *Paston Letters and Papers of the Fifteenth Century*, 2 vols. (Oxford: Clarendon Press, 1976), vol. I, p. 461.

[2] Ibid., vol. I, p. 580. A goshawk is a large, short-winged hawk, of the genus *Accipiter*; a 'sowyr' or 'sore' hawk is a young hawk that has not yet moulted for the first time, and a tiercel or tercel is a male hawk of any kind, but usually a peregrine falcon; 'provyd' suggests one that has been trained.

Paston – still stuck in London, looking for replacements – was asking after 'lykly men *and* fayre condycioned *and* good archerys'. He was willing to take on up to four, and 'they shall have iiij m[a]rke by yere *and* my levere [livery]', though he will never, he swears, 'cherysshe' them as he did the 'knaves' who left.[3] Wood, however, had been by no means just a soldier, or a keeper of horses. The oldest surviving Robin Hood play, a fragment packed onto half of one manuscript page and now in the Wren Library at Trinity College, Cambridge, has the same provenance as the Paston papers. Linked with one of the oldest and most brutal of the ballads, 'Robin Hood and Guy of Gisborne', it also features the sheriff of Nottingham. Household accounts appear on the back of this page, not to mention a very fine bright green dragon, and some graffiti that editors pass over in embarrassed silence. Few people doubt that this is the Paston entertainment (or what remains of it) in which for three years William Wood performed. For what kind of audience, whether village, or predominantly domestic is less clear. Still, the manuscript ought to remove any suspicion that Paston was only speaking figuratively when he talked about his truant retainer playing St George, and Robin Hood and the sheriff. Wood leaving Paston's service and taking himself off to 'Bernysdale' is more problematic.

'The woodland of the renowned Barnsdale Forest, where it is said that Robin Hood lived as an outlaw',[4] as John Leland described it when he later, during the reign of Henry VIII, rode through what he believed to be the place, lay at a considerable distance from Norfolk, in the West Riding of Yorkshire. It (and Inglewood in Cumberland) later became eclipsed by Sherwood Forest as a setting for the Robin Hood legend but, in early ballads, Barnesdale predominates over the more southerly and thickly wooded Sherwood, near Nottingham. Whoever was responsible, around 1400, for compiling much older material to form the centrally important 'Gest of Robyn Hode' put him in Barnesdale while preserving the outlaw's identification with Nottinghamshire as well. Was John Paston merely indulging in a sour joke when he said that William Wood, his pretend Robin Hood, had left him 'and goon into Bernys-dale'? In *Robin Hood: a Mythic Biography*, Stephen Knight suggests that he was.[5] It is entirely possible, however, that Wood may quite literally have disappeared into Barnesdale, where outlaws were robbing travellers at the time, and have

---

[3] Ibid., vol. I, p. 463.

[4] John Chandler (ed.), *John Leland's Itinerary: Travels in Tudor England*, (Gloucester: Alan Sutton Publishing Ltd., 1993), p. 522.

[5] Stephen Knight, *Robin Hood: A Mythic Biography* (Ithaca: Cornell University Press, 2003), p. 10.

done so, moreover, because he could not resist turning a fiction – one that he had already become accustomed to acting out for the Pastons – into something real. The impulse has parallels, both on the stage and off.

Almost a century and a half later, whoever wrote *Tom a Lincoln*[6] created a dramatic hero who abandons his un-glamorous shepherd's life in Lincolnshire and travels north to Barnesdale, in order to live like Robin Hood. In *A Health to the Gentlemanly Profession of Servingmen*, a pamphlet printed in 1598, the author (identified only as J. M.) states that liveried servants dismissed by their master will almost never support themselves by agricultural or other manual labour; they prefer to 'make . . . appearance at Gaddes Hill, Shooters hill, on Salisburie playne, or Newmarket heath'[7] – to live, in other words, as highway robbers, fleecing passers-by. J. M. too was writing well over a century after John Paston, and William Wood left rather than being dismissed, but the observation is still worth taking into account. Wood had re-entered Paston's service in 1469, having walked out on him at least once before. We are not informed about the season of year on the previous occasion, but in 1473, it was mid-April, coming up to May Day, the time when Robin Hood plays and shows were customarily performed. April, as it happens – 'well-nigh May'[8] – is also the moment in Richard Brome's comedy *A Jovial Crew* of 1641 when Squire Oldrents' steward Springlove leaves his master to vanish into 'wild woods',[9] highways and commons with a disreputable band of associates. Springlove's defection, like William Wood's, is not his first, and although Oldrents certainly 'cherishes' him, this time he too has had enough.

Neither Brome nor the author of *Tom a Lincoln* can conceivably have read the Paston letters. Springlove joins a peripatetic society of beggars who are voluntary dropouts, not officially outlawed men. Still, the underlying paradigm is recognizably the same. Near the end of the 'Gest of Robyn Hode', Robin accepts not only King Edward's pardon, but his request that

---

[6] *Tom a Lincoln*, ed. G. R. Proudfoot, Malone Society Reprints (Oxford: Oxford University Press, 1992), lines 269–72, 292–300, pp. 9–10. *Tom a Lincoln* was originally a popular romance by Richard Johnson (*fl.* 1592–622). Its two parts were entered into the Stationers' Register in 1599 and 1607, and it was reprinted many times in the seventeenth century. The dramatization survives, incomplete, in MS; it is subscribed 'Morganus Evans', but the author has not been identified. In the *Oxford Dictionary of National Biography*, Proudfoot suggests that it probably dates from the second decade of the seventeenth century. The play is further discussed below.

[7] J. M., *A Health to the Gentlemanly Profession of Servingmen or The Servingmans Comfort* (London, 1598), in ed. W. C. Hazlitt, *Inedited Tracts: Illustrating the Manners, Opinions, and Occupations of Englishmen During the Sixteenth and Seventeenth Centuries: Now First Published from the Original Copies with a Preface and Notes* (New York: Burt Franklin, 1868), p. 164.

[8] Richard Brome, *A Jovial Crew*, ed. Ann Haaker (London: Edward Arnold Ltd., 1968), 1.1.152.

[9] Ibid., 1.1.196.

he and his companions 'leve the grene wode / . . . And come home, syr, to my courte, / And there dwell with me'.[10] Robin lasts only fifteen months as a royal servant, not only because he freely spends all his money 'to gete hym grete renowne',[11] while his men (except for Little John and Scathlocke) gradually desert him and sneak back to Barnesdale and their old life, but because 'Yf I dwell lenger with the kynge, / Sorowe wylle me sloo [slay; strike, cast down]'.[12] (Little John had come to a similar conclusion earlier in the 'Gest', after a brief attempt to serve in the Sheriff of Nottingham's household.) Paston's William Wood was a real, historical person, Brome's Springlove only a dramatic character. The behaviour of both, however, across some two hundred and seventy years, is governed by the Robin Hood story, a story in which no one, to this day, can properly disentangle fiction from fact.

* * *

Thanks to the work of John Bellamy, J. C. Holt, Maurice Keen, Stephen Knight, J. R. Maddicott and others, we probably now know most of what we are going to know about real mediaeval outlaws.[13] As a power in the land, something distinct from a few stray and disorganized unfortunates, they seem to have originated in England with certain landed Saxons who had been driven from their estates by the Normans. Some of the dispossessed took refuge in fens and forests, living (as one thirteenth-century historian later reported) by hunting, robbing only when they had to, but continually laying traps and ambushes for the hated Normans. Hereward the Wake, who operated from the fens of East Anglia, was the most famous

---

[10] R. B. Dobson and J. Taylor (eds.), *The Gest of Robyn Hode*, in *Rymes of Robyn Hood: An Introduction to the English Outlaw*, 2nd edition (Gloucester: Alan Sutton Ltd., 1989), 'The Seventh Fytte', stanza 414–5, p. 109. Dobson and Taylor describe the 'Gest' as 'incomparably the fullest source for the late medieval Robin Hood legend to survive' (p. xv). It runs to nearly 14,000 words, in four-line stanzas divided into eight 'fyttes', and brings together a number of stories (including many of the themes, characters, and motifs which will become familiar) rather than operating as a single narrative. The earliest surviving copy to which an approximate date can be ascribed is the *Lytell Geste of Robyn Hode*, printed by Wynkyn de Worde before 1534; some earlier fragments survive. See the survey of sources and additions, and an account of the text, in Dobson and Taylor, pp. 71–4. The 'Gest' is number 117 in the *English and Scottish Popular Ballads*, ed. Francis James Child (1882–98).
[11] Ibid., 'The Eighth Fytte', stanza 434, p. 110.   [12] Ibid., 'The Eighth Fytte', stanza 438, p. 111.
[13] See John Bellamy, *Crime and Public Order in England in the Later Middle Ages* (London: Routledge & Kegan Paul, 1973); John Bellamy, *Robin Hood: An Historical Enquiry* (London: Croom Helm Ltd., 1985); J. C. Holt, *Robin Hood* (London: Thames and Hudson Ltd., 1982); Maurice Keen, *The Outlaws of Medieval Legend* (London: Routledge & Kegan Paul Ltd., 1961); Stephen Knight, *Robin Hood: A Complete Study of the English Outlaw* (Oxford: Blackwell Publishers, 1994); Knight, *Robin Hood: A Mythic Biography*; J. R. Maddicott, 'The Birth and Setting of the Ballads of Robin Hood', in *The English Historical Review* 93 (1978), 276–99.

of these, his harassment of the Conqueror mythologized in epic narratives, ballads and songs. Later, Fulk Fitzwarin and Eustace the Monk, two outlaw leaders living during the reign of King John, also generated a complex of legends and romance tales. Facts, however, cling to these men after the fantasies have been stripped away. All three were historical individuals, enmeshed in a particular context, a particular moment of time, and they confronted a particular king. All were upper class.

The case of Robin Hood is very different. Fifteenth- and sixteenth-century chroniclers refer to him as though he had been a real person, without agreeing about when he lived and under which king (Henry II, Richard I, John or Edwards I to III) and with what part of England he should be associated, why he was outlawed, and whether he was a yeoman, a dispossessed aristocrat, like those who fought for Simon de Montfort at the Battle of Evesham, or even (by 1569, in Richard Grafton's *Chronicle at Large*) a noble earl. Nor are they by any means unanimous in his praise, although on the whole his reputation, like his behaviour, tends to improve with time. Historians today go on trying to track down the original of Robin Hood, but with singular lack of success. It is not that individuals with that name cannot be found in thirteenth- and fourteenth-century records, but that there are far too many of them, and none quite right. By the mid-fourteenth century, moreover, the possibility cannot be ruled out that any particular 'Robertus Hudus' has taken his name from the ballads, rather than providing their source.

The popularity of Robin Hood, and the power of his legend, far exceed that of Hereward, Fitzwarin or Eustace the Monk. Yet despite the presence of Robin Hood place names not just in the north, but in virtually every county of England, and the colossal amount of literature generated over the centuries by the stories, he is (paradoxically) a man who has never had a face of his own. When the 'Gest' first broke into print, probably from a press at Antwerp, in the early years of the sixteenth century, it carried on its first page a supposed picture of Robin: mounted, dressed as a forester, bearing a longbow and sheaf of arrows. Readers who thought this image looked familiar were quite right; it had already appeared a decade or so before, as a depiction of Chaucer's Yeoman, in Pynson's edition of *The Canterbury Tales*. When William Thackeray reprinted Martin Parker's *True Tale of Robin Hood* in 1687, he reused the title-page image from its first edition in 1632, which had depicted three figures – presumably Robin Hood, Will Scarlet and Little John – in plumed and broad-brimmed hats, with a sword and a pike as well as a longbow. But he had already made use of the same image for numerous editions of *Adam Bell,*

Clim of the Clough and *William of Cloudsdale*, three quite different outlaws, from 1667 onwards.[14]

In innumerable film redactions, Robin Hood does of course have an individual face: that of the actor who happens to be playing the part, whether Douglas Fairbanks, Errol Flynn or Kevin Costner.[15] But even here, there is an unusual latitude about his physical type – very different, for instance, from the case of Sherlock Holmes – another fictional character whose devotees yearn to propel him into the real. No director in his right mind would ever cast as Holmes an actor who was fair-haired, short and snub-nosed. With Robin Hood, on the other hand, the longbow and the standard forester's outfit of Lincoln green are the only essentials. Given that in the traditional stories, he is more often than not worsted in physical combat – by the Potter, Little John, the curtal friar, the Pinder of Wakefield or England's King – there is not even any requirement that he be particularly burly or physically strong. Almost invariably, the task of waylaying travellers and forcing them back to an *al fresco* meal that will not come cheap falls to Little John, Scarlet and the rest. Robin stays quietly in the centre of the forest, waiting to see what the day will bring. When he does leave the greenwood, he often does so in disguise, submerging his own, outlawed identity in that of a potter, a butcher or, in the Guy of Gisborne ballad, a man he has just killed.

It was just this featureless, almost anonymous, quality that made it easy for Robin Hood to be absorbed in the course of the fifteenth century into the May games, where Maid Marian was already present as a summer queen. As an annual May Lord, the Green Man, even a representative wodewose,[16] he could be universalized, while retaining definable outlines and a story, as Fitzwarin or Hereward the Wake could not. But he harboured another and ultimately more important potentiality. 'Robin Hood' was also a kind of costume, hanging vacant and untenanted by the wall, one into which other men increasingly felt impelled to fit their own identities and acts. The 'hood' of Robin's surname obviously hides and conceals; in that sense, as Robert Pogue Harrison points out in *Forests: The Shadow of Civilization*, it resembles the canopy of the forest itself.[17]

---

[14] The work had first appeared in the 1530s; earlier editions had depicted them as Jacobean gallants.

[15] Douglas Fairbanks, Jr., *Robin Hood* (1922), dir. Allan Dwan; Errol Flynn, *The Adventures of Robin Hood* (1938), dir. Michael Curtiz, William Keighley; Kevin Costner, *Robin Hood: Prince of Thieves* (1991), dir. Kevin Reynolds.

[16] See Chapter 3.

[17] Robert Pogue Harrison, *Forests: The Shadows of Civilisation* (London: University of Chicago Press, 1992), p. 79.

But *hood* (taken back to its Indo-European root) also means something that covers, or shelters and in this case, not just Robin Hood himself, but a host of other people who put it on. Some of these were real, others are characters in sixteenth- and seventeenth-century plays, and the relationship between them is complex.

The various gentry gangs who operated from wooded parts of England (in the case of the Coterels, in Sherwood itself) during the fourteenth and early fifteenth centuries resembled the Mafia more than they did those earlier, dispossessed Saxons who had become objects of popular celebration. These later forest-dwellers were involved in, and encouraged, family feuds; they were often retained by local magnates and corrupt ecclesiastics, even on occasion by the king. They poached the king's and other people's deer, practised extortion and robbed, but certainly with no intention of levelling out economic inequalities. Nobody felt strongly inclined to mythologize their leaders – except, interestingly enough, the leaders themselves. The most revealing document here is the letter that in 1336 was received by Richard de Snaweshill, the unhappy chaplain of Huntingdon:

> Lionel, King of the rout of raveners [gang of plunderers, ravishers] salutes, but with little love, his false and disloyal Richard de Snaweshill. We command you, on pain to lose all that can stand forfeit against our laws, that you immediately remove from his office him whom you maintain in the vicarage of Burton Agnes; and that you suffer that the Abbot of St. Mary's have his rights in this matter and that the election of the man whom he has chosen, who is more worthy of advancement than you or any of your lineage, be upheld. And if you do not do this, we make our avow, first to God and then to the King of England and to our own crown that . . . we shall hunt you down, even if we have to come to Coney Street in York to do it. . . . And if you do not take cognizance of our orders, we have bidden our lieutenant in the North to levy . . . great distraint upon you . . . Given at our Castle of the North Wind, in the Green Tower, in the first year of our reign.[18]

This, as Harrison shrewdly points out, is 'the logic of comedy at its most rudimentary level . . . that of the absurd'.[19] It is also, however, the letter of someone simultaneously affirming his allegiance to the Crown, God and an uncorrupted holy church – things that for Robin Hood too are sacred – and setting up an alternative, fantasy kingdom, with himself as monarch, that vies with, and even threatens to usurp, the real. The 'Green Tower' may be a forest thicket; his 'Castle of the North Wind' only a wood where

---

[18] Ibid., p. 78.   [19] Ibid., p. 78.

he endures the bleak air. For Lionel, in the strange game he is playing, they are integral parts of a rhetoric that deploys what only one man in England had the right to use in earnest: the first person plural of an anointed king. In terms of genuine, consequential and quite illegal action, however, there can be no doubt that Lionel *is* in earnest.

This bogus 'kingship' in the woods, the establishment of a rival forest commonwealth with its own monarch and laws, is something that was going to re-appear in a number of sixteenth- and seventeenth-century plays. Other outlaws, meanwhile, tended to adopt a less grandiose style. Robert Stafford, for instance, a most *un*holy chaplain whose followers harried, poached and murdered in Surrey and Sussex between 1417 and 1429, called himself 'Frere Tuck'. Was he the original of Robin Hood's fictional companion? Tuck first appears in conjunction with Robin Hood in the Paston fragment, but the two characters might have been associated earlier, in plays or poems that have not survived. Stafford perhaps borrowed the name from these, or from literature in which the irregular friar enjoyed a quite independent existence. In any case, he did well for himself. When he finally became too old to go on living in the greenwood, Stafford purchased a pardon from the king out of his ill-gotten gains, and ended his days in comfort.[20]

The *victims* of outlaws such as Stafford sometimes reached for a Robin Hood comparison, like those Derbyshire men who petitioned Parliament in 1439 for redress against Piers Venables and his supporters, said to have gone 'into the wodes in that county like it hadde be Robyn Hode and his meynee [followers, retinue]'.[21] Only, however, towards the end of the century do miscreants begin to be recorded who have themselves assumed the name and distinguishing attire of the ballad hero: rebels in 1497, again in Derbyshire, who dressed as Robin Hood and took to the woods; one Robert Marchall (alias 'Robin Hood') who caused a riot by appearing at Willenhall in Staffordshire on Trinity Sunday 1498 at the head of more than a hundred men (one hundred being the traditional number of Robin's meinie); or the priest of Wednesbury, also in Staffordshire, who claimed to be 'Robin Hood' in 1499, when he and his lieutenant forcibly liberated several of their companions, arrested and charged with murder after a skirmish on the previous day, and neatly imprisoned the mayor of Walsall in their place.

---

[20] Roger B. Manning, *Hunters and Poachers: A Cultural and Social History of Unlawful Hunting in England 1485–1640* (Oxford: Clarendon Press, 1993), pp. 21, 64.
[21] As quoted by Knight in *Robin Hood: A Complete Study of the English Outlaw*, p. 25.

The Walsall affair is especially interesting because it replays an incident in the 'Gest' that also occurs in several of the ballads: the springing from prison of condemned associates of Robin (sometimes even of Robin himself) by the loyal forest fraternity. The Wednesbury priest did not impersonate Robin Hood on the day of the original disturbance; that only happened afterwards, when circumstances reminded him of the ballad episodes, and encouraged him to act them out. The use of Robin Hood's name as a generalized cover for social protest and dissent has been well documented by Buchanan Sharp, in his book *In Contempt of All Authority*, and by Peter Stallybrass, in an essay entitled 'Drunk with the Cup of Liberty'.[22] This discussion is more concerned, however, with something not unrelated, yet different: with real individuals who insist upon re-enacting specific parts or circumstances of the Robin Hood story. That seems to have happened a good deal, and over a long space of time: at Walsall; again at Edinburgh in 1561, when the mob rioted after the suppression of the Robin Hood May games, robbed strangers, and forced the gaol to release their imprisoned leader; or when Thomas Bright of Carnebrook in Yorkshire cast himself, in 1621, as 'Robin Hood', his chief follower as 'Little John', and the rest as his 'merry men', before riding out to poach the Earl of Pembroke's deer.[23] That used to cause perplexity, there being little official animus, at that date, against the Robin Hood games, or much need to 'revive' them. 'Greenleaf', however, is the name Little John invents for himself in the 'Gest', when he temporarily serves, and then betrays, the forces of law and order as personified by the sheriff of Nottingham. As with Paston's William Wood, it looks like another case of Robin Hood 'pagentes' sliding disconcertingly into the real.

* * *

Not all these impersonators were men up to no good. Henry VIII, that passionate slayer of deer in royal parks, and curtailer of other men's hunting privileges, was nonetheless on excellent terms with Robin Hood. In 1509, he and eleven nobles, carrying bows and arrows and clad in Kendal green, 'lyke outlawes or Robyn Hodes men', appeared without warning in the Queen's chamber. Katherine, 'abashed' (according to Hall) at 'the

---

[22] Buchanan Sharp, *In Contempt of All Authority: Rural Artisans and Riot in the West of England 1586–1660* (London: University of California Press, 1980); Peter Stallybrass: 'Drunk with the Cup of Liberty': Robin Hood, the Carnivalesque, and the Rhetoric of Violence in Early Modern England', *Semiotica* 54 (1985), 113–45.

[23] Manning, *Hunters and Poachers*, p. 22.

straunge sight',[24] seems not to have known what to do with the role of Maid Marian, forced so suddenly upon her. She was more at ease seven years later, when she and Henry were waylaid (in the most deferential fashion) on May morning, as they rode on Shooter's Hill, by a man calling himself 'Robyn hood' and two hundred archers of the King's guard, who bore them off to the greenwood 'to se how the outlawes lyue', and to breakfast ('Then said Robyn hood, "Sir, outlawes brekefastes is venyson"')[25] in a carefully prepared bower. They were not, needless to say, relieved of any cash.

Historical impersonations of Robin Hood, and the acting out of his stories, whether by royalty or rogues, bear in important ways upon the real subject of this chapter: a number of attempts by characters in sixteenth- and seventeenth-century plays to do this too, in what for them (although not for us) are non-fictional circumstances. This means paying only brief attention to those early Robin Hood folk dramas that survive from what must originally have been a much larger corpus – the Paston fragment, *Robin Hood and the Friar*, or *Robin Hood and the Potter* – or even to those Elizabethan and Jacobean plays in which he appears in his own person as a character: Anthony Munday's two-part *Downfall and Death of Robert Earl of Huntingdon*, and his *Look About You*, the anonymous *George a Greene*, or Jonson's *The Sad Shepherd*. More interesting here are those dramas where characters with distinct identities of their own elect to put on Robin's hood.

George Peele's *Edward I*, a chronicle history of about 1591, is in some ways the strangest. Driven into exile in the Welsh mountains by King Edward, Lluellen, the rebellious Prince of Wales, together with Elinor, his betrothed, his cousin, Rice ap Meredith, and Hugh ap David, a friar, decide that since they are obliged to rob passers-by in order to live, they may as well 'get the next daie from *Brecknocke* the booke of *Robin Hood*'[26] and use it to fit themselves into the framework of the tales. Lluellen announces that he will sell his gold chain to clothe them all properly in green:

> ile be maister of misrule, ile be *Robin Hood* . . . cousin *Rice* thou shalt be little
> *Iohn*, and hers Frier *David* as fit as a die for Frier *Tucke*, now my sweet *Nel* if
> you wil make up the messe with a good hert for Maide marian and doe well

[24] Edward Hall, *The Union of the Two Noble and Illustre Families of Lancastre and York* (London, 1550), 'The ii yere of Kyng Henry the Viij', fol. vi[v] (a6[v]).

[25] Hall, *Lancastre and York*, 'The vii yere of Kyng Henry the Viij', fol. lvii (k3).

[26] George Peele, *King Edward the First* (1593), ed. W. W. Greg, The Malone Society Reprints (Oxford: Oxford University Press, 1911), lines 1293–4.

with *Lluellen* under the greene wood trees, with as good a wil as in the good townes, why *plena est curia*.[27]

Once in the forest, where other men join them, Lluellen is pleased to discover that the Robin Hood stories, judging from their own success in realizing them, were probably true, not just a pack of 'Bedlams' tales. Like Shakespeare's Duke Senior, he even tries to celebrate the outlaw life. Yet his little 'Common-wealth', as he calls it, has its problems.

Although Nell puts a brave face on it in her lover's presence, she dislikes having 'to passe the wearie time away'[28] as Maid Marian, dutifully making garlands while the men are out waylaying travellers from Brecknocke. To make matters worse, Lluellen without knowing it harbours a couple of vipers in his bosom. Friar David ap Tuck, as he now calls himself, craftily stays behind in the forest camp after Robin has gone in order to 'licke his marrian',[29] a plan that misfires only because Mortimer, the earl of March, is also lingering for the same purpose. The lovesick Mortimer, a newcomer to this society, has penetrated it by playing its game; he introduces himself as the Potter, another important figure in the tales. Neither the legendary Potter, however, nor Tuck ever betrayed Robin – that was reserved for Nottingham's sheriff, or the Prioress of Kirklees.[30] Circumstances are already wrenching the old stories in new, and unexpected directions. These old stories may not be lies, as Lluellen once suspected, but neither when re-enacted do they run quite true.

Mortimer, predictably, is not the only outsider who decides to participate in Peele's very special play within the play. England's King Edward is also familiar with the 'Gest of Robin Hood', and with the part reserved for him: 'as I am a Gentleman, / Ile have one merrie flirt with little *Iohn*, / And *Robin Hood*, and his *Maide marrian*'.[31] Like his prototype in the 'Gest', the king, although not wearing a monk's disguise, arrives in the greenwood incognito. When it comes to a trial of physical strength, he too knocks Robin down, and earns the outlaw's personal respect: 'his courage is like to the Lion, and were it not that rule and soveraigntie sets us at jarre, I could love and honour the man for his valour'.[32] Everything else in the scenario is tellingly different.

[27] 'The court is complete'. Ibid., lines 1299–305.   [28] Ibid., line 1426.   [29] Ibid., line 1421.
[30] In the 'Gest', the Prioress of Kirklees kills Robin Hood under the pretext of bleeding him for the good of his health. See Dobson and Taylor, *Rymes of Robin Hood*, The Eighth Fytte, stanzas 451, 454–5 (pp. 109–10), and also the later 'Robin Hoode His Death' and 'Robin Hood's Death and Burial', ibid., pp. 134–9.
[31] Peele, *King Edward the First*, lines 1707–8.   [32] Ibid., lines 2122–4.

Lluellen, who has never shared the original Robin Hood's loyalty to the English crown, knows exactly who his opponent is by the time they come to blows. Edward, once he has Lluellen down, intends to rid himself of this troublesome Welsh nationalist by killing him on the spot. The only reason he doesn't do this is that Mortimer, the pretend potter, has abruptly switched allegiances, and so has David of Brecknock, Lluellen's brother, but purportedly an adherent of the king. If Edward slays Lluellen, David (who has Mortimer at a similar disadvantage) will kill *him*. Stalemate, and also a parting of the ways that abruptly ends the Robin Hood game. Peele's Robin, unlike the one in the 'Gest', does not ride merrily back to London, horns blaring, arrows flying, beside a king now wearing outlaw green himself, to whom he has formally been reconciled. He remains in Wales and then, defeated by the English in battle, makes his next appearance as a severed head rammed onto the end of a spear. Lluellen's brother David exits on a hurdle, being dragged to the place of execution, while the Friar and Maid Marian are left to make a hasty composition with the enemy.[33]

As a dramatist, Peele seems to have been drawn both to forest settings and Pirandellian effects. His *Arraignment of Paris* takes place in a wooded vale on Mt Ida, introduces the 'country gods' Faunus, Pan and Sylvanus, and ends with a startling rupture of dramatic illusion as the object of discord, the golden ball which will burn Troy, is awarded to Queen Elizabeth in the audience as the embodiment of Venus, Juno and Pallas all in one. In *The Old Wive's Tale*, three pages separated from their master and lost in a romance forest had taken refuge in the solitary cottage of a smith, only to find themselves mysteriously precipitated there into 'England's wood', a second forest even stranger and more dreamlike than the first, in which characters in the tale the smith's wife is telling materialize to act it out themselves. *Edward I*, however, is unique. No other dramatist ever juxtaposed the material of the ballads and the 'Gest' with brutal political reality quite as overtly as Peele, although Shakespeare produced one very powerful glancing shot.

Falstaff's wistful notion in *1 Henry IV*, that when Hal becomes king, the consequential word 'thief' will be abolished in favour of such harmless circumlocutions as 'Diana's foresters, gentlemen of the shade, minions of the moon' (1.2.23–9), strongly suggests that Shallow's deer in *The Merry*

---

[33] Ibid., line 2629SD. See also Edwin Davenport, 'The Representation of Robin Hood in Elizabethan Drama: *George a Greene* and *Edward I*', in ed. Lois Potter, *Playing Robin Hood: The Legend as Performance in Five Centuries* (London: Associated University Presses, 1998), pp. 45–63.

Wives are not the first or only ones he has poached. Certainly the Falstaff who addresses Bardolph as 'Scarlet' and Nym as 'Little John' in a context of deer-stealing and general thievery during the first scene of *The Merry Wives*, is casting himself, however fleetingly, as Robin Hood (1.1.173). The most resonant association, however, occurs in 5.3 of *2 Henry IV*, although Falstaff neither makes it himself nor understands what it means. As the wine and the healths circulate in that Gloucestershire orchard where Silence, Shallow and his man Davy sit down to enjoy 'a last year's pippin of mine own grafting', in the company of Bardolph, Falstaff and his page, and Justice Silence becomes more and more convivial in his cups, a theatre audience is likely to remember that the last place in this play where a group of men drank together 'friendly' was Gaultree Forest. The Act 5 scene looks back to Gaultree, and an act of expediency all the more chilling for being cloaked behind a familiar social ritual, while also casting shadows ahead. At the beginning of Act 5, Davy had asked Justice Shallow to countenance 'an arrant knave', William Visor of Woncot, against Clement Perkes a'th' Hill, on the grounds that 'the knave is mine honest friend' (5.1.38–51). Now, as Davy thinks of venturing to London for the first time, he and Bardolph pledge mutual loyalty and support. 'The knave will stick by thee', Shallow assures Bardolph and, when Bardolph promises to do the same, Shallow declares, 'Why, there spoke a king' (5.3.65–9). The irony here, as Shakespeare prepares for what we have known all along must happen – the rejection of Falstaff by Henry V – is unmistakable. But there is one last turn of the screw. The scraps of song from Silence which have punctuated this scene throughout are all of one kind, except the very last. Pistol has already burst in, and Falstaff is trying to make sense of his tidings, when Silence suddenly erupts with the line 'And Robin Hood, Scarlet and John' (5.3.103), just before passing out. This, uniquely among Silence's fragments, is not part of a drinking song. The anonymous author of *George a Greene*, a Henslowe property enormously popular during the 1590s, had already drawn upon the ballad from which it comes, *Robin Hood and the Pinder of Wakefield*, in a comedy Shakespeare and his audience must have known well. In that play, Robin Hood, Scarlet, Little John and the Pinder of Wakefield, all sit down in the final scene to do something Falstaff and his cronies never will; they drink together, in affection and trust, with England's king.

* * *

In the mid-fifteenth century, when Walter Bower, continuing Fordun's *Scotichronicon*, implicitly identified Robin Hood as a noble follower of

Simon de Montfort, deprived of his lands after the Battle of Evesham,[34] it registered as an isolated inconsistency among accounts that otherwise had been unanimous in assigning the outlaw to the yeoman class:

> Lythe and listin, gentilmen,
> That be of frebore blode;
> I shall you tel of a gode yeman,
> His name was Robyn Hode.[35]

That is how the 'Gest' itself begins and, apart from Bower, no one disputed it until the sixteenth century. When John Major, in his Latin *History of Greater Britain* of 1521, called Robin *princeps*, in the course of stressing his courtesy to women, persecution of rich clergy, and relief of the poor, he almost certainly intended the outlaw's nobility to be only figurative.[36] But one must never underestimate the strength of what Freud called 'the family romance'. Towards the middle of the sixteenth century, John Leland was claiming that Robin Hood had been outlawed for debt, and that he was of noble blood.[37] Richard Grafton, writing in 1569, went even further; Robin was an earl who 'so prodigally exceeded in charges and expences . . . that he lost or sould his patrimony and for debt became an outlaw'.[38] By the time of William Warner's account, in *Albion's England* – an account increasingly favourable to Robin Hood in successive editions between 1586 and 1602 – something new had been added to Robin's venerable associations with the May Lord, the green man, and the wodewose; he is now a '*Tymon*

---

[34] Walter Bower, *Scotichronicon*, vol. V (Books 9 and 10) ed. Simon Taylor, D. E. R. Watt, Brian Scott (Aberdeen: Aberdeen University Press, 1990), pp. 354–7. 'Moreover all those who supported Simon in that battle were outlawed and disinherited . . . The greater part of the disinherited infested the roads and streets and became robbers . . . At this time there arose from among the disinherited and outlaws and raised his head that most famous armed robber Robert Hood . . .' (p. 355). His identification with the forest is explicit: 'Robertus Hode inter frutecta et dumeta silvestria exulabat' (Robert Hood was an outlaw among the woodland briars and thorns) (pp. 356, 357). The editors note that the identification of Robin Hood with those disinherited for following Simon de Montfort is 'a plausible suggestion for which there is no supporting evidence' (p. 470).

[35] The opening of the First Fytte of the 'Gest', in Dobson and Taylor, *Rymes of Robin Hood*, p. 79.

[36] 'foeminam nullam opprimi permisit, nec pauperum bona surripuit, verum eos ex abbatum bonis ablatis opipare pauit. viri rapinam improbo, sed latronum omnium humanissimus & princeps erat' (he allowed no woman to be oppressed, nor did he pilfer the goods of the poor; in fact, he fed them splendidly with the goods he stole from the abbots. I disapprove of robbery, but of all brigands, he was the prince, and the most compassionate), John Major, *Historia majoris Britanniae* (Paris, 1521), fol. 55ᵛ (G7ᵛ).

[37] Of the monastery of Kirkley in Yorkshire, Leland notes that it is '*ubi Ro: Hood nobilis ille exlex sepultus*' (where the noble outlaw Ro[bin] Hood is buried). John Leland, *Antiquarii de rebus Britannicis collectanea*, vol. I, ed. Thomas Hearn (London: Richardson, 1770), p. 54.

[38] Richard Grafton, *A Chronicle at Large and Meere History of the Affayres of England* (London, 1569), 'This Second Volume, Beginning at William the Conqueror' (1568), p. 85.

of the world', a man who retired in disgust to the forest after bankrupting himself through his generosity to ungrateful friends.[39]

Excessive liberality, verging upon waste, is perhaps the easiest to forgive of human vices. In *The Downfall and Death of Robert Earl of Huntingdon*, Anthony Munday's two-part Robin Hood play of 1598, only Robin's enemies (themselves obsessed with money and property in a way he and the lion-hearted King Richard disdain) continually harp on the Earl's extravagance. As all these carpers are treacherous and grasping, the accusation does him little harm. Like so many of the young prodigals in those Jacobean city comedies that Thomas Middleton and others were shortly to write, Munday's Robin Hood has been undone by a scheming uncle to whom he rashly mortgaged his land. Unlike the later Follywits and Wit-goods,[40] however, he manifests a goodness so alarming that Doncaster actually makes it an excuse for poisoning him. He hates the banished Earl of Huntingdon,

> Because so many loue him as there do,
> And I myselfe am loved of so fewe.
> Nay, I haue other reasons for my hate:
> Hee is a foole, and will be reconcilde
> To anie foe hee hath: he is too milde,
> Too honest for this world, fitter for heaven:
> Hee will not kill these greedie cormorants,
> Nor strippe base pesants of the wealth they haue:
> He does abuse a thieves name and an outlawes,
> And is indeede no outlawe nor no theef,
> He is unworthy of such reuerent names.
> Besides, he keepes a paltry whinling girle,
> And will not bed, forsooth, before he bride. . . .
> He saies his praiers, fasts eues, gives alms, does good:
> For these and such like crimes sweares Doncaster,
> To worke the speedie death of Robin Hoode.[41]

In a way, Doncaster is right. Certainly, Munday's Robin Hood bears little resemblance to Lionel, King of the rout of Raveners,[42] Piers Venables,[43] or

---

[39] William Warner, *The First and Second Parts of Albions England. The Former Revised and Corrected, and the Latter Newly Continued and Added*, 2nd edition (London, 1589), p. 118. See the discussion of Shakespeare's *Timon* in Chapter 3, pp. 63–6.

[40] The spendthrift anti-heroes of Thomas Middleton's *A Mad World My Masters* and *A Trick to Catch the Old One*, respectively.

[41] Anthony Munday, *The Death of Robert Earl of Huntingdon* (1601), in ed. John C. Meagher, Malone Society Reprints (Oxford: Oxford University Press, 1965), lines 308–27.

[42] See p. 76.

[43] Another outlaw, compared by his contemporaries to Robin Hood, quoted in Holt, *Robin Hood*, p. 150.

to his original in the early ballads or the 'Gest': that sturdy thief who, for all his ironic courtesy and veneration of the Virgin Mary, was capable in one story not only of impaling the decapitated head of an opponent on the end of his longbow, but mutilating the face with a knife, 'That he was never on a woman borne, / Cold tell who Sir Guye was'.[44] Munday's plays really look forward to the nostalgic, sentimentalized Sherwood of Leigh Hunt, John Keats and John Hamilton Reynolds[45] and beyond them to Thomas Love Peacock's *Maid Marian* (1822), or Tennyson's play *The Foresters* (1892).[46]

Ben Jonson was a far greater poet and dramatist than Anthony Munday. Yet *The Sad Shepherd*, his Robin Hood pastoral, left unfinished when its author died in 1637, evokes a Sherwood even more wistfully golden. Munday's banished Earl had extracted money from carefully selected travellers – usurers or priests – but Jonson's Robin Hood and his band rob no one at all. Their legal right to kill the stag on which they and the shepherds of Belvoir feast is hastily passed over, while the witch of Papplewick, the only person ever to mention the word 'outlaw', is so curst and malevolent as almost to make the designation suspect. Robin and his associates seem, in fact, to live in Sherwood as if they were official forest rangers, comfortably equipped and scrupulously managing the woods.

It was neither in Munday or Jonson, but in Elizabethan and Stuart plays where the Robin Hood paradigm remains visible below the surface, even though explicit reference to it is non-existent or slight, that the strains and contradictions inherent in the historical and ballad material were most interestingly explored. With two exceptions, Frapolo in James Shirley's *The Sisters* of 1641, and the Captain in a dramatization of Sidney's *Arcadia* attributed to Shirley when it was published in 1640, all these outlaw leaders are by birth well above yeoman rank. In this respect, although they derive immediately from the late tradition encouraged by Bower, Major, Leland and Grafton, they are also throwbacks to Hereward, Fitzwarin or the fourteenth-century robber gangs. Through them, paradoxically, we are made to remember that neither Robin Hood literature nor the character himself enjoyed a uniformly good press in the period. It is also possible to

[44] Dobson and Taylor, 'Robin Hood and Guy of Gisborne', in *Rymes of Robyn Hood*, stanza 42, p. 144.

[45] Leigh Hunt, 'Ballads of Robin Hood', first published in *The Indicator* in 1820; John Keats, 'Robin Hood: To a Friend', published in *Lamia, Isabella, The Eve of St Agnes, and Other Poems* (1820); John Hamilton Reynolds, various sonnets in *The Garden of Florence* (1821).

[46] Tennyson's play, with music by Arthur Sullivan, was first produced in New York in 1892, and in London in 1893, after Tennyson's death.

see, in the later Jacobean and Caroline examples, how certain very contemporary social and political issues begin to form and re-shape the Robin
Hood myth.

It is easy to forget that the earliest written reference to Robin Hood, in
Langland's *Piers Plowman*, is disparaging. Sloth, foolishly keen on the
poems, can't manage to learn the Lord's Prayer: 'I kan noght parfitly my
Paternoster as the preest it syngeth, / But I kan rymes of Robyn Hood and
Randolf Erl of Chestre, / Ac neither of Oure Lord ne of Oure Lady the
leeste that evere was maked'.[47] Against popular enthusiasm for the outlaw
hero have to be set all the reservations of the chroniclers: Bower describing
Robin as a 'famous murderer',[48] and even John Major – who wrote while
Henry VIII was gaily masquing in Kendal green – carefully asserting that
although Robin may have been the most humane and chief of robbers, the
robberies themselves 'I condemn'.[49] Grafton maintains a similar balance,
and so does Warner: although a victimized '*Tymon* of the world', Robin
was not 'devoutly' so, 'And therefore praise I not the man'.[50] This list could
easily be extended – particularly if you begin to take into account the
disapproval of the clergy, or of people like the antiquarian John Smyth of
Nibley, when he compared the long poaching war involving the Berkeley
and Dudley families between 1576 and 1596 to 'the lawles daies of
Robinhood'.[51]

The only overt reference to Robin Hood in *The Two Gentlemen of
Verona* comes from the third outlaw, who swears 'By the bare scalp of
Robin Hood's fat friar' when proposing Valentine as 'a king for our wild
faction' (4.1.36–7). As with Justice Silence's scrap of song in *2 Henry IV*, the
allusion is more than casual; the reverberations it sets off extend throughout the outlaw scenes, helping to focus their inconsistencies. The outlaws'
concern as to whether Valentine has 'the tongues' seems initially curious.
It looks less like a need to waylay travellers in more than one language – like
Robin Hood, Valentine will sit alone in the centre of the forest while his

---

[47] William Langland, *The Vision of Piers Plowman*, ed. A. V. C. Schmidt, 2nd edition (London:
Everyman, 1995), Passus V, lines 395–7, p. 82.
[48] See p. 83; Bower, *Scotichronicon*, vol. 5, p. 355.
[49] See p. 83; Major, *Historia* fol. 55ᵛ (G7ᵛ). Henry VIII's masquing is discussed pp. 78–9.
[50] Warner, *Albions England*, p. 118.
[51] John Smyth of Nibley, *The Berkeley Manuscripts: The Lives of the Berkeleys, Lords of the Honour,
Castle and Manor of Berkeley, in the County of Gloucester from 1066 to 1618, with a Description of the
Hundred of Berkeley and of Its Inhabitants*, ed. Sir John Maclean, 3 vols. (Gloucester: John Bellows,
1883), vol. II, p. 269. Smyth's comment here relates specifically to an earlier feud in the reign of
Henry VIII; it broke out again in Elizabeth's reign, after the death of the earl of Leicester. Ibid.,
pp. 296–7.

men bring likely victims to him – than a rather endearing wish for a leader both civilized and cosmopolitan. To Valentine's stipulation that the band should 'do no outrages / On silly women or poor passengers', the third outlaw replies with apparent indignation: 'No, we detest such vile base practices' (4.1.69–71). Yet not only will Valentine later admit that he still has 'much to do / To keep them from uncivil outrages' (5.4.16–17), but Silvia when rescued by Proteus never denies his claim that the first outlaw, supposed to escort her back to Valentine while the others scour the woods for Eglamour, was about to violate her 'honour'. Nevertheless, at the end, Valentine recommends to the Duke that these banished criminals be forgiven and recalled, and the Duke, like King Richard or Edward II in the 'Gest' and the ballads, immediately agrees.[52]

It can be tempting to include, among the various dramatic uncertainties and confusions of *The Two Gentlemen of Verona*, the conflicting descriptions of its outlaws. This particular contradiction, however, whether what Valentine's men practice is 'an honourable kind of thievery', as Speed calls it (4.1.39), or something altogether more brutal, was by this time an inherent part of the Robin Hood myth. It is paralleled, moreover, in too many other contemporary plays to look either accidental or merely inept. In Thomas Heywood's *The Four Prentises of London*, for instance, first performed around 1600, Charles, son of the banished Earl of Bulloigne, becomes (at their urgent and admiring request) the leader of outlaws whose captain he has killed. Immediately he, like Valentine, sets about the task of converting them to honourable thievery:

> Well, I must have you now turne honest Theeves,
> Hee that commits a rape, shall sure be hang'd:
> Hee that commits a murder, shall be murdered
> With the same weapon that did act the deed.
> Hee that robbes pilgrims, or poore Travellours,
> That for devotions sake doe passe these Mountaines,
> Hee shall bee naked tyed to armes of Trees,
> And in the dayes heate stung with Waspes and Bees.
> Yee slaves, Ile teach you some civility.[53]

Charles intends not only to enforce Robin Hood's rules, but 'in these Forrests make a Common-wealth', of which he will be king. His attempts at 'civil nurture' fail. As one man mutters, 'what a foole is our Captaine, to

---

[52] This episode, and *The Two Gentleman of Verona* more generally, are discussed at greater length in Chapter 6.
[53] Thomas Heywood, *The Four Prentises of London. With the Conquest of Jerusalem* (London, 1615), C4.

prescribe Lawes to Out-lawes? If we would have kept the Lawes before in
the City, wee needed not to have beene driven now to leade our lives in the
Country'.[54] Not only does the first woman who enters the forest narrowly
escape rape; the two outlaws sent to guide the old Earl, their captain's
father, on his way as a pilgrim to the Holy Land, plot to murder him for his
gold and fling the body 'into some cole-pit'. Yet only a few minutes later,
when Tankred, Prince of Italy, makes the familiar royal excursion into the
forest, talking about the reported 'valour' and 'brave deeds of these rude
foresters', and wishing he could win them to his service, he receives the
same assurance that Valentine gave the Duke of Milan:

> We have reform'd these villaines since we came,
> And taught them manners and civility:
> All rape and murder we repay with death:
> Amongst us does not live a ravisher.[55]

And everyone is forgiven.

A not dissimilar division of attitude can be seen in the anonymous *Tom
a Lincoln*.[56] Its eponymous hero, a foundling brought up by a kindly old
shepherd, is really (as it turns out) a lost son of King Arthur. When, like
Paston's William Wood, he gathers followers about him and heads north
to Barnesdale, he calls himself 'the Red-Rose Knight', declaring that 'wee
for knightwhoods prowesse shalbe Crownde / . . . And those that passe
shall yeld, stay, fight, or dy',[57] aligning himself with a mediaeval romance
tradition oddly mingled with Robin Hood associations. (His men are not,
for instance, to despoil any 'poore men of theyr treasure'.) The locals
complain, but the King, impressed by a certain 'bright Nobility' in
Tom's 'youthfull folly', rapidly translates him to court, where his rise is
meteoric. Just before this happens, however, we see the other side of the
coin. The foundling's old foster father journeys to Barnesdale and remon-
strates with him: "Tis dishonourable, gentle boy / to spend thy tyme in
spoiles & Robbery / depriving men of that wch they obtaine / wth toyling
labour, & heart piercing paine'.[58] His words falling on deaf ears, he dies.

* * *

Even in the improbable world of *The Four Prentises*, that 'cole-pit' in which
the thieves plan to conceal the Earl's body suddenly jars. All romance forests
are by definition pre-industrial. They can accommodate wild men, outlaws

---

[54] Ibid., C4.   [55] Ibid., E1.   [56] See p. 72.   [57] *Tom a Lincoln*, lines 267–71, p. 9.
[58] Ibid., lines 538–41, p. 16.

and deer, a hidden castle, perhaps a solitary charcoal-burner or smith, but certainly not coal and ironworks, blast furnaces, smelting houses and strip mines.[59] These, however, did exist in many Elizabethan and Jacobean forests, woodland which, of course, they gradually destroyed. In 1612, mayhem broke out in the Forest of Dean when James I granted the Earl of Pembroke a monopoly there on the digging of ironstone and coal. This monopoly not only involved a far more drastic, large-scale exploitation of mineral resources; it abolished the privileges of the local forest dwellers, rights based on ancient custom rather than law, but regarded by the free miners of Dean as inviolable. When, on 5 August, a group of men crying 'God save the King!' set fire to wood that had been cut and corded for Pembroke's use, the Privy Council ordered the immediate arrest of what it termed 'these Robin Hoods'. No one, however, in an impoverished but tightly-knit community, reputedly including highway robbers, would identify or turn them in.[60] The struggle between the Crown and the free miners of Dean continued throughout James' reign and into that of Charles, exploding again with particular fury in 1631 and 1632, when attempts were made to enclose portions of the forest where iron ore was to be found. When the Sheriff of Gloucester arrived to apprehend the rioters, he found that they had vanished into the woods and, as in 1612, the locals wouldn't tell. The conflict was still going on at the outbreak of the Civil War.

Censorship made it impossible for anyone to write a play dealing directly with the Forest of Dean, or with unrest in any other English forest, which were castigated in 1607 as particular 'nurseries of beggars'.[61] But the Robin Hood tradition, with all its ambiguities, did offer undercover ways of commenting on these things. In the later part of James' reign, and under Charles, plays featuring outlaws tended to become more and more politicized and complex. In Philip Sidney's *Arcadia*, the outlaws who capture Musidorus and Pamela had been a leaderless rabble, treated with contempt, and slaughtered without remorse.[62] For James Shirley, dramatizing Sidney's romance in 1640, such dismissiveness was no longer possible. These men

---

[59] 'Coal-pit' was also used at this time to refer to a charcoal-burner's pit; it is unclear from the context whether this, or a mineshaft, is referred to here.

[60] Sharp, *In Contempt of All Authority*, p. 191.

[61] See Joan Thirsk and J. P. Cooper (eds.), *Seventeenth-Century Economic Documents*, (Oxford: Clarendon Press, 1972), p. 107.

[62] They are initially described as 'a dozen clownish villains ... so forwasted that they seemed to bear a great conformity with the savages' (Book 3, p. 177), and subsequently as 'a rascal company', the 'scummy remnant' of a previous rebellion (Book 4, p. 265); their killing by Musidorus is recounted inventively and satirically (pp. 266–8). Sir Philip Sidney, *The Old Arcadia*, ed. Katherine Duncan-Jones (Oxford: Oxford University Press, 1999).

now have a Captain; not everything they do and say is foolish, and far from being annihilated, they end up as official guards to the royal prisoners before returning, pardoned, to their homes. Here, and in a number of other plays, the ambivalence of the Robin Hood paradigm was being exploited in ways that extended the legend, but also put it under increasing strain.

Individual dramatists reacted in different ways. In 1621, John Fletcher's play *The Pilgrim* featured a distinctly unsavoury outlaw chief. The banished gentleman Roderigo robs everyone except his friends, and anyone who might have influence with the king. His followers, far from being heroes to the local poor, gobble up their food and ravish their wives and daughters. These forest-dwellers are feared and detested alike by the citizens of Segovia and the peasants outside the walls, all of whom long for the Governor to march against them. It is all purposefully anti–Robin Hood, except at moments when the archetype, too strong to be suppressed entirely, suddenly breaks through. These outlaws may have robbed churches in the past; as soon as their leader proposes to murder the pilgrim, they unanimously refuse 'to lay violent hands on holy things'.[63] And, at the end, when the King forgives Roderigo, the Governor forgets his intended expedition and issues the usual general amnesty.

In Philip Massinger's *The Guardian* of 1633, the topicality (and the Robin Hood paradigm) become more overt. Severino, a nobleman banished from Naples for killing his brother-in-law in a duel, is unlike the hero of the ballads and the 'Gest' in that he hates his present way of life: 'Quiet night that brings / Rest to the labourer, is the Outlaws day, / In which he rises early to do wrong'.[64] Yet his followers – explicitly said to imitate 'the courteous English thieves' – gladly accept from him a charter of behaviour socially far more responsible than Roderigo's. Some articles are traditional; scholars, soldiers, labourers, the poor and all women are to pass unmolested. Cheating shopkeepers and vintners, usurers, especially those taking advantage of a bond or mortgage 'from a prodigal', are lawful prize. But Severino has a particular eye for two new classes of victim: 'The grand Incloser of the Commons, for / His private profit, or delight', and 'Builders of Iron Mills, that grub up Forests, / With Timber Trees for shipping'.[65] *The Guardian* sophisticates its Robin Hood material throughout. Severino's wife, Iolante, eventually joins him in the forest, to be ceremonially garlanded and hailed as

[63] John Fletcher, *The Pilgrim*, in ed. A. R. Waller, *The Works of Francis Beaumont and John Fletcher*, 10 vols. (Cambridge: Cambridge University Press, 1907), vol. V, 2.2, p. 175.

[64] Philip Massinger, *The Guardian*, in eds. Philip Edwards and Colin Gibson, *The Plays and Poems of Philip Massinger*, 4 vols. (Oxford: Clarendon Press, 1976), vol. IV, 2.2.35–7.

[65] Ibid., 2.4.94–5.

its queen, but *we* know even if he does not that this Maid Marian has just tried to cuckold him. At the end, when Alphonso, king of Naples rides into the greenwood in disguise, to meet and test Severino, that test no longer takes the form of a simple game of buffets. In a complicated replay of the famous episode in the 'Gest' involving Sir Richard at the Lee,[66] the king pretends to be a father whose three heroic sons, after freeing thousands of Christian galley slaves from the Turks, were themselves made captives. The gold taken from him by the outlaws would be enough to ransom them, but not their shipmates, and without them they refuse to go free. Severino's men rebel momentarily when he at once offers up the entire three-year accumulation of outlaw treasure. The king, however, overlooks this when he reveals himself and declares that 'pardon' is the word for all.

Most interesting of all, perhaps, is the way the doubleness of the Robin Hood material came to be exploited during the years of insurrection and war leading up to the Restoration. Frapolo, the outlaw leader in James Shirley's *The Sisters* of 1642 (the year that the theatres closed), is like Shirley's earlier Captain in not being a gentleman. He ends up, however, impersonating the Prince of Parma, and doing it so well that, until Frapolo himself abandons the game because 'I can hold out no longer', the Prince himself is baffled and confused. This is part of Frapolo's final speech:

> 'Tis time your prince were dead; and when I am
> Companion to my father's dust, these tumults,
> Fomented by seditious men, that are
> Weary of plenty, and delights of peace,
> Shall not approach, to interrupt the calm
> Good princes after death enjoy. Go home,
> I pray; depart: I rather will submit
> To be depos'd, than wear a power or title
> That shall not all be dedicate to serve you:
> My life is but the gift of heaven, to waste it
> For your dear sakes. My people are my children,
> Whom I am bound in nature and religion
> To cherish and protect.[67]

As Martin Butler pointed out in *Theatre and Crisis*,[68] this sounds uncannily like the voice of Charles I, articulating here everything expressed by his role

---

[66] In the Seventh Fytte of the 'Gest', in Dobson and Taylor, *Rymes of Robin Hood*, pp. 104–9.
[67] James Shirley, *The Sisters*, in *Six New Playes: The Brothers, The Sisters, The Doubtfull Heir, The Imposture, The Cardinall, The Court Secret* (London, 1653), Act 5, p. 56.
[68] Martin Butler, *Theatre and Crisis 1632–1642* (Cambridge: Cambridge University Press, 1984), pp. 264–5.

as Philogenes or Lover of his People, in the last court masque before the war: Davenant's *Salmacida Spolia* of 1640. What is one to make of it in the context of *The Sisters*? Is Charles, like Frapolo, perhaps a criminal beneath all the rhetoric of love and concern? Would he – ought he to – be prepared to sacrifice himself for his subjects' good? Shirley later fought on the Royalist side, but his own masque, *The Triumph of Peace* in 1634, had not been uncritical of Charles. In 1653, he was to write another masque, *Cupid and Death*, for Cromwell. *The Sisters* tantalizes, but Shirley refuses to be drawn.

1642 was by no means the last time that a Stuart monarch was associated with Robin Hood, or with life in the forest. 'Robin Whood Revived', a cavalier song written shortly after the Battle of Worcester in 1651, casts the young Charles II as Robin Hood throughout. Charles' enforced sojourn in the hollow oak even allowed him to become a kind of royal wodewose, or Green Man. In John Tatham's civic pageant, *The Royal Oak*, performed in the year of Restoration, the woodland god Sylvanus fleetingly costumed him for this role: 'the pendant leaves his head enshadow'd round / Not only to conceale but to be Crown'd'.[69] But it is part of the adaptability of the myth, and the facelessness of its hero, that Robin Hood could be a Roundhead too. In 1661, the burghers of Nottingham itself, which had just returned a notorious regicide to the first Restoration parliament, reversed the casting. The little play of *Robin Hood and His Crew of Soldiers* is a hasty demonstration of loyalty: a reminder, as the Messenger from London hands out royal pardons to the former insurgents and their leader, that whatever his past misdemeanours, the legendary Robin could always be counted on to kneel down before the rightful king. As such, it is a testimony not just to his continuing vitality, but to the fact that, almost two centuries after Paston's servant William Wood rode away into Barnysdale, the Robin Hood legend was still refusing to disentangle itself from fact.

---

[69] John Tatham, *The Royal Oake and Other Various and Delightfull Scenes Presented on the Water and the Land*, (London, 1660), p. 12.

CHAPTER 5

The Forest and the City

In Robert Browning's last collection of verse, *Asolando*, published in 1889, there is a sequence called 'Bad Dreams'. 'Bad Dreams III' begins, 'This was my dream: I saw a Forest / Old as the earth, no track nor trace / Of unmade man'.[1] Here, the dreamer confronts a vast primal wilderness, one that baffles any human gaze: 'space immeasurable', 'trees that touch heaven', 'enormous growths that bar / Mine eye from penetrating past / Their tangled twine'. Within that tangle, something at least potentially human seems to dwell, 'royally lone, some brute-type cast / I' the rough, time cancels, man forgive', but its exact nature is impossible to make out. Then, in the second stanza, the scene shifts abruptly. Now, the dreamer explores 'a lucid City / Of architectural device / Every way perfect'. 'Bright marbles, dome and spire, / Structures palatial, – streets which mire / Dares not defile'. This place, obviously created by human hands, and designed for human beings to inhabit, has only one unsettling feature; there aren't any people *in* it. The City simply stands there, pristine, complex, immaculately ordered and beautiful, but silent: empty of all life, whether human, animal or vegetable. Or it does until the third and final stanza:

> Ah, but the last sight was the hideous!
> A City, yes, – a Forest, true, –
> But each devouring each. Perfidious
> Snake-plants had strangled what I knew
> Was a pavilion once: each oak
> Held on his horns some spoil he broke
> By surreptitiously beneath
> Upthrusting . . .

The shining City fights back against this wild invasion; cracked pavements, 'as with teeth', grip and mutilate the huge weeds forcing a way through

[1] John Pettigrew (ed.), 'Bad Dreams III', in *Robert Browning: The Poems*, 2 vols. (Aylesbury: Penguin, 1981), vol. II, l. 109–11, p. 884.

them to the light. But it is clear which side will win – and it is not going to be the City. 'Oh, Nature – good! Oh, Art – no whit / Less worthy!', the poem concludes. 'Both in one – accurst!'[2]

Browning's nightmare vision of a death struggle between the forest and the city is hallucinatory and extreme. But something like this has gone on from time immemorial all over the world. 'They say the Lion and the Lizard keep / The Courts Where Jamshyd gloried and drank deep',[3] Fitzgerald lamented in the *Rubáiyát of Omar Khayám*. The city of Rome presents the archetypal historical example of such antagonism and inter-change between the urban and the wild. According to Virgil and Livy, Rome initially came into being as Alba Longa, a city established by a son or grandson of Aeneas who was known as 'Silvius' because he had been born in the forest. That sylvan designation remained attached to all the kings of Alba Longa down to Romulus, the man who first enclosed the seven hills of Rome within a single wall, pushing back the forests to a degree unequalled by any of his Silvian predecessors, and bestowing upon the metropolis he had thus created his own name. Romulus, however, was not only the child of a woman called 'Rhea Silvia'; he and his twin brother, Remus, cast away and abandoned at birth, had been suckled by a wild but compassionate she-wolf, and they spent their youth ranging just those forests that Romulus, the city-builder, was later to clear and destroy. Later Romans, historical rather than legendary, would compound this original betrayal, managing to deforest a great deal of the Mediterranean and regions well beyond it, only for the woods, later, to avenge themselves when the Vandals and the Visigoths, men from the great forests of the north, swept down upon this shining city and burnt and pillaged it. In their wake, the wilderness for a time returned, grass rooting itself in the streets and in the Forum, weeds and young trees prying apart the masonry of once-proud civic buildings.

London too, another legendary Trojan foundation, was a city carved out of forests whose vestiges surround it to this day. They, in their original vastness, are what Marlow, in Conrad's *Heart of Darkness*, is chiefly remembering when, before telling his scarifying tale of Mr Kurtz's activ-ities in the Belgian Congo, he observes to his listeners as they sit on a small boat anchored in the Thames estuary, with the lights of London and its

[2] Ibid., pp. 884–5.
[3] Edward Fitzgerald, *Rubáiyát of Omar Khayyám: With a Persian Text, a Transliteration and a Close Prose and Verse Translation by Eben Francis Thompson* (Worcester: The Commonwealth Press, 1907), p. 30.

commercial river traffic visible all around them, that 'this also has been one of the dark places of the earth'.[4] Conrad's Marlow was looking back, evoking what he calls 'those very old times, when the Romans first came here' and found only savage forest, sandbanks and marsh. Richard Jefferies, in his novel, *After London*, published in 1885, had bleakly looked ahead, imagining the great metropolis annihilated by some indeterminate disaster – famine, plague or cosmic mishap. After that calamity, grass invades first, then weeds, followed in the usual order by briars and brambles and, in their wake, saplings taking root and growing until London has disappeared beneath dense woodland and the Thames, poisoned by the centuries of human effluvia festering beneath it, is transformed into a fetid and deadly marsh.

Nothing as drastic as this happens, or even threatens to happen, in the group of early modern plays with which this chapter is concerned. All, however, assume the forest to be alien and 'other', existing in a complicated, often problematic, relationship with the city. That is so even (perhaps especially) when the two places are contiguous and the forest well-known. Or, as is far more common in England than on the continent, where tracts of forest have come to harbour a few small urban settlements in their midst. As the Mariner in Lyly's *Galatea* reassures the two shipwrecked pages, 'there be woods hard by', but 'at every mile's end, houses'.[5] Such proximity, however, neither prevents some very odd things from happening in these circumambient woods nor guarantees that their denizens will necessarily be restricted to animals, birds and the occasional human. (The goddess Diana and her nymphs, not to mention Venus, Cupid and Neptune, all reside or turn up in *Galatea*'s Humberside forest. And there is a hungry sea-monster, with an appetite for virgins, en route.)

Forests tend to be places where (sometimes for better, often for worse) events occur that would be surprising, or even impossible, in the cities where people normally congregate. Yet the two locales can merge, even seem to exchange identities, and not just in the literal sense. In his book, *The Fall of Public Man*, the sociologist Richard Sennett proposed as the most fundamental definition of the city, the thing most distinguishing it from the village or town, the country hamlet or great house, that it is 'a place where strangers

[4] Joseph Conrad, *Heart of Darkness*, in ed. Samuel Hynes, *Joseph Conrad: The Complete Short Fiction: Heart of Darkness and Other Tales*, 4 vols. (London: Pickering and Chatto Ltd., 1993), vol. III, p. 3.
[5] John Lyly, *Galatea*, ed. George K. Hunter; *Midas*, ed. David Bevington (The Revels Plays) (Manchester: Manchester University Press, 2000), 1.14–5. See the discussion of *Galatea* in Chapter 2, pp. 40–42.

are likely to meet'.[6] But the forest too is a place where strangers continually meet. Some are people who have either elected (as Shakespeare's Timon does) to uproot themselves and seek a life in the woods. Others have been forced, for one reason or another, to flee there, like Rosalind and Orlando, Duke Senior and his followers, in *As You Like It.* None of these new residents have any way of predicting who or what they may encounter after they arrive. And there are always ordinary travellers, people taking a short cut through the forest, on their way to some destination on the other side, who fall unexpectedly into the hands of outlaws, or lose their way and need to be rescued by a fortuitously met hermit, an isolated charcoal-burner, or (as in George Peele's Elizabethan play *The Old Wive's Tale*) a smith.

Newcomers in the forest not infrequently project an image of the urban world with which they have been familiar upon the wild. So, Arden's deer, in Duke Senior's imagination, become 'native burghers of this desert city' (2.1.23), an idea to which the melancholy Jaques, with his talk of poor bankrupts and their 'fat and greasy' fellow 'citizens' (2.1.55) in the antlered herd, has already given more elaborate expression. It is rare now to superimpose the urban upon the wild in this way, largely because so few forests and forest communities are left. Its obverse, however, is often evoked, when major cities are characterized (or deplored) as 'urban jungles'. There are precedents for that superimposition, too, in sixteenth- and seventeenth-century drama. 'Dost thou not perceive', Shakespeare's Titus says, 'that Rome is but a wilderness of tigers?' (3.1.53–4). In *Timon of Athens* too, the city becomes 'a commonwealth of beasts' (4.3.348), enclosing wolves, paling savagery *in*, not out. That is why Timon himself, on his way to exile in the forest, suggests that its walls should dive into the earth and disappear. Which is the urban, which the wild? That antagonism, however, is by no means a constant in drama of the period. Particularly interesting here are three Elizabethan and Jacobean plays in which London and some of the forests in its immediate environs are, as places, quite distinct, but their relationship is basically harmonious. The first was not only set, but actually performed within the bounds of Waltham (now Epping) Forest, before a very special audience which had journeyed there from London. The second makes use of several towns on the road north from London in the neighbourhood of Enfield Chase before moving, climactically, into that woodland at night. The third moves from London to Waltham Forest and back again.

* * *

[6]   Richard Sennett, *The Fall of Public Man* (New York: Alfred A. Knopf, 1974), p. 39.

Three years after *The Princely Pleasures at Kenilworth*, that very costly extravaganza,[7] Robert Dudley, Earl of Leicester provided another, and more modest, outdoor entertainment for the Queen. The scriptwriter this time was his own nephew, Philip Sidney. Sidney's *The Lady of May*, as it came to be called in the eighteenth century, was published posthumously in 1598, as an untitled after-piece to his *Arcadia*. It had been performed in May 1578, not at Kenilworth in Warwickshire, but at Wanstead, the Essex manor within Waltham Forest that Leicester had acquired a year before. Waltham, some ten miles north of London, was a royal forest, subject since the twelfth century to Forest Law. Elizabeth herself, like many of her predecessors, liked to hunt in it. It was huge – some 60,000 acres – but within it were villages or small towns with their schools and churches, together with farms, isolated cottages, lodges for forest officials, and a few aristocratic estates such as Leicester's. The wooded parts (where the deer congregated) were mostly pollarded – this was very much a 'managed' forest – although some timber trees were allowed to reach full height. These areas were liberally interspersed with heath, pasture and with smaller clearings, or 'launds', among the trees. There was some arable land, but sheep-farming in the larger open spaces was far more important to the economy of the region. Immemorial common rights, whether to gather fuel, or to put cattle and horses or feed pigs during certain months in the woodland itself made the administration of this great area – variously owned, but over which royal jurisdiction always hovered – ceaselessly problematic. And proximity to London and its thriving black market for venison didn't help.

A contemporary map of the general area exists in John Norden's *Speculum Britanniae: An Historical and Chorographical Description of Middlesex and Hertfordshire*, first published in 1593 and again in 1723 (with only superficial alterations to the maps). London, the central conglomeration on the Thames, is conspicuous. Greenwich, from whose palace Elizabeth set out on her visit to Leicester, appears on the bottom right. Wanstead itself, in Essex, is marked by Norden with his symbol for 'Houses of the Nobilitie' – in this case Leicester's – and also with the one for a parish. Virtually the whole of Essex, as the large-letter designation at the top right indicates, was then subsumed within 'Waltham Forest', although some differentiating names, derived from particular human settlements, identified certain tracts of it: hence (among others) Hainault, Epping, Chingford and Walthamstow forests, all of them, like

---

[7] See the discussion in Chapter 3, pp. 60–61.

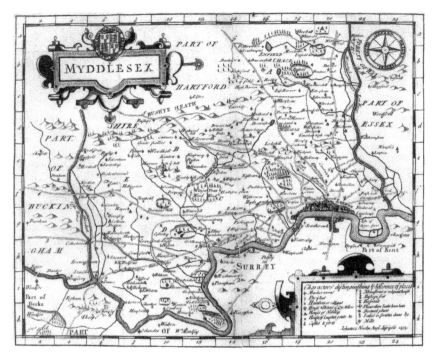

Figure 11. Middlesex, from John Norden, *Speculum Britanniae: An Historical and Chorographical Description of Middlesex and Hertfordshire* (1723)

their encompassing parent forest, under Forest law. Norden's map also marks Enfield Chase and its surrounding towns: Enfield, Edmonton and Waltham Cross, just across the river Lea, and, much further away, Windsor Forest and Great Park down in Berkshire on the far left.

In the spring of 1578, Elizabeth left her royal palace at Greenwich on the outskirts of London to visit Wanstead House. A former royal hunting lodge, it had been greatly enlarged by Leicester, who also increased the acreage of the private park which had existed there since 1512. Wanstead House would undergo several further architectural transformations before being demolished in 1823, but its garden seems to have been laid out before the East Front, and to communicate with the larger area of the park. It was while walking (with her train) in that garden, on May Day, that the queen found herself suddenly accosted by 'one appareled like an honest man's wife of the country', and implored to settle the contention between a shepherd and a forester, rivals for the hand of the country woman's daughter, the Lady of May.[8] Although the resolution of the fictional dilemma was left for Elizabeth herself to dictate, the entertainment itself gently urges her to prefer Therion, the vigorous forester, to the shepherd Espilus, and in doing so, the active above the contemplative life. Whether because she wasn't listening with sufficient attention or (more likely) because she cannily recognized that she was being coerced into support for Sidney's and Leicester's ambitions to take an active part in the religious wars on the continent, she finally gave her verdict in favour of the passive and inoffensive Espilus, thus throwing the end of the entertainment into a modest degree of disarray.

According to the 1598 text of *The Lady of May*, it was when Elizabeth's guided perambulation of Wanstead Garden led her into its 'grove'[9] that she encountered the country woman and her problem. The grove, however, was not where the main action of *The Lady of May* was scheduled to occur. 'Your own way', according to the country woman, 'guides you to the place'.[10] Exactly where that second 'place' might have been remains unclear. The queen can scarcely have been expected to set out on a cross-country hike. On the other hand, she needed at least enough time to read – or have read aloud to her – the verse supplication handed over by her female petitioner, and it was only after this had happened that she found herself no longer in a single, confined garden grove, but facing something arboreally more extensive: 'woods', from which there issued first 'a confused noise', and then six shepherds and six foresters contending violently for possession of the Lady of May, being haled about between them, and accompanied by one 'Master Rombus', described as 'schoolmaster of a village thereby'.[11] Elizabeth had presumably left Leicester's garden and entered his park. The 'woods' she actually confronted may have been contained within the perimeters of this park, but they are more likely to have been adjacent, permitting access for the actors through one or more gates. In Sidney's fiction, the May Lady herself entertains no uncertainty in the matter. The 'gentleman', she tells Elizabeth, who 'seeks to do you all the honour he can in this house ... is but our neighbour, and these be our own groves'.[12] In effect, a fictional version of Waltham Forest at large, woodland, pasture and villages, the 'integrated determination of all [which] topographical region', as the schoolmaster ponderously puts it, has elected this year's May queen, is being conjured up to surround the far

[8] Arthur F. Kinney (ed.), *Renaissance Drama: An Anthology of Plays and Entertainments*, (Oxford: Blackwell Publishers Inc., 1999), pp. 38–44; lines 3–4 (p. 38).
[9] Ibid., line 2 (p. 38).   [10] Ibid., line 35 (p. 39).   [11] Ibid., lines 57, 62–3 (p. 39).
[12] Ibid., lines 144–7 (p. 40).

more limited private setting in which Leicester's entertainment actually took place.

The affluent shepherd Espilus claims (and no one contradicts him) that he owns rich pasture and two thousand sheep. This quantity of livestock is matched exactly by Therion the forester: 'two thousand deer in wildest woods I have'. The forester, however, owns neither these deer nor, as far as one can tell, any land, which is why Espilus can dismiss him as 'one that hath no wealth'.[13] Therion and his companions merely look after the royal forest and its game, as officers of the crown, and it is to Elizabeth that all its beasts of the chase – although not for the most part its land – actually belong. The fact that he is supposed to be protecting the royal deer does not, however, prevent Therion from occasionally and quite illegally making off with one himself: 'stealing me venison out of these forests' as the May Lady happily confesses.[14] The foresters of Waltham were prone to this kind of intermittent theft, as court records of the time attest, some of the deer ending up for sale in London. Elizabeth in 1578 may or may not have relished the joke, but it conceivably influenced her final choice of Espilus over Therion. Alternatively, she could simply have become so accustomed to the literary convention that foresters, unlike shepherds, are by nature lustful and savage as to doubt the wisdom of actually marrying one, whatever the prompts in Sidney's text. The rivalry between shepherds and foresters in *The Lady of May*, and the long literary tradition in which shepherds, almost by definition, are tranquil and orderly people, and foresters, by contrast, libidinous and unruly (like those who pursue the unfortunate Florimell in Book 3 of Spenser's *Faerie Queene*)[15] is a long-standing one. The two occupations became polarized very early on, not so much reflecting the real competition that did sometimes exist between the maintenance of pasture and of woodland, than because they were seen respectively to embody the contemplative and the active life, the gentle and poetic as opposed to the uncouth, savage or (even) mad.

This frequently antagonistic relationship between foresters and shepherds would be explored in other plays of the period; in the anonymous *The Maid's Metamorphosis* (1600), for instance, where the ranger Silvio and Gremulo the shepherd engage in a long debate over the advantages of their respective ways of life as they compete for the favour of Eurymine, the beautiful girl they have found wandering in the forest. The setting, half

---

[13] Ibid., lines 221, 223 (p. 41).   [14] Ibid., lines 169–70 (p. 40).

[15] Edmund Spenser, *The Faerie Queene*, ed. Thomas P. Roche (London: Yale University Press, 1978) Book IV, Canto i, stanzas 15–18; Canto iv, stanzas 46–50; Canto v, stanzas 5–25.

fictional, half real, of *The Lady of May* bears immediately, however, upon at least one later sixteenth-century play designed not (like Sidney's) for a single very special *al fresco* performance, but for London's commercial theatres. Shakespeare's *Love's Labour's Lost*, although never (as far as one knows) performed in a park like Leicester's at Wanstead, could easily have been staged in one. Nothing anywhere in this text indicates an indoor scene. The royal court of Navarre, a great house said now to be 'silent' (2.1.24) and 'unpeopled' (2.1.88) in consequence of the king's three-year vow of abstinence and study, is only a shadowy presence, unvisited and remote. According to Don Armado, it possesses a formal, 'curious-knotted garden' (1.1.246), north-west from the building and giving on the park, but neither that garden nor the house itself is ever required in the comedy, which unfolds either within the park or in those adjacent fields where Navarre has hastily put up tents to accommodate the Princess of France and her companions. Within the park, locals such as constable Dull, the school-master Holofernes and Nathaniel the curate walk freely, but it is clear that they live in what *The Lady of May* had called 'a village thereby'. No shepherds are mentioned, but there certainly are deer – and a forester to look after them – although the game here is harboured within the park itself, not 'in wildest woods'. Shakespeare may not have seen either Wanstead, or a manuscript copy of *The Lady of May* when he wrote *Love's Labour's Lost* around 1596. Still, the two settings have a good deal in common and, for members of his London audience, they would have seemed familiar, even though Shakespeare's is supposedly French, and the other lay only a short distance from their own city.

* * *

Early in the reign of King James, two plays employing either Waltham Forest or Enfield Chase, across the county border, as settings appeared in rapid succession. One of them, although it has become a staple of Renaissance drama courses and is still occasionally performed, began life as a disaster. The other, although almost forgotten today, was overwhelmingly popular in its own time. In October 1607, *The Merry Devil of Edmonton* was entered in the Stationers' Register with no indication of author, and published (again anonymously) in the succeeding year as having been acted 'sundrie times' by the King's Men at the Globe. It ran through no fewer than five subsequent quarto editions, the last of them in 1655, by which time it had not only enjoyed a royal performance before King James, but succeeded in getting itself attributed to Shakespeare.

In 1616, Ben Jonson was pleading (rather wearily) with audiences at Blackfriars to accord his own devil play (*The Devil Is an Ass*) something like the approval given to what he called 'Your dear delight, *The Devil of Edmonton*'.[16] The second play, Beaumont's *The Knight of the Burning Pestle*, composed about 1607, probably for the Children of the Queen's Revels at Blackfriars, and certainly for a private theatre, waited until 1613 for an edition. The publisher described it then as having been unfairly but 'utterly rejected' by its audience.[17] Not until 1635 when it was finally performed again by Queen Henrietta Maria's Men at the private house in Drury Lane was a second quarto called for, after which, the author's name having finally become attached to the play, it was absorbed into the second Beaumont and Fletcher Folio of 1679. A good deal of speculation has come to surround the original misfortune of *The Knight of the Burning Pestle*, a comedy that now seems both original and entrancing. It certainly makes fun of London's citizen class, but in one of the private theatres, before a fashionable audience, that ought not to have mattered (and it was hardly unusual in so doing). Although far less attention has been paid to it, the enormous popularity of the now-neglected *Merry Devil*, even after the appearance of most of Jonson's and Shakespeare's greatest comedies, also seems puzzling. Some possible and partial explanation might be found, however, in the setting of the two plays, which make use of particular tracts of woodland near London with which many members of the audience at both the Globe and Blackfriars were familiar.

Whoever wrote *The Merry Devil of Edmonton* had a striking interest in locality. The plot of this comedy may be somewhat fanciful; its topography is not. An obsession with place manifests itself immediately in the Prologue. Edmonton, the Globe audience was reminded, the birthplace and abode of Peter Fabell, the eponymous merry devil, lies 'not full seven mile from this great famous Citty', and there, 'Fixt in the wall of that old antient Church, / His monument remayneth to be seene; / His memory yet in the mouths of men'.[18] The dramatist had clearly looked at the memorial, as had John Norden, who mentions it in his Middlesex volume, while expressing scepticism that Fabell really had (as claimed) vanquished the 'Devell by pollicie', Satan (he observed) being 'deceite it selfe; and hardly

[16] Ben Jonson, *The Devil Is an Ass*, ed. Anthony Parr, *The Cambridge Edition of the Works of Ben Jonson* (Cambridge: Cambridge University Press, 2012), vol. IV, Prologue line 22, p. 482.

[17] Francis Beaumont, *The Knight of the Burning Pestle*, ed. Michael Hattaway (London: Ernest Benn Limited, 1969), Walter Burre's letter, line 6, p. 3.

[18] C. F. Tucker Brooke, *The Merry Devill of Edmonton*, in *The Shakespeare Apocrypha* (Oxford: Clarendon Press, 1967), Prologue lines 13 and 18–20, p. 265.

deceived'.[19] In *The Merry Devil* itself, Fabell's necromantic exploits are confined to the Induction, in which he outwits his diabolic familiar Coreb, who has come to claim his soul after the appointed seven years, by trapping him in a magic chair. (Fabell also seems to be a fellow of Peterhouse, and has been accustomed to commute between Edmonton and his academic commitments at Cambridge through the agency of Coreb, who conveniently whisks him through the air. The other fellows appear not to have noticed. Neither this, however, nor any other magical improbability, plays a part in the plot of the comedy.) After the Induction, Fabell relies on nothing but his own wit and inventiveness in ensuring that his former tutorial pupil Raymond Mounchensey gets to marry Milliscent Clare, the girl he loves, despite her father's opposition. The only supernatural manifestations are those invented by the fears of four ordinarily very down-to-earth poachers as they try to evade the forest rangers and kill a buck after dark in Enfield Chase.

John Norden speculated that the county of Hertfordshire derived its name from 'the passage of Deere' formerly called 'hartes', but now 'stagges', through this heavily forested region, 'fitte' (as he says) 'for the fostering of suche kinde of wilde beastes'.[20] The places that matter in *The Merry Devil* are Edmonton (on the bottom-righthand corner of Norden's map), in Middlesex, then Enfield and the town of Waltham Cross, all north of it, and Enfield Chase lying to the west. Eastwards, Waltham Abbey, Cheston Nunnery and Waltham Forest also figure. The play is meticulous about who among its (not inconsiderable) cast of characters lives where and about tracing their movements within the district: Fabell and Smug the smith both live in Edmonton, and the Mounchesney family on estates just outside it; Blague is the host of the George Inn at Waltham, in which town Banks the miller also resides, and the raffish Sir John is vicar of Enfield church. Sir John spells out the geography plainly: 'Neighbour Banks of Waltham, and Goodman Smug, the honest smith of Edmonton, as I dwell betwixt you both at Enfield, I know the taste of both your ale houses, they are good both, smart both'.[21] Among other members of the gentry, the wealthy Sir Ralph Jerningham and his son live within 'the forest', Enfield Chase itself, as does Brian, the forest officer, at the upper lodge there. The lodges of Enfield Chase, however isolated their position

[19] John Norden, *Speculum Britanniae. Description of Middlesex* (Amsterdam: Theatrum Orbis Terrarum Ltd., 1971), p. 18.

[20] John Norden, *Speculum Britanniae. The Description of Hartfordshire* (Amsterdam: Theatrum Orbis Terrarum, 1971), p. 1.

[21] Tucker Brooke (ed.), *The Merry Devill of Edmonton*, 2.1.11–5.

Figure 12. Hertfordshire, from John Norden, *Speculum Britanniae: An Historical and Chorographical Description of Middlesex and Hertfordshire* (1723)

within the woods, were not simple rustic buildings. The surviving East Lodge there has obviously been altered after the time of the play, but remains indicative nonetheless of the considerable style in which forest keepers with Crown appointments might live. It would be an entirely plausible intended refuge for Milliscent Clare and her lover, Raymond Mounchensy, who describes Brian as his friend. The Clare family itself, Sir Arthur, his wife, his daughter Milliscent and his son, live on their estates in the region of Waltham, but far enough away for the entire party to arrive at the George Inn there on horseback to sort out Milliscent's marriage – the women, according to the stage direction, not only wearing cloaks, but 'safeguards', protections for their clothing against muddy country lanes – and they have planned to stay over-night in Waltham.

Only three localities are actually staged, as opposed to being talked about, in *The Merry Devil*: the George Inn, together with a rival inn across the street, and Banks' house, all at Waltham; then the nunnery at Cheston (briefly) and crucially, for all of Act 4, the woods of Enfield Chase, together with Enfield Church on their outskirts. Woods in drama of the period are, almost by definition, places of confusion and misunderstanding, and that certainly is true here as Milliscent, her lover, the two friends who have helped her to escape from Cheston nunnery, her irate father and his friend, the four poachers Banks, Blague, Smug and Sir John, plus Brian the keeper with his servant and dog all blunder about the Chase in the dark, continually mistaking one another's purposes and identity. Enfield Chase exists now only in the much-diminished form of Hadley Wood, which can just be glimpsed before the train tunnels under it on the Cambridge to London line, but at the time of the play it was extensive. Some of them lose their way specifically near Potters Gate, now Potters Bar, also a railway station on the Cambridge line. It all ends happily enough in Act 5, with almost everyone assembled back at The George, Milliscent married to Mounchesny by Sir John, her father reconciled to the match and (Smug having managed somehow to carry off the buck he killed in 'Brians walke') a sumptuous wedding breakfast of illegally procured venison about to be served. Brian the keeper is, for obvious reasons, absent at this gathering. So, oddly enough, is Banks, the fourth transgressor against Forest law. That may be because the dramatist decided he had already sailed too close to the wind by giving one of his poachers this name, even if he was camouflaged as a miller in Waltham. John Banks, deputy bailiff of the Manor and Chase of Enfield at the time had, with his son, become so notorious for deer-stealing from the very forest he was supposed to oversee that in 1609, a public enquiry would be set up to look into his depredations.

Although it has a certain charm, *The Merry Devil of Edmonton* is not a play likely to be revived today. Its enormous success in its own time surely had much to do with the delight of its original Globe Theatre audience at seeing such an intricate and sprightly comic plot, even if it was all supposed to be happening long ago, before the Protestant Reformation, superimposed upon terrain they could recognize immediately, and indeed knew well. As Peter Fabell says in Act 1, the thoroughfare out of London by way of Tottenham Cross, extending north through Edmonton, Enfield and Waltham, was much frequented not only by carriers of various kinds transporting goods and provisions to and from the metropolis, but by ordinary Londoners on a day's outing, including what he calls 'the franke and merry London prentises, / That come for creame and lusty country cheere'.[22] Those very apprentices, to the despair of London's strait-laced

---

[22] Ibid., 1.3.143–144.

civic authorities, spent a considerable amount of time at public playhouses like the Globe. At Blackfriars, on the other hand, when *The Knight of the Burning Pestle* made its unlucky debut, the higher prices meant that the only apprentices present are likely to have been Beaumont's fictional characters Jasper and Ralph, the latter indentured to the grocer, George, and his wife Nell, equally fictional citizens who clamber onto the stage at the beginning and wreak havoc with the plot of the play the company is trying to perform.

George and Nell are extremely proud and defensive of London citizens and tradespeople like themselves, and angrily aware that at private theatres such as Blackfriars, they were likely to become objects of mockery. But they also, especially Nell, have a well-developed if unsophisticated taste for romance fiction, the wilder and more improbable the better. That is why they insist on introducing their apprentice Ralph into the play as a knight errant bearing the arms of the Grocers' Company, and propelling him into a series of bizarre adventures that lead from London into Waltham Forest and then (after a brief excursion to Moldavia) back to London again. It is unclear just why *The Knight of the Burning Pestle* was such a signal failure in 1607. Walter Burre, its publisher in 1613, writes vaguely in his prefatory letter about the audience's 'want of judgement, or not understanding the privy mark of irony about it', 'merely literal interpretation or illiterate misprision'[23] and defends the play as printed from any charge of being parasitic upon Cervantes' *Don Quixote*, which had appeared in Sheldon's English translation in 1612. That last assertion was disingenuous; not only had a manuscript translation of Cervantes' great novel begun to circulate in 1605, in good time for Beaumont to have read it, its influence on his play is obvious. As for 'not understanding the privy mark of irony', it was surely unmistakable. Far more likely is the possibility that Beaumont's audience understood it all too well and resisted it, not in terms of the dramatist's satiric treatment of citizens, but because they disliked his parody of romance.

The genteel Blackfriars audience was steeped in works such as Sidney's *Arcadia* (printed in multiple editions in the 1590s) and Spenser's *The Faerie Queene* (1590, 1596), and in 1607, the memory of Elizabeth's Accession Day tilts, with all their neo-mediaeval chivalric display, was still green. It was a cult that King James' eldest son and heir, the charismatic Prince Henry, took seriously and it was about to manifest itself in court masques, particularly those, like *Prince Henry's Barriers* (January 1610) and *Oberon*

---

[23] Beaumont, *Knight of the Burning Pestle*, Walter Burre's letter, lines 4–5 and 21–2, p. 3.

(January 1611), devised by Ben Jonson and Inigo Jones as part of the year-long festivities surrounding Henry's installation as Prince of Wales in June 1610; Henry himself both tilted and performed in the *Barriers*. Ben Jonson might have grumbled about the contemporary taste for Spenser, Sidney and Iberian romances such as *Palmerin de Oliva* and *Amadis de Gaul*, but he indulged it in these masques for Prince Henry and also in some of his later masques. Beaumont's audience may also have reacted as adversely as they did to *The Knight of the Burning Pestle* because of the parodic use it makes of Waltham Forest, a place they knew: a treatment wholly different from that accorded Enfield Chase in *The Merry Devil*. In creating this double image – Waltham Forest as his Blackfriars' audience knew it on excursions out of London, and the fantastic forests of Iberian and French romance – Beaumont was not just treading in the footsteps of Cervantes. He was carrying to a comic extreme something visible to greater or less degree in most of those plays by his contemporaries which utilize woodland settings: a deliberate blurring of the symbolic with the literal, the fictional with the real.

Almost all of Acts 2 and 3 of Beaumont's play take place in what Humphrey, the dreadful suitor of Luce, the London merchant Venturewell's daughter, exaggeratedly calls 'the wild Waltham Forest', lying he says 'some ten miles off'[24] from the city. Luce has feigned will-ingness to marry him, but only if he carries her off there so that she can pretend to have experienced a romantic elopement. In fact, she has arranged to be rescued in the forest by the man she really loves, her father's apprentice Jasper. As usual in forest plays, a number of people converge upon what Ralph, the knight of the title, persists in calling this 'desert': not only Humphrey, Luce and Jasper, but Jasper's mother, Mistress Merrythought, and her favourite son Michael, and Ralph himself with his attendant 'squire' and 'dwarf'. Predictably, chaos results as they stumble across one another in the woods, a confusion exacerbated by the fact that Ralph, who encounters all of them, is living in an imaginary chivalric world of his own devising. He also tangles with the Host of the Bell Inn at Waltham's Town End, in the midst of the forest, who asks him to pay for his night's lodging. This is incomprehensible to Ralph, for whom the inn is a lonely castle whose courteous owner is accustomed to welcome knights errant astray in the woods without any thought of reimbursement. Rescued from his predicament by George and Nell, who rush forward to settle the bill, Ralph then moves on (prompted by the malicious invention of the

[24] Beaumont, *Knight of the Burning Pestle*, Act 2, line 59, p. 37.

innkeeper) to undertake what the latter describes as 'the great venture' of this wilderness: battle with that 'furious fiend'[25] the huge giant Barbaroso, said to dwell in a nearby cave, where he keeps many good knights prisoner. Because not only the supposed Barbaroso (actually Waltham's barber-surgeon), but his customers, primed by the Host of the Bell, all join in the pretense, this lunatic adventure ends surprisingly well for Ralph and his attendants, who set off happily afterwards for Moldavia.

All this is wonderfully comic. But it also ridicules folk, fairy tale and romance motifs that are deeply engrained in Western literature generally, and which (in terms of the lonely house in the woods) remain potent. Giants tend to inhabit forests, as Orgoglio does in Book 1 of *The Faerie Queene*,[26] or the unnamed giant in Davenant's late masque *Britannia Triumphans* (1638),[27] but it is the isolated forest dwelling itself, almost always come upon as a surprise, that was and still is truly resonant. Such dwellings take a variety of forms. In the illustration for the month of November from the Duc de Berry's 'Book of Hours', the hunters low down in the foreground, bloodily despatching a wild boar at the end of their chase, do not even glance up at the crenellated and oddly spectral white castle in the distance, separated from them by thick forest. They may or may not know of its existence. But it is just the kind of place that the lonely traveller through such woods is likely to come upon unexpectedly. Beaumont's Ralph is looking for this, for the golden castle in the middle of Henry VIII's pageant 'Forrest Salvigne',[28] or for what Gawain (like many another mediaeval traveller) finds in the fourteenth-century alliterative poem *Sir Gawain and the Green Knight*: a warm and apparently welcoming castle in the midst of a wild and inhospitable forest.[29] Gawain's castle isn't altogether what it seems, but then dwellings so situated rarely are, whether it is the chateau in which Beauty's father, lost in the woods, takes refuge in 'Beauty and the Beast', or the palace of Comus that springs up to receive the Lady in Milton's *Masque at Ludlow Castle*.[30] Such places don't need to be grand to be uncanny. They can be small, like the ginger-bread cottage of

[25] Ibid., Act 3, lines 215–9.   [26] Spenser, *Faerie Queene*, Book I Canto viii, *passim*.

[27] The stage direction describes it as 'a vast Forest, in which stood part of an old Castle kept by a Giant, proper for the Scene of the Mock *Romansa* which followed'. The design was by Inigo Jones, *Britannia Triumphans a Masque* (1638), B4ᵛ. See Figure 1.

[28] See the discussion in Chapter 2, p. 28.

[29] *Sir Gawain and the Green Knight*, ed. J. R. R. Tolkien, E. V. Gordon (Oxford: Clarendon Press, 1925), fit 2, line 767f, p. 24.

[30] '*The scene changes to a stately palace, set out with all manner of deliciousness*', 'A Masque Presented at Ludlow Castle', in John Milton, *The Complete Shorter Poems*, ed. John Carey (revised second edition) (Harlow: Pearson Education Limited, 2007), 657SD, p. 213.

the wicked witch in *Hansel and Gretel,* or the humble forest dwelling of the smith Clunch in Peele's play *The Old Wive's Tale,* which looks perfectly homely and normal until (as the good-wife begins to tell her story) the cottage walls suddenly dissolve, and the be-nighted pages her husband has brought home find themselves surrounded by a forest far more weird and irrational than that in which they originally went astray. (This new one harbours the castle of a malicious sorcerer, a magic well, and a keeper of the crossroads who is a man by day but is transformed into an animal at night, becoming 'the white bear of England's wood'.)[31] Forests in themselves tend to be alien and disturbing; oddly enough, a single, supposedly human habitation discovered in their midst (a village is an altogether different and more comforting matter) renders them even more sinister. This is brilliantly realized in Walter de la Mare's haunting poem 'The Listeners' ('"Is there anyone there?" said the Traveller, / Knocking on the moonlit door; / And his horse in the silence champed the grasses / Of the forest's ferny floor'),[32] and still exploited for all it's worth, as it is in David Lynch's television series *Twin Peaks* (1990–1), John Fowles' novel *The Magus* (1966) or the closing sequence of *The Blair Witch Project* (1999), with its eerie ruined house, to give just a few, very different, examples.

Ralph, although the most extreme, is not the only character in *The Knight of the Burning Pestle* who behaves like someone living in a book. Luce may be trying it on when she persuades both her father and her credulous suitor Humphrey that she must be abducted and transported to 'the wild Waltham Forest', but her preferred lover Jasper is not when, having taken possession of her there according to plan, he decides when they become lost after a night spent wandering in 'the darkness of this wild unpeopled place' that he must 'try her, that the world and memory / May sing to aftertimes her constancy'. Luce wakes from sleep to find him standing over her with drawn sword, announcing that he means to kill her in order to be revenged on her father Venturewell, who has turned him out of doors. Although Luce passes this test with flying colours ('Strike; I am ready, / And, dying, still I love thee'), the outcome is calamitous: Luce is rescued against her will by Venturewell and Humphrey, leaving Jasper in despair over his own folly.[33]

Beaumont was parodying the whole tradition of women lured into a forest and threatened there with death, rape or both. It had a considerable history

---

[31] George Peele, *The Old Wives Tale*, ed. Patricia Binnie (Manchester: Manchester University Press, 1980), line 169, p. 45.

[32] Walter de la Mare, *Collected Poems* (London: Faber and Faber, 1979), lines 1–4.

[33] Beaumont, *Knight of the Burning Pestle*, Act 3 lines 72–3 and 103–4, pp. 61–2.

already in English drama. Robert Greene's *James IV* (c. 1590), had left the
queen of Scotland wounded and bleeding after being attacked by an assassin
in the forest. The reason why the beautiful Eurymine in *The Maid's
Metamorphosis*[34] becomes the object of contention between a forester and
a shepherd is that she has been abandoned in the woods by hired murderers
who, when it came to it, found themselves (as is often the case) unable to do
the dastardly deed. Thomas Heywood's character Bella Franca has a narrow
escape from rape in the woods in *The Four Prentises of London*, as does Silvia
in Shakespeare's *The Two Gentlemen of Verona*.[35] Shakespeare's Tamora, in
Titus Andronicus, taps knowingly into this tradition when she claims (falsely)
that Bassianus has attempted to murder her in a lonely forest vale, the same
forest, described as 'ruthless, dreadful, deaf and dull', in which Titus'
daughter Lavinia, Bassianus' wife, will genuinely be raped and mutilated
by Tamora's own sons Chiron and Demetrius (2.1.127).

Beaumont and Fletcher's collaborative play *Philaster, or Love Lies
a-Bleeding* (probably 1609), is especially interesting here. Apparently their
first real theatrical success, it includes a forest scene in which the princess
Arethusa, who has strayed away from the royal hunting party, is savagely
wounded by her lover Philaster, because he believes (quite wrongly) that he
has surprised her indulging in wanton familiarities with her page.
The scene (which has been identified as the work of Beaumont, not
Fletcher)[36] was sufficiently arresting not only to give the play its sub-title,
but to appear, on the title page, as the reader's introduction to the first
quarto of 1620. (There are considerable textual problems with this initial
edition, which may derive from an unreliable theatre prompt-book.)[37]
In the second and more reliable quarto (1622), however, the so-called
'country gentleman' seen beside the wounded Arethusa, while Philaster
lurks on the right in a bush, is demoted in rank, becoming a simple
'countrey fellow'. This matters, not only because it accords better with
the character's earthy, no-nonsense style of speech, but because it high-
lights Beaumont's inability, even after the failure of *The Knight of the
Burning Pestle*, and in a very different kind of play, set in Sicily, to refrain

---

[34] See p. 100   [35] See pp. 86–8.
[36] For a succinct account of Beaumont and Fletcher's collaboration and a breakdown (drawing on the
work of Cyrus Hoy) of their particular contributions to *Philaster*, see Francis Beaumont and
John Fletcher, *Philaster*, ed. Suzanne Gossett (London: Methuen Drama, 2009), 'Introduction',
pp. 14–20.
[37] See Gossett, 'Introduction', pp. 76–99. The problems with Q1 most likely arose from censorship
following its revival in 1619. Gossett prints parallel passages from Q1 and Q2 as Appendix 1,
pp. 272–317.

Figure 13. Francis Beaumont and John Fletcher, *Philaster* (1620)

from launching one quick satiric dart at this particular plot device. The countryman is devastatingly sensible about the romantic excesses of his supposed social betters, including Arethusa herself, who attempts *not* to be rescued from death at her lover's hands because (she insists implausibly) these are 'our private sports, our recreations'. ('God uds me', her defender replies, 'I understand you not; but I know the rogue has hurt you'.)[38]

* * *

The frequency with which forests turn out to spell trouble for women in sixteenth- and early seventeenth-century plays is on the one hand quite explicable but, on the other, presents a paradox. Although wild men, hermits, and the occasional (and usually lascivious) satyr tend to call forests 'home', woodland is famously the haunt of that 'Queen and huntress, chaste and fair',[39] the goddess Diana, and her train of virgin followers. It also harbours, in European folk and fairy tales, a wide variety of lesser female spirits, some beneficent, others alarming to encounter. A number of these figures appear in Philippe Barrier's *Forêt Légendaire*. Forests, more-over, as Barrier points out, have a tendency in themselves to register in the male imagination (and in French grammar) as female.[40] They spell other-ness: something dark, secret, irrational and difficult to see clearly or control, as fields and open country are not. The immemorial human hostility to them is at least partly sexual. That female gendering may help to explain why, throughout the seventeenth and eighteenth centuries, both in England and France, men trying to defend a particular forest against government legislation designed to exploit it and restrict its tradi-tional common use often felt impelled to signal their identification with the place by disguising themselves, on their protest outings, as women.[41]

Although in the many original maps illustrating Drayton's enormous chorographic poem *Poly-Olbion*, composed between 1612 and 1622, the emblematic figures representing streams and rivers are, as in Drayton's poem, predominantly female, they *can* also be personified as male, as with the Thames and the Lea in Figure 14, and also the Humber in the north of England. In explicitly marrying the Trent to the Humber, and making Isis the bride of Thames in his poem, Drayton was probably remembering Spenser's elaborate celebration, in Book 4 of *The Faerie Queene* (1596,

[38] Beaumont and Fletcher, *Philaster*, in eds. C. F. Tucker Brooke and Nathaniel Burton Paradise *English Drama 1580–1642*, (Boston: D. C. Heath and Company, 1933), 4.3.95–7, p. 748.

[39] Ben Jonson, *Cynthia's Revels*, ed. Eric Rasmussen and Matthew Steggle, *Cambridge Edition of the Works of Ben Jonson* (Cambridge: Cambridge University Press, 2012), vol. I, 5.1.1 (p. 525).

[40] See Philippe Barrier, *Forêt légendaire: Contes, légendes, coutumes, anecdotes, sur le forêts de France* (Paris: Christian de Bartillat, 1991).

[41] See Natalie Zemon Davis, *Society and Culture in Early Modern France* (Stanford: Stanford University Press, 1975), pp. 147–50. Zemon Davis discusses examples from France and England; in 1641, the leaders of men rioting against the enclosure of forest land in Wiltshire dressed as women and called themselves 'Lady Skimmington' (p. 148).

Figure 14. Middlesex and Hertfordshire, from Michael Drayton, *Poly-Olbion* (1612)

reprinted in 1609), of the wedding of Thames and the 'lovely' Medway.[42] Forests in these seventeenth-century illustrations, however, are invariably female. That is unmistakably the gender of Enfield Chase in Drayton's map, and elsewhere of Arden or Waltham, Hatfield or Sherwood forests, just as it is when Drayton describes woodland, or actually makes it speak. Although his rivers speak too, or rather babble to one another, to the landscape and to the towns by and through which they flow, and where they often merge, his forests are qualitatively different. They are far more isolated and, on the whole, more reticent. Theirs is a strictly celibate and exclusive sisterhood of trees making infrequent contact with one another across geographical space; that they are almost always represented carrying a bow and arrows underscores their association with the huntress Diana.

Drayton's forests have long accepted the presence within and around them of human habitations and of wood pasture where flocks can graze. As Arden herself puts it in *Poly-Olbion*,

---

[42] Spenser, *Faerie Queene*, Book IV Canto xi, stanzas 8–53.

> But, of our Forrests kind the quality to tell,
> We equally partake with Woodland as with Plaine,
> Alike with Hill and Dale; and every day maintaine
> The sundry kinds of beasts upon our copious wast's,
> That men for profit breed, as well as those of chase.[43]

The idea, still sometimes voiced by critics of pastoral, that the mingling of forests and pasture, sheep and deer, is literary and artificial, an eclectic arcadian landscape, ignores the reality that, in England, this combination was not only possible, but practical and fairly widespread. Fact, not simply literary tradition, encouraged sixteenth- and early seventeenth-century English dramatists to mingle foresters with shepherds, timber trees with grazing, in play after play. Simon Forman, watching a performance of *The Winter's Tale*, would have seen no reason to question the co-existence, however uneasy, of sheep and wild animals (like the bear that devours Antigonus) in the same locale.[44] Certainly the present-day shepherds of Transylvania do not: men who continue, every summer, to take village flocks up to the high pastures of the Carpathian mountains, a practice known as transhumance, and struggle heroically to bring roughly the same number of sheep back down with them in October, despite the depredations of both bears and wolves living in the dense forests by which these pastures are ringed.

For obvious reasons, the shepherds of Transylvania do not take their wives and families with them when they migrate temporarily to the high pastures. They leave them in the villages below, subsisting in the mountains from June until the autumn as a lonely, self-sufficient, all-male community. That is a pattern alien on the whole to the gentler landscape of Britain,[45] where not only sheep-cotes but rural hamlets with their schools and churches have tended to cluster in the purlieus just outside a forest, or even in certain open spaces within, allowing shepherds sometimes to rub shoulders with foresters, domestic animals with game. Yet, even in Britain, it is true that, in the innermost depths of a wood, areas remote from villages or country hamlets, women are a rare (and usually mythological) presence. It is unusual, for instance, for sylvan outlaw communities anywhere in the world to include a woman, although many are capable of victimizing one if they come upon her lost in the forest or simply passing through. Although the forest itself may often strike men not only as female, but troublingly so,

---

[43] Michael Drayton, *Poly-Olbion*, in ed. John Buxton, *Poems of Michael Drayton*, 2 vols. (London: Routledge & Kegan Paul Ltd., 1953), 13th song, lines 34–8, p. 587.

[44] See the discussion of Forman and *The Winter's Tale* in Chapter 2, p. 45.

[45] It was historically practiced in some parts of Wales and Scotland.

its human inhabitants, outlaws and foresters, as well as the isolated char-
coal-burners, woodcutters and smiths located there by the necessities of
their trade, tend to be aggressively male. Only one woman, the beautiful
Draupadi, shares the forest exile of the Pandavas in *The Mahabarata*, the
great Sanskrit epic.[46] Robin Hood's Maid Marian, too, is significantly
alone. A very late addition to his legend, she is never given companions of
her own sex within Sherwood, either in the ballads or the plays. Ben
Jonson's unfinished pastoral, *The Sad Shepherd, or a Tale of Robin Hood*
may seem at first to be an exception; in fact it is not. The shepherdesses
who appear in that play are merely guests of Robin and Marian, day-
trippers from the Vale of Belvoir, outside the forest, and it is in the open, or
champaign, country there that they reside, and to which they will, presumably, return. 'People bred among woods', John Norden noted in his
early seventeenth-century *Surveyor's Dialogue*, 'are naturally more stub-
borne and uncivil, than in the Champaign Countreys': '*Rudes & refractarij
Silvicole*',[47] he calls them. 'But woodes', he added, with palpable relief, 'are
commonly most desert'.[48] Even Drayton's personified forests recognize
themselves as gravely endangered, as deserts becoming, as it were, yet more
deserted. About all that Waltham Forest can say to cheer up her 'dear sister
Hatfield', who is seriously worried about rapacious men 'Who having sold
our woods, doe lastly sell our soyle', is that 'though we go to wracke in this
so general waste, / This hope to us remains, we yet may be the last'.[49]
In this, she was largely right.

---

[46] *The Mahābhārata*, abr. and trans. John D. Smith (London: Penguin, 2009), Book 2, 68f.; Book 3 *passim*.

[47] John Norden, *The Surveiors Dialogue: London 1618* (Amsterdam: Theatrum Orbis Terrarum Ltd., 1979), p. 221.

[48] Ibid., p. 221.   [49] Drayton, *Poly-Olbion*, vol. II, 19th song, lines 48, 61, 65–6, pp. 630–1.

CHAPTER 6

Let the Forest Judge

In Chaucer's 'The Knight's Tale', Palemon, who has escaped from prison with the help of an anonymous friend, takes temporary refuge among the 'thikke' bushes of a nearby grove of trees. By chance, his cousin Arcite – now his rival in love – rides out early that May morning to the same grove where (thinking himself alone) he proceeds to soliloquize about his own misfortunes, including his passion for Emelye, the woman Palemon also despairingly adores. Before Arcite begins, the narrator comments: 'But sooth is seyd, go sithen many yeres, / "That feeld hath eyen, and the wode hath eres"'.[1] Chaucer was right about the antiquity of this proverb. It had been familiar in the classical world: 'Campus habet lumen, et habit nemus auris acumen'. (The open country has eyesight and the forest sharp ears.) There are innumerable later French and German versions of the saying as well. In *The Canterbury Tales*, Chaucer's narrator is primarily drawing attention to the fact that although Arcite believes he is alone, Palemon, lurking unsuspected and invisible in the undergrowth, overhears every word he speaks. That is one way of using the proverb, but it is by no means the only, or even necessarily the central, interpretation. It is entirely possible for the forest itself to listen, through its own ears, not through those of any human presence within it. Even so, the 'feeld' – the open champaign country – can sometimes quite autonomously see.

There is a traditional American folk song which warns: 'O do not cross the hay-fields, the hay-fields, the hay-fields, / O do not cross the hay-fields, when sinks the blood-red sun'.[2] The reason why it would be inadvisable to

---

[1] Geoffrey Chaucer, 'The Knight's Tale', in ed. F. N. Robinson, *The Works of Geoffrey Chaucer*, 2nd edition (London: Oxford University Press, 1957), l. 1521–2, p. 32.

[2] 'The Reaper's Ghost' was written by the singer and song-collector Richard Dyer-Bennet. The sleeve notes of the album on which he recorded it in 1962 state: 'In 1935, in an English pub, I overheard two men speaking of a supposedly haunted field nearby. It appeared that in the time of their grandfathers a local farmhand vanished under peculiar circumstances. He was seen crossing a hayfield at sunset, passed behind a pile of hay, did not come into view on the other side, was not to be found behind the

cross these fields at sunset, when they are deserted (as subsequent stanzas make clear), is because now, in high summer, when the grass has been cut and stands about in isolated hay-ricks to dry, there is something ghostly and malign concealed in one of those ricks. You can't see it, but in flat, open terrain which leaves you visually exposed, whatever it is can see you, map your progress, emerge and grab you: an agoraphobic nightmare, in effect. Dense woodland does not induce agoraphobia. The presence of massed trees is far more likely to seem stifling, menacing in a wholly different, claustrophobic way. People who walk alone in such places are usually more apprehensive about being heard than about being seen: the crack of a dry twig carelessly trodden underfoot that suddenly goes off like a rifle-shot, or a collision with overhanging branches that audibly betrays your presence. It may be game, possibly gamekeepers, that you don't want to alert, or predatory animals, including other humans. But it can also seem that the forest itself listens and has a capacity, for better or worse, to remember what it has heard and even respond.

In *The Two Noble Kinsmen*, Shakespeare's late collaborative play with John Fletcher, based on *The Knight's Tale*, Chaucer's proverb does not figure in the equivalent Palemon and Arcite scene, inevitably perhaps, given the absence of any narrative voice. Shakespeare, however, clearly knew about the sentient forest. 'You have said', Touchstone replies to Rosalind in Act 3 of *As You Like It* after she accuses him of being a medlar, a fruit rotten before it is half-ripe, 'but whether wisely or no, let the forest judge' (3.2.119–22). Prince Charles, it is said, occasionally talks to trees. If that constitutes an eccentricity, it is not one in which he has ever been alone. Tree cults of various kinds were widespread in antiquity and lingered on in Europe well beyond that period, the individual great oak as an object of human worship and subject of address being, in particular, one of the relics of paganism that Christianity found it hardest to eradicate. The Druids play their part here. But Henry Vaughan in the seventeenth century, William Cowper in the eighteenth and John Clare in the nineteenth made remarkable poems ('The Timber', 'Yardley Oak', and 'To a Fallen Elm') out of conversational encounters with a huge and venerable tree – fallen in the first and third cases, still upright but hollow to the core in the second – trees whose consciousness, in both cases, is assumed to be present and possible to communicate with. This chapter, however, is concerned less with the imagined responsiveness of individual trees than

hay, and was never seen again. The spirit moved me to put the story into ballad verse and set it to music, and I did so that very night'. *Richard Dyer-Bennet 10* (Dyer-Bennet Records 1962).

with the forest conceived of as an intelligent whole, something older and far more complicated than Tolkein's Ents.

The Birth of Merlin: Or, the Childe Hath Found His Father, that Jacobean play of indeterminate date mentioned in Chapter 2, purportedly the work of Shakespeare and William Rowley, and later absorbed into the Shakespeare apocrypha, is a farrago of Arthurian pseudo-history and diabolism, in which Shakespeare himself can have had no hand. Still, the play exploits that same idea of the listening forest which Touchstone also invokes. In Act 2 of *The Birth of Merlin*, an exasperated country clown enters a forest with his appropriately named sister, Joan Go-too't, who is 'great with childe'. Joan has made her brother accompany her there because, she says, during 'the last great hunting'[3] she met in these same woods a richly dressed courtier by whom, after his many protestations of fidelity and love, she allowed herself to be seduced. Unfortunately, she omitted to ask his name. But, she says, he frequents 'these woods, / And these are witness of his oaths and promises'.[4] The clown is less than sanguine about the testimony of trees in a paternity case, but nevertheless, when she begs him to 'enquire this Forrest', he consents to do so, although in two different ways. First, 'Ile make Proclamation; if these Woods and Trees, as you say, will bear any witness, let them answer'. (Silence.) Then, 'If there be any man that wants a name will come in for conscience sake, and acknowledge himself to be a Whore-Master, he shall have that laid to his charge in an hour he shall not be rid on in an age.'[5] To the first appeal, the forest itself had made no reply. The second does elicit a verbal although, as it turns out, not very satisfactory human response.

Prince Uter, that future Uther Pendragon who will be the father of King Arthur, is also seeking in these woods someone whose name he does not know: in his case, a woman of dazzling beauty by whom he was smitten when he recently encountered her there. They had no sexual congress, but like the clown's sister, the prince is searching frenziedly for an anonymous beloved, and he too seems to believe that the forest itself (as he says) 'heard my vows and oathes' and can be summoned as witness and judge. Indeed, he goes so far as to imagine that now, if only he could 'tell her beauties' at length, the trees would 'bend their tops' in acknowledgement, and their leaves weep.[6] Meanwhile, he asks them once again to record his lovelorn protestations. The Go-too'ts and the prince, despite the social gulf between

---

[3] William Shakespeare and William Rowley, *The Birth of Merlin: Or, the Childe Hath Found His Father*, in ed. C. F. Tucker Brooke, *The Shakespearean Apocrypha* (Oxford: Clarendon Press, 1967), 2.1.14.
[4] Ibid., 2.1.37–8.   [5] Ibid., 2.1.50–7.   [6] Ibid., 2.1.71–83.

them, make the same appeal to a sentient forest. All are in for a nasty surprise, although scarcely one for which the forest can be held responsible. The father of Merlin, Joan's unborn child, was not of course Prince Uter, although it is he who innocently appears in answer to the clown's second summons. Her lover was actually an incubus – the devil himself in courtly disguise – while the woman Uter longs for will very awkwardly be revealed, when he does meet her again, as his own brother's wife.

In responding to the clown's halloo, Prince Uter is initially perplexed as to whether the voice he heard was that of another human, or merely a mocking echo of his own. This kind of uncertainty often afflicts people who raise their voices when alone in a wood. Echo, however, tends to be a disappointment, as she is when Thomas Dekker's character Old Fortunatus, in his 1599 play of that name, enquires 'tel me how thou cal'st this wood?', only to be fobbed off with 'This wood'.[7] His further, more anguished question, 'which is my best way out?', receives the even less helpful, if predictable reply: 'best way out'.[8] After which, hopelessly lost, he respectfully asks permission of a large tree to lie down under it, and takes refuge in sleep.[9] Fortunatus seeks practical guidance. It is possible, however, for characters in early modern plays to desire far more sophisticated communication with the forest, and to be less than pleased if Echo gets in the way.

Walter Montagu's pastoral, *The Shepherds' Paradise*, received its first and apparently only performance early in 1633, at Somerset House, the London residence of Charles I's French queen Henrietta Maria. The play had sets and costumes by Inigo Jones, seems to have lasted more than seven hours and was acted by an all-female, courtly cast, some of them taking breeches parts. In Act 5, the heroine Bellesa, played by Henrietta Maria herself, wanders into a forest: 'Enter Bellesa in a wood called Love's Cabinet'.[10] Her intention is, as she says, to consult it as to whether she ought to confess to her tutor Moromante – actually a prince in disguise – that she loves him. Her reasons for seeking advice from its trees are interesting. Here, she says,

> where all things look so pleasingly, and so well pleased, as you must be all in love with one another: ... Whither but unto you should I repaire for company? To your so pure innocence as ill can ne're come so neere, as to be withstood. For in your veine [sic] runneth water instead of blood.

---

[7] Thomas Dekker, *Old Fortunatus*, in ed. Fredson Bowers, *The Dramatic Works of Thomas Dekker* (Cambridge: Cambridge University Press, 1953), 1.1.5–7.
[8] Ibid., 1.18–9.   [9] *Old Fortunatus* is also discussed in Chapter 2, p. 30.
[10] Walter Montagu, *The Shepherds' Paradise* (London, 1659), K3ᵛ.

My breath is yet so innocent it will not blast your tenderest purity. And I will trust you as to take counsell of you in the discovery of my thoughts of love, you are the fitter because you cannot speake. For you may answer me by instinct, as you seeme to entertaine one another, and not speak.[11]

Just what kind of non-verbal response Bellesa is asking of the forest is unclear. At this point, however, Eccho intervenes in the usual way, turning her last word into an imperative: 'Speake', only to be rejected by Bellesa. 'Alas *Eccho*', she says, 'you are too generally free to be trusted. You will answer any body, and that they please'.[12] Rather like Robert Frost, in his poem 'The Most of It', who also repudiates Echo, she wants from the forest not what Frost calls one's 'own love back in copy speech, / But counter-love, original response'.[13] Frost has to be content with the sudden, ambiguous appearance of a deer, a huge buck that swims the stream in front of him, lands 'pouring like a water-fall', forces its way through the underbrush and wordlessly disappears. Bellesa, despite her original mistrust, finds herself obliged to make a confidante of Eccho and follow her counsel – which turns out to be more or less what she wanted to hear anyway.

There are, of course, other ways of making the forest speak, most of them suspect. The ancient oaks surrounding the temple of Zeus at Dodona, in Thessaly, were said to be endowed with the gift of prophecy and to deliver oracular pronouncements. Priests artfully concealed behind the trees probably provided them with a voice, but this myth of arboreal articulacy passed into Greek literature, especially in poems dealing with the voyage of the Argonauts. Jason's ship, the Argo, was said to contain either in its prow or its keel a beam cut by Athena from one of the sacred oaks in the forest of Dodona. It could and did speak, crucially alerting the heroes to dangers ahead. Far more enduring, however, and widespread is the humbler practice of carving messages, names or love poems into living bark, or hanging them from trees. A patently fraudulent way of making the forest say what you want it to say – and even memorize it if you insist upon incising your words in the trees themselves – the habit goes back at least to the first century BC, and probably much further. The Latin poet Propertius, in the first book of his elegiac poems for Cynthia, suggested that forest oaks and pines had often listened sympathetically to his outpourings of love and – just as Joan Gotoo't and Prince Uter later think – could bear witness to it. But to make

---

[11] Ibid., K3ᵛ.   [12] Ibid., K3ᵛ.
[13] Robert Frost, 'The Most of It', in ed. Edward Connery Lathem *The Poetry of Robert Frost*, (London: Jonathan Cape, 1971), lines 7–8.

doubly sure of their testimony, he admits, he has often recorded Cynthia's name in their bark.[14]

By the time Andrew Marvell wrote his poem, 'The Garden', around 1650, both this real-life practice and its deployment in literature had become commonplace in England as well as across Europe. Ariosto's *Orlando Furioso*, in which Orlando runs lunatic in the forest as a result of seeing his beloved Angelica's name linked in tree-carvings with that of another man, spawned in itself alone a number of literary offshoots and imitations, including Robert Greene's play, *Orlando Furioso*, of 1591. That is why Marvell could have so much fun reflecting on the insensitive habits of lovers and assuring his own 'fair trees' that 'wheres'e'er your barks I wound, / No name shall but your own be found',[15] in full consciousness, of course, that (apart from the fact that trees would certainly prefer not to be mutilated in this way at all) there is something risible, even grotesque, about forcing them to advertise the species name – oak, elm, beech and so on – that human beings have arbitrarily attached to them. It scarcely allows the forest to speak for itself.

Nor does that other, related and equally venerable trope, probably most familiar now in the form given it by Duke Senior, in *As You Like It*, when he claims to prefer his forest exile, 'exempt from public haunt', to 'painted pomp', and happily to find 'tongues in trees, / Books in the running brooks, sermons in stones, / And good in every thing' (2.1.3, 15–17). Even the courteous lord Amiens, the Duke's faithful companion in banishment, sounds slightly sceptical about these supposed woodland communications: 'Happy is your Grace, / That can translate the stubbornness of fortune / Into so quiet and so sweet a style' (2.1.18–20). And indeed, a minute later, Duke Senior is ruefully acknowledging the intrusiveness of his presence in Arden, where, in order to sustain life, he and his former courtiers are obliged to kill its fallow deer, 'native burghers of this desert city', as they themselves are not (2.1.23). The Duke never suggests that he or anyone else has legal or territorial rights over vert and venison in this forest. If anything, the implication is that Arden's deer belong to no one but themselves. As wild animals, they are free citizens, not property, an argument that, as it

---

[14] Propertius, *Elegies*, ed. and trans. C. P. Goold (Cambridge, MA: Harvard University Press, 1990), Book 1, Elegy 18, lines 19–22, p. 101. 'Vos eris testes, si quos habet arbor amores, / fagus et Arcadio pinus amica deo. / ah quotiens vestras resonant mea verba sub umbras, / scribitur et teneris Cynthia corticibus!' (You trees will be my witnesses, if trees know any love, Beech and Pine, beloved of the god of Arcady. Ah, how often my words echo beneath your shade, and Cynthia's name is written on your delicate bark!)

[15] Andrew Marvell, 'The Garden', in ed. Nigel Smith, *The Poems of Andrew Marvell* (London: Pearson Education Ltd., 2003), l. 22–4, p. 156.

happens, was greatly exercising Coke and other lawyers in the period, particularly as it affected areas outside the royal domain. The melancholy Jaques goes much further than the Duke in deploring their unkindness to the deer, and will later anticipate Marvell by scolding Orlando for marring trees by cutting love poems into their bark. He also manages nonetheless to turn the wounded and herd-abandoned stag into a 'bankrupt' ignored by 'fat and greasy citizens', that very urban phenomenon (2.1.55–7). The whole play quietly undermines the idea of tongues in trees, books in brooks, and sermons in stones, revealing it for what it is: a wishful projection of the civilized upon an environment which may be for the deer but cannot be for human beings like the Duke and his followers, an 'assign'd and native dwelling place' (2.1.63).

* * *

In 1599, when Shakespeare wrote *As You Like It*, he had already availed himself of a forest setting in four previous plays: *The Two Gentlemen of Verona, Titus Andronicus, A Midsummer Night's Dream* and probably *The Merry Wives of Windsor*. He would have recourse to staged woodlands afterwards too, not only in the collaborative *Two Noble Kinsmen*, but in *Timon of Athens, Cymbeline* and (very briefly but importantly) in *Macbeth*. Gaultree Forest in *Henry IV Part 2*, despite the unusual scene heading at the beginning of Act 4 – 'within the forest of Gaultree' – is more problematic, there being not the slightest indication in the quarto or Folio texts that Prince John's betrayal of the rebels takes place in a wooded locale as opposed to that extensive 'plaine' specified in the third book of Holinshed's *Chronicles*, within the bounds of the royal forest of Gaultree in Yorkshire. This open space, clearly too big to be a 'laund', was probably, in fact, Shipton Moor. In the other plays, there is no doubt as to the immediate presence of trees, to be conjured up, for the most part, by the audience's imagination. But these woodlands receive a variety of characterizations and treatments, some registering in their particular dramatic context as influences more potent than others.

The Two Gentlemen of Verona, perhaps Shakespeare's very first play, is not remarkable for its geographical accuracy. That much later and infamous sea-coast of Bohemia about which Ben Jonson had so much fun pales into insignificance beside the confusion here as to the relative positions of Verona, Milan and Mantua, the first two endowed with sea-ports they have never had, while the city of Mantua scarcely seems obvious as a stopping-off place in any direct line between. Still, it is towards Mantua, the young

Shakespeare tells us, that the banished Valentine directs his weary steps when trudging home from Milan to Verona, and his itinerary appears also to be that of Silvia and her unreliable escort, Eglamour, with Proteus and the disguised Julia, then Silvia's father and Thurio behind them in energetic pursuit. All these characters find a forest in the way, one through which they are obliged, it seems, to pass, and where almost all of them fortuitously meet. This woodland, apparently about three leagues from Milan, but undiscoverable on any map, exists tangibly in Shakespeare's comedy both as a place to journey through, and as a refuge for outlaws, men banished from the cities in which they have committed various crimes, who prey upon such travellers. In itself, it is almost entirely featureless. Shakespeare mentions no keepers or lodges, no caves to live in, no deer or hunting, no brooks or species of trees. The place is significant all the same as an unaccustomed locale in which people come to understand themselves and others – sometimes very abruptly – in entirely new ways, something that would not have been possible either in Verona or Milan.

This note is first struck casually at the beginning of Act 5, when the Duke informs Proteus that his runaway daughter and Eglamour have recently been glimpsed by one Friar Laurence, 'as he in penance wander'd through the forest' (5.2.38). Friar Laurence never appears as a character in *The Two Gentlemen of Verona*. His recourse, however, to the forest as a place of penance and self-examination is significant. There is something teasingly symbolic about Valentine's predicament when taken prisoner there by the outlaws; he can either, they tell him, consent to be their master and chief, or they will kill him. The choice itself is not unique to this play; it recurs in Heywood's *The Four Prentises of London*.[16] But in relation to Valentine, it is special. This, after all, is the man whose 'braggadism' in love (as Proteus described it) back in Act 2 (2.4.164), when Valentine callously suggested that Julia might just about be worthy to carry his own lady Silvia's train, was as unattractive as his snide connivance in the Duke's plan to entrap the 'nice and coy' Milanese lady who supposedly spurns her ruler's aged eloquence (3.1.82–3). Only in 'this shadowy desert, unfrequented woods' (5.4.2), a place to which he has become strangely reconciled, does the Valentine of Act 5 achieve a measure of control over irrationalities and passions set to destroy him if he cannot keep them in order. This is not entirely easy. The outlaws try to obey, but tend to break out, making 'their wills their law' (5.4.14). Still, at the end, Valentine can

---

[16] See Chapter 4, pp. 87–8.

speak for them – which also means speaking for himself – when he claims that they 'are reformed, civil, full of good, / And fit for great employment' (5.4.156–7). They can be reintegrated into society, and so can he.[17] The last scene of *The Two Gentlemen of Verona* is notoriously problematic, and dramatically uncertain in its handling of Proteus' sudden repentance and Valentine's over-generous offer to his friend: 'All that was mine in Silvia I give thee' (5.4.83). It is clear, however, that the other revelations here – that Eglamour, that 'perfit gentle knight' is really a coward, Thurio someone who never cared for Silvia anyway, and Julia as the girl Proteus really loves – could have been crafted nowhere else. 'One feast, one house, one mutual happiness' is promised at the end of *The Two Gentlemen of Verona* and although these things will not be realized there, they are the gift of the forest (5.4.173).

The forest in Act 2 of *Titus Andronicus*, that other very early play, could scarcely be more different. For one thing, it keeps shifting not only its character, but even its definition. We know roughly where it is – somewhere on the outskirts of imperial Rome – but never quite what. Aaron's description of these woods as 'ruthless, dreadful, deaf, and dull' (2.1.128) suggests a forest both sentient in its ruthlessness and callous, able to close its ears to cries for help it does not want to hear, choosing to make no response. That is something that Lavinia, her husband, Bassianus, and the two sons of Titus, all fatally ensnared within it, will discover for themselves. Tamora's 'L'Allegro' and 'Il Penseroso' diptych in Act 2 – the radiant and leafy glade where she intends to disport herself with Aaron abruptly transformed into 'a barren detested vale' (2.3.93) into which light never penetrates – is only the most extreme example of something that keeps happening throughout the hunting scenes. And these woods have agreeable 'walks', administrative sub-sections driven through them, a keeper's lodge on 'the north side' (2.3.255). Sometimes called a 'forest', sometimes 'woods' or a 'chase', at one moment the place even becomes a 'park', a paled-in and carefully managed space for deer, in which the mutilated Lavinia is found wandering like a stricken doe, 'that has receiv'd some unrecuring wound' (3.1.90). Deer, however, are apparently not the only quarry to be found here. Shakespeare must have been entirely aware not only that panthers are not indigenous to Italy, but that a simultaneous hunt for such an animal and for a red deer stag, par force, with hounds, could have happened – if at all – only as a bizarre

---

[17] See Chapter 4, pp. 86–7.

stage-managed entertainment inside the Coliseum.[18] Undeterred, as he would be later when he introduced a lioness into Warwickshire Arden, he opted nevertheless for symbolism over literal truth.

The 'palace wood, a mile without the town' (1.2.101–2) in *A Midsummer Night's Dream* is, by contrast, remarkably stable and consistent, the only uncertainty surrounding it being a matter of its precise location with respect to Athens. In 1.1.165, it had been significantly further: 'a league without the town'. Puck refers to it once as a 'forest'; otherwise, it is uniformly a 'wood', and never a chase or a park. A royal hunting preserve, no one actually lives in it, except perhaps for the forester Theseus summons in 4.1.103. Puck's customary habitat is the country village. Even the fairies are transients, merely passing through. The wood is large enough to get lost in, especially at night, as Lysander and Hermia discover when trying to get to the other side. But, although hunting in it is clearly a royal prerogative, ordinary Athenians seem to enter it freely and without trespassing, whether to exchange school-girl confidences, as Hermia and Helena once did, to observe the rites of May, or secretly rehearse a play. In itself, it has no influence over its visitors; even love-in-idleness, the magical flower which causes all the confusion, doesn't grow there, but has to be fetched by Puck from afar.

Queen Elizabeth may or may not have been responsible for *The Merry Wives of Windsor*, commissioned (or so the legend has it) because she wanted to see Falstaff in love. The play is, of course, anomalous among Shakespeare's other comedies not only because of its focus on the two already-married women featured in its title, but for its firmly located, bourgeois English setting, at Windsor, just outside London. Like the slightly later *Merry Devil of Edmonton* and *The Knight of the Burning Pestle* (discussed in the previous chapter), this play is topographically precise in ways that would have been familiar both to its original audience and to Shakespeare himself as a resident London dramatist. It bristles with local reference, not only to Windsor itself, with its royal forest (where commoners, as it happened, had long-established grazing and other rights) and to its attached parks, but to other nearby and well-known places: Frogmore, Datchett Mead, Brentford, Eton and Windsor Old Town, near Frogmore. Something approximating to this kind of geographical particularity marked Shakespeare's English histories, where Falstaff, Pistol and the rest of his seedy entourage, not to mention Justice Shallow, had initially

---

[18] See Anne Barton, *Essays, Mainly Shakespearean* (Cambridge: Cambridge University Press, 1994), p. 361.

appeared. But it was and would remain distinctly a new and unique departure in his comedy.

Certainly the wooded landscape evoked at the end of *The Merry Wives* is very different from the ones in *The Two Gentlemen* or the *Dream*, and not just because (unlike them) this was a park, and one in which members of Shakespeare's audience might themselves have walked on occasional excursions out of London. They could even indeed have enjoyed a pint beforehand at the Host's Garter Inn. At least there seems to have been a real hostelry bearing that name in Windsor at the time. There was also a Windsor family with the surname 'Ford'. Herne's Oak is more problematic. A huge tree bearing that appellation stood for some time (it finally died in 1790) on the right of the footpath leading from Windsor itself, through the park, to Datchett. Almost certainly, however, it acquired its name from Shakespeare's play, not the other way round. As for Herne the Hunter, no one has yet been able to track down a specific source for this 'old tale' (as it is described in *The Merry Wives*) of a one-time keeper here in Windsor Forest, who

> Doth all the winter-time, at still midnight,
> Walk round about an oak, with great ragg'd horns.
> And there he blasts the tree, and takes the cattle,
> And makes milch-kine yield blood, and shakes a chain
> In a most hideous and dreadful manner.   (4.4.30–4)

Mistress Page may be properly sceptical of such a story, as handed down by what she calls 'the superstitious idle-headed eld', her husband immediately points out that even now 'there want not many who do fear / In deep of night to walk by this Herne's oak' (4.4.36, 39–40). Yet Herne's oak probably stands in Windsor's Home Park, in close proximity to the town and its castle, and within sound of its bells.

Although one might like to know more about just why Herne haunts the scene of his former employment, it is clear that he is a malign spirit. Putting spells on beef cattle, making dairy cows yield blood (both, in fact, enjoyed pasturage in the park and even in the forest itself) and withering trees are misdemeanours of a kind more serious than Robin Goodfellow's pranks in *A Midsummer Night's Dream*, which went no further than occasionally spoiling the beer and butter, simply for the fun of it, misleading travellers and impairing the dignity of elderly village gossips telling tales. Witches might be prosecuted for less. Herne's 'chain' he presumably drags with him at midnight from Hell. But behind the idea that he sometimes walks not simply with horns but (in the quarto edition of the play) entirely in the shape of a great stag, the apparent restriction of his appearances to midnight and winter-time, and his association with a huge oak, the Druid and fairy tree of Celtic religion, there lurks a complex of ideas, many of them pagan in origin; Cernunnos, the Celtic stag-deity, and the troubling metamorphosis of humans into animals (were-wolves, the bestial shapes of Circe's multiple victims, or the unfortunate Actaeon) together with all those legends of huntsmen unable to leave the chase – sometimes because them made the mistake of joining it when they should have been at Mass – doomed participants in a spectral 'wild hunt' that careers perpetually not just through forests, but across the sky.

Falstaff is presumably cajoled into assuming two of Herne's attributes, his chain and (if Mistress Quickly can manage it) a buck's head and horns, because he has been persuaded that this time, his tryst with both Mistress Ford and Mistress Page will not be interrupted, any night stroller in the park, even a jealous husband, being guaranteed to flee at the ghastly sight. In fact, Falstaff will find himself ambushed by a group of fairies, including their supposed queen, and by elves, goblins, a satyr and Hobgoblin, all emerging either from the castle ditch or from a nearby sawpit used for cutting up timber. This cast of characters is richly suggestive of what the community of Windsor possesses, however sceptical the attitude of some of its members, in the way of supernatural lore. The exact mix (like the locale) is distinct from that of either Lyly's *Galatea* or Jonson's *The Sad Shepherd*. Yet, all three plays, written by three very different dramatists, for different audiences and theatres, and across the span of half a century, have in common a contemporary English wood: a place (unlike the imaginary wood near Athens in *A Midsummer Night's Dream*, or *As You Like It*'s memory of the lost greatness of Ardennes/Arden) that could be visited, and identified on a map. Hunting, predictably, features in all three, but so (whether bogus or real) do fairies. *Galatea* mingles indigenous Humberside fairies with its classical gods, while 'in the stocks of trees, white fays do dwell, / And span-long elves, that dance about a pool' in Robin Hood's witch-haunted Sherwood.[19] Shakespeare's supernatural here, however gentle or ridiculous, is still a judgemental manifestation: Windsor taking upon itself to make the forest speak, of its own accord, chastising 'sinful fantasy', 'villainy' and the 'bloody fire' of lust and greed (5.5.93–100).

The Herne the Hunter episode reaches back to archetypal stories like the one Barrier relates from the forest of Paimpont in Brittany, about the young charcoal-burner who falls asleep while his elder brothers are away

---

[19] Jonson, *The Sad Shepherd*, 2.8.52–3 (p. 471).

and lets the fire in their kiln go out, sees a great conflagration further away in the woods at midnight and, desperately seeking it out, is abducted by wood-nymphs and haled into the presence of the god of the oak trees, who allows him to take home a burning brand from his brazier, on condition that he uses it well and never seeks him again. Not only does the charcoal-kiln miraculously re-light, the boy finds next morning a huge ingot of gold among the cinders, which he promptly takes to Paris, sells and, without ever telling his brothers or assisting any of his impoverished woodland neighbours, buys himself a chateau, and a grandiose life-style. When the chateau later mysteriously burns down, taking all his wealth with it, he imprudently goes back to the god of the oaks in Paimpont. This time, the fire-brand he tries to remove consumes him alive.[20] Nothing so drastic happens to Falstaff, who gets off with a few pinches and candle-burns, plus a humiliation softened by the discomfiture of some of his tormentors when they discover that Anne Page has stolen off to marry Fenton after all. Yet the punishment inflicted on him, however blundering and improbable its human agents, is traditional and authentic as a judgement handed out by the forest.

* * *

The Merry Wives stands alone among Shakespeare's plays before 1599 in giving its forest a precise geographical location and a proper name. The woods in *Titus Andronicus, The Two Gentlemen of Verona* and *A Midsummer Night's Dream*, however evocative in themselves, had been endowed with neither of these things. The sylvan situation in *As You Like It*, the next woodland play he wrote, just before the turn into the seventeenth century, is different, and more complex. Shakespeare's Oxford editors were surely wrong to introduce the French spelling 'Ardennes' into their text throughout. That spelling is present neither in the 1623 Folio (the only authority for this play), nor in Lodge's *Rosalynde*, Shakespeare's prose source. The Ardennes, in French Flanders, was (like Brocéliande) one of the greatest and most mythical of all European forests, although it too had been gravely diminished by Shakespeare's time. The name itself was Celtic and, in both its French and English spellings, it meant a great wood, or 'forest', as Camden pointed out in his *Britannia* of 1586, a work Shakespeare certainly knew.[21]

---

[20] See Philippe Barrier, *Forêt légendaire: Contes, légendes, coutumes, anecdotes, sur les forêts de France*, ed. (Paris: Christian de Bartillat, 1991), pp. 55–6.

[21] William Camden, *Britain, or a Chorographicall Description of the Most Flourishing Kingdomes England, Scotland, and Ireland, and the Ilands Adjoyning* ... (English trans. of the 1586 edn., London, 1610), pp. 287–8.

(Even so, he must have been aware, although he never, it seems, chose to make use of the fact, that the word 'Avon' means 'river'.)

Thomas Lodge, a life-long Londoner and likely to have been familiar with nearby Waltham and Windsor forests, handles his distinctly foreign Arden in interesting ways. The place here is clearly the French one, despite its English spelling, but Lodge moved it considerably south from its actual position, to an indeterminate locality somewhere between the cities of Bordeaux and Lyons. This Arden harbours within its depths two very different kinds of outlaw; there are the genuine and savage ones, who live in caves, and indulge whenever they can in robberies, abductions and rapes. Then, quite separate from them, is Gerismond, the rightful king of France, who shelters there after his overthrow by Torismond, together with a few faithful companions. Apart from these two groups of outlaws, no one in Lodge's tale actually seeks out the forest. It simply happens to be in their way. Rosalynde and her friend Alinda, both banished by Torismond, are fleeing from Paris in the hope of finding shelter and anonymity at a safe distance. Rosader (Shakespeare's Orlando) with his servant Adam Spencer and (later) his brother Saladyne, Shakespeare's Oliver, are trying to get from the city of Bordeaux to Lyons and, in Saladyne's case, still further afield after that, into Italy. All five may be happy to leave the dangerously exposed area of the vineyards and travel more obscurely through the wooded outskirts of Arden, despite the danger even there from outlaws and wild beasts. None, however, intend to penetrate the depths of the forest. Rosalynde and Alinda are rescued by the shepherds Coridon and Montanus on a grassy plain and find habitation in the former's country cottage before that can happen. The men, however, travelling more boldly, lose themselves, mistaking some of the various 'by-waies' of Arden for the main route through to Lyons, and so arrive at what Lodge calls 'the desert', the largely unpopulated 'thicke of the forrest' where the two groups of outlaws – the royal ones and the rascals – live in uneasy conjunction.[22]

Lodge differentiates these two outlaw groups in ways that go beyond their morality and their birth. The exiled king Gerismond does not inhabit a cave, but a more comfortable forester's 'lodge'. He has, moreover in his gift, as it seems, other dwellings of the same kind, one of which he bestows upon Rosader and Adam Spencer when they join him and his companions. Wild this place may be, but Gerismond nevertheless conducts himself there exactly as though he were a chief forester in royal employ. When

[22] See Thomas Lodge, *Rosalynde, passim*, in ed. Geoffrey Bullough, *Narrative and Dramatic Sources of Shakespeare's Plays* (London: Routledge and Kegan Paul, 1958), vol. II.

Rosader makes known to him that he is the son of the late Sir John of Bordeaux, the former king promptly engages him as one of his forest rangers, equipped not only with a lodge of his own, but with an administrative 'walk' to govern and patrol, and even the forest 'bill' requisite for such employment. This was a special forestry knife, in use since the fifteenth century, with a blade about a foot long, three to four inches wide, and a six-inch handle, designed to be wielded in one hand and used – inter alia – for such routine woodland tasks as coppicing.[23] As Lodge's narrative unfolds, Arden begins, its lion and 'lymon trees' notwithstanding, to look more and more like London's Waltham. No one ever complains about the fact that Gerismond and his foresters feast on venison they have killed, but then (compassion for hunted animals left aside) no one really could. Gerismond is a rightful king, not, as in Shakespeare, merely an exiled duke. Like Waltham, and unlike Arden, the Ardennes was a royal forest, and so its game properly belongs to him.

When Shakespeare sat down to transform Thomas Lodge's *Rosalynde* into *As You Like It*, another forest invaded his consciousness. Although never apparently a royal domain, Warwickshire's Arden had also been vast, spilling over into the counties of Worcestershire and Staffordshire. Like its French namesake, however, this once-greatest (it has been said) of English forests had long been in retreat by Shakespeare's time.[24] Unlike Lodge's Arden, Shakespeare's does not interpose itself on the road to or from anywhere else, whether Paris, Bordeaux, Lyons or Italy. There are no other place names in *As You Like It*. We are told neither where the ducal court of the usurper Frederick might be situated, nor the location of Oliver's estates. Oliver himself, moreover, and his brother Orlando, are no longer sons of John of Bordeaux, but of Sir Roland de Boys, the surname (as it happens) of an actual Warwickshire family which held the manor of Weston-in-Arden, and the French original of which – de Bois – although telling, yields nothing more localized than 'of the wood'. The dubious Oliver Martext may be vicar of 'the next village', but that village has no name (3.3.43–4). The effect overall is to focus attention, considerably more concentrated than in Lodge, upon Arden itself, the forest and its 'skirts' and 'purlieus' where Corin's churlish master has the cottage that Rosalind and Celia buy. Shakespeare also purposefully changed the name 'Montanus', that of Phebe's disconsolate shepherd lover in

[23] N. D. G. James, *An Historical Dictionary of Forestry & Woodland Terms* (Oxford: Basil Blackwell Ltd., 1991), pp. 17–8.
[24] See the discussion in Chapter 1, pp. 8–9.

Lodge, to 'Silvius', while Lodge's 'Rosader' became 'Orlando', remembering Ariosto's forest lover, another man concerned with inscriptions on trees. Both alterations increased the play's woodland associations.

He omitted Lodge's wicked outlaws, the villains who try to abduct Alinda and sell her as a concubine to her own father, King Torismond, in Paris. It is Duke Senior, in *As You Like It*, who is obliged to dwell, as they had, in a cave. There are no forest lodges here, no assigned walks, and no forest 'bills', employments or other indications that the Duke and his followers manage Arden professionally, as opposed simply to enduring its winter winds and (out of necessity) poaching its venison from time to time. (If they were attempting to 'manage' the forest, Audrey's lethally voracious troop of goats, for one thing, would not be permitted to put a hoof in it.) One stage direction, in the seventh scene of Act 2, specifies that they enter 'like outlaws'; others introduce them 'dressed as foresters'. In both cases, costume would primarily have conveyed their status: liveries like the 'vj grene cottes for Roben Hoode' mentioned in Henslowe's 1598 inventory of costumes owned by the Admiral's Men at the Rose, where Anthony Munday's two-part *Downfall and Death of Robert Earl of Huntingdon* had in that year been performed.[25] Shakespeare's liveries, however, may have changed from brown to green in the course of the play. That venerable theatrical tradition which makes *As You Like It* begin in winter and end in spring has usually had recourse to Amiens' songs in 2.7 – 'Blow, blow thou winter wind' and 'Under the greenwood tree' with its persistent refrain: 'Here shall he see / No enemy / But winter and rough weather' – counterpoised with Act 5's vernal 'in spring-time, / The only pretty ring time' (5.3.19). It was one of the more seductive features of the Golden Age that it enjoyed perpetual spring. But it is worth remembering that although Lincoln or Kendal green is the colour normally associated with Robin Hood and his men, that is because in the Sherwood of the ballads and Robin Hood plays, the year also seems permanently arrested – in June:

> In somer, when the shawes be sheyne [woods are bright]
> And leves be large and long,
> Hit is full mery in feyre foreste
> To here the foulys song.[26]

[25] *Henslowe's Diary*, ed. R. A. Foakes and R. T. Rickert (Cambridge: Cambridge University Press, 1961, 2002), p. 317.
[26] 'Robin Hood and the Monk', in eds. R. B. Dobson and J. Taylor *Rymes of Robyn Hood: An Introduction to the English Outlaw*, 2nd edition (Gloucester: Heinemann Ltd., 1989), lines 1–4 (p. 115).

That is how the oldest surviving Robin Hood ballad begins, a formulaic opening that its successors repeat time and again.[27] Even in one of those early ballads, Robin could promise the Pinner of Wakefield that, if he agrees to join him in the forest, 'Thou shalt have a livery twice in the year, / The one green, the other brown'.[28]

That offer was entirely realistic. Not only outlaws, but poachers and the forest wardens concerned to keep an eye out for them as well as for the game, did in fact clothe themselves in green during the summer months, then in brown when the leaves turned colour and began to fall, the better to camouflage themselves at both times of year as they moved quietly about the woods. Shakespeare may well have directed the Lord Chamberlain's Men to make use of that fact. If so, it was not the only reality he introduced into a forest often mis-described as quite mythical, a purely imaginary place of pastoral love-making and song. Drayton's personified Arden was accurate in complaining not only about the wholesale felling of her trees, but about enclosure, a change already effected there by the late sixteenth century. Whereas Lodge's Coridon and Montanus feed their two flocks of sheep on common pasture, and fold them there together at night, Shakespeare's Corin, by contrast, talks about 'bounds of feed', private grazing that is the property of his master (2.4.83). Coridon, moreover, had been a leasehold tenant of his cottage, with a small amount of arable land attached to till, and presumably the right both to 'shear' and to sell the 'fleeces' he derives from his landlord's capital investment in sheep. Shakespeare changed all that in ways reflecting the actualities of life in the Warwickshire Arden in which he had grown up. The Corin of *As You Like It* is a humble wage-earner, not a tenant, an agricultural labourer allowed a bed in the cottage that his 'churlish master' not only owns, but in which he resides, although in the comedy, he is said just at present to be away. That, as Corin says apologetically to Rosalind and Celia, is why there is very little that he can rustle up for them there just now by way of food. As agrarian histories like V. H. Skipp have established, Corin's social slide from tenant farmer to mere hired man was something actually happening in Arden, and at an alarming rate, towards the end of the sixteenth century, and Shakespeare's play reflects it.[29]

'No forest', Oliver Rackham has written in his book *The Last Forest*, about the one surviving at Hatfield, 'was really complete without

---

[27] See Chapter 4.

[28] 'The Jolly Pinder of Wakefield', in Dobson and Taylor, *Rymes of Robyn Hood*, p. 148.

[29] V. H. Skipp, 'Economic and Social Change in the Forest of Arden', *Agricultural History Review* 18 (suppl.) (1970), 84–111.

a hermit'.[30] Shakespeare, or at least the Shakespeare of *As You Like It*, appears to have thought so too. There is no equivalent in Lodge for that 'old religious man' who so happily encounters Duke Frederick in 'the skirts of this wild wood', which the usurper is penetrating in order to put his elder brother 'to the sword', and suddenly converts him 'both from his enterprise and from the world' (5.4.158–62). Lodge's King Torismond had no intention of entering Arden. He was simply defending his possession of the throne in battle with the twelve peers of France, somewhere in the vicinity of that forest, and in this battle was killed. Nor had Lodge any real equivalent to that shadowy double of Shakespeare's woodland hermit, Rosalind's supposed uncle, mentioned three times in *As You Like It*, and said to be 'a great magician, / Obscured in the circle of this forest', his art 'profound' and yet 'not damnable' (5.4.33–4, 5.2.61). This uncle is, on the one hand, a convenient fiction, invented by Rosalind as Ganymede initially to explain to a credulous Orlando why her accent (as he observes) is 'something finer than you could purchase in so removed a dwelling', (3.2.341–4) then reintroduced in Act 5 to prepare for the 'strange things' she is about to do in order to bring about her own and the play's happy ending. But this magician, as the Berkeley family papers rather surprisingly reveal, was also disconcertingly real. The original of Rosalind's uncle was a conjuror known as 'old Bourne', and about the twenty-third year of Elizabeth's reign, approximately 1581, when Shakespeare was in Stratford and about to marry Anne Hathaway, he was alive and well, and 'then dwelling in the forrest of Arden in Warrwickshire'.[31]

Old Bourne survives now only in the records kept by John Smyth of Nibley, steward at the time of the great Berkeley estates, who compiled a history of the family. According to his cautious account, Lady Katherine Berkeley, the wife of his own employer Lord Henry, was so imprudent at just this time as to consult Bourne. He does not reveal the nature of her enquiry, but his description of Bourne as a 'conjurer, witch, or foreteller of events, and of the periods of Princes lives'[32] provides a clue. She sent her query into Warwickshire by way of a sealed letter entrusted to John Bott, a servant of hers, with instructions that he should see the document burned

[30] Oliver Rackham, *The Lost Forest: The Story of Hatfield Forest* (London: J. M. Dent & Sons Ltd., 1989), p. 61.

[31] John Smyth of Nibley, *The Berkeley Manuscripts: The Lives of the Berkeleys, Lords of the Honour, Castle and Manor of Berkeley, in the County of Gloucester from 1066 to 1618, with a Description of the Hundred of Berkeley and of Its Inhabitants*, ed. Sir John Maclean, 3 vols. (Gloucester: John Bellows, 1883), vol. II, pp. 379–80.

[32] Ibid., p. 379.

as soon as Bourne had read it, and the magician's reply returned to her in another sealed letter. Bott dishonestly opened the Lady Katherine's communication en route from Gloucestershire, delivered its substance by word of mouth, and brought back a written answer, the seal of which (for obvious reasons) he did not dare to break. Her own letter he secretly kept. Then, a few years later, when he was dismissed by Lord Henry for falsifying accounts, he tried to blackmail the Berkeleys with it. The attempt failed, for reasons fascinating in themselves and for what they reveal about intrigues and counter-intrigues below stairs in a great Elizabethan household. More pertinent here, however, is the demonstrable existence of Rosalind's uncle in Shakespeare's real-life Arden, and the way his memory surfaces in a play which again and again seems determined, whether through nomenclature, hermits, imaginary magicians, love madness or stag-hunts, to include almost everything a self-respecting forest ought to have, even a wild man.

Unlike Lodge's Saladyne, Shakespeare's Oliver seeks Arden as a desperate place of refuge after his banishment. It is not, for him, simply a place to travel through. And when Orlando finds him asleep in Act 4 under what from the meticulous description of it – 'mossed with age', its 'high top bald with dry antiquity' – is a so-called 'stag-headed oak' like those still visible in Windsor Forest, and menaced there by a serpent and a starving lioness, he has been transformed, almost unrecognizably, from a wealthy landowner into 'a wretched ragged man, o'ergrown with hair' (4.3.106). Oliver looks far less savage than this when he presents himself later to Rosalind and Celia, having been cleaned up and generally civilized in appearance by his forgiving rescuer and brother. But the verbal snapshot of the wild man sleeping under the oak has nonetheless made its point, adding one further ingredient to a forest which Shakespeare seems to have been determined to endow with as many traditional sylvan elements as possible.[33]

Even more than in *The Two Gentlemen of Verona*, the happy ending of *As You Like It* is the gift of the forest. At the end of the comedy, moreover, these woods are not left deserted, as would seem to be the case in *The Two Gentlemen of Verona*. Indeed, Arden never really was a desert, in the sense of being essentially 'unpeopled' (except by a few outlaws), even if newcomers such as Rosalind and Celia, or Orlando and Adam understandably all begin with that misconception. It takes time for the presence of native forest dwellers, and even communities, to be found out. When Duke

---

[33] On wild men, see Chapter 3.

Senior and all but one of his followers, as well as Orlando and Rosalind, Touchstone and Audrey, Oliver and Celia finally depart, Corin, Silvius and Phebe, Martext the hedge-priest and the dim-witted William who says he was born 'i' the forest' will remain (5.1.22). So, from the look of it, will Jaques. Critics have often expressed surprise that Shakespeare should assign to Jaques at the end, as opposed to his social superior Duke Senior, the formal words of prediction and farewell which dismiss all the major characters into their respective futures, and that these words should seem so accurate and just. Jaques, after all, has been consistently mocked and corrected in the course of the play by Touchstone, by Rosalind and Orlando, and even by the Duke himself. Yet he has also operated to a large extent as the voice of the forest, deploring the slaughter of its deer, the marring of its trees with carvings, and insisting that the Duke and his followers 'do more usurp', in Arden, 'than doth your brother that hath banished you' (2.1.27–8). We never hear what Jaques might have to say about Orlando's despatch of the 'suck'd and hungry lioness', with her 'udders all drawn dry', who threatens the sleeping Oliver (4.3.114, 126). Orlando had, of course, to act as he did. Nevertheless, in changing Lodge's male lion to a famished lioness, whose death will inevitably condemn her helpless cubs to slow starvation, Shakespeare quietly reinforces the one attitude of Jaques' that the play as a whole does not undercut, his sense of the destructive intrusiveness of humans who take up a temporary life in the depths of the forest entirely on their own terms. Hermits, solitary old religious men and such convertites to their way of life as the former Duke Frederick are likely to be less ecologically damaging. It is to them, declining either to join in the dance at the end, or to accompany those who do participate in it when they return to court and town, that Jaques now plans to go, pausing only to exchange some last words with the Duke at what he calls (with a telling emphasis) 'your abandon'd cave' (5.4.196).

* * *

Jaques was a character Shakespeare added to his source. He did not exist in Lodge. In *Timon of Athens* later, what Shakespeare strikingly introduced into the story handed down by Plutarch, Lucian and others was the forest itself. In none of these previous accounts had Timon sought the woods after his downfall in Athens.[34] Only Shakespeare makes Timon tear off his clothes and go to live in the forest as a solitary wild man. Once there, he neither attempts to 'manage' his sylvan environment, nor avail himself of

---

[34] See Chapter 3, pp. 63–6.

its game. He eats only roots, nuts and berries, and drinks fresh water from the forest springs, a 'hundred' of which, he claims, 'break forth' within a mile of his cave (4.3.418). He keeps an axe as well as a spade in his cave, and winter's cold compels him to make some use of trees as a source of firewood, but he certainly does not inflict his feelings on their bark. When Apemantus is so insensitive as to enquire, when visiting the sylvan exile, whether the former plutocrat of Athens might perhaps be expecting 'these moist trees / That have outliv'd the eagle' (4.3.223–4) to act as body-servants, or the brooks to deliver hot drinks on cold mornings, Timon's disgust is extreme. The man who can identify with the feelings of an oak stripped bare by autumn winds does indeed perceive the forest as sentient, but not in the ways Apemantus so crudely suggests. For him, moreover, unlike the oak, there will be no renewing spring. 'Nothing', with its underlying sense of *nemus*, that ancient word for a forest, may indeed for a strictly limited time seem to give Timon everything he now requires. His life there has been far more stripped and extreme than anything one can imagine Jaques embracing after the end of *As You Like It* and he appears at least to tire even of it. The earlier play can be seen, however, to point forward to the later.

Simon Forman, who felt oddly impelled when he saw *Macbeth* at The Globe to replace Shakespeare's blasted heath at the beginning with a wood, through which he thought he saw Macbeth and Banquo ride, has not been alone in this.[35] Akira Kurosawa's classic version of *Macbeth*, known in England and America as *Throne of Blood* (1957), is not in fact called that in Japanese. The original title, *Kumonosu-jō*, can approximately be translated as 'Cobweb Castle', and it refers to a castle that stands as so often (like those in *Sir Gawain and the Green Knight*, 'Beauty and the Beast' or in the duc de Berry's Book of Hours), in the heart of a dense forest. It is from Cobweb Forest that Kurosawa's castle derives its name. Yet the forest is not entirely natural; it has been deliberately planted near the castle to act as a defence. Castle and forest are bound to each other, the forest in part the product of human design and construction, the castle made from forest materials (emphasised, especially in the final sequence, by the wood-based score and sound-effects). In Kurosawa's film, Washizu/Macbeth and Miki/Banquo are initially shown astray in the 'natural labyrinth' (as it is described) of Cobweb Forest, a place of spiderously interwoven trees and branches and twigs, before they encounter the weird sister, in this case, a forest spirit, lurking in its depths, its appearance heavily influenced by the

---

[35] See Chapter 2, pp. 45–6.

ghost figures of Noh drama. This forest apparently moves at the end against the castle without any human assistance whatever, a movement heralded by a flight of terrified birds. Although it seems, in the final lethal arrow storm, that the forest itself is fighting against Washizu/Macbeth, a final sequence does show that, as in Shakespeare's play, the trees, or their branches, have been moved by human hands. Yet the sense of the forest itself as an autonomous agent of justice remains.

That was not quite the situation in Shakespeare's play. There, a logical explanation had already been provided, the need, as Malcolm carefully explains, for each of his soldiers to 'hew him down a bough / And bear't before him' as they approach Macbeth's stronghold the better to conceal the size of this invading army. Even the most partisan proponent of the bare stage, or of the stage pillars as the default means of staging the forest, cannot ignore the Folio stage direction at the beginning of 5.6: 'Enter Malcolm, Siward, Macduff, and their army, with boughs', nor Malcolm's subsequent instruction that the soldiers should only now 'your leavy screens throw down' (5.4.4, 5.6.1). These tree branches are inescapably present as stage properties. That, however, is by no means all they are. There is no way of telling if Shakespeare had read or knew about the early fifteenth century Scottish *Chronicle of Andrew Wyntoun*. If he had, he would have learned there that Macbeth's mother, like Joan Go-too't in *The Birth of Merlin*, was said to have conceived him as the result of a chance encounter in a forest with an anonymous fine gentleman who was, in fact, the Devil.[36] He betrays, however, no knowledge of this rather scabrous story, scrupulously following Holinshed in his insistence that Malcolm's soldiers marched against Dunsinane as a moving wood. In doing so, he invested that disturbing image with meanings far more complex than those in his source: the forest invading the city, the urban attacked (as so often) by the alien wild, but also and conversely, as in the traditional rites of May morning, when tree branches were customarily carried into houses and towns, the forest not as an enemy but as a symbol of renewal. Birnam too is a sentient forest, visually realized on Shakespeare's stage, not just in Kurosawa's film, as a punitive but also an autonomous, just and ultimately benevolent judge.

---

[36] *The Chronicle of Andrew Wyntoun*, in ed. Bullough, *Narrative and Dramatic Sources of Shakespeare's Plays*, vol. VII, pp. 476–7.

Afterword: Anne Barton (1933–2013)

by Peter Holland

In 1953, *Shakespeare Quarterly*, then, as now, one of the two leading academic Shakespeare journals in the world, published an article concisely titled '*Love's Labour's Lost*'.[1] The list of contributors identified the author as 'Miss Bobbyann Roesen, a Senior at Bryn Mawr', who 'is the first undergraduate to contribute an essay to *Shakespeare Quarterly*. She attended the Shakespeare Institute at Stratford-upon-Avon in the summer of 1952 and hopes to pursue graduate studies in Renaissance literature at Oxford or Cambridge'.[2] Looking back forty years later, the former Miss Roesen, now Anne Barton, had 'a few qualms and misgivings' about reprinting the article in a collection of some of her pieces. As usual, her estimate of her own work was accurate, if too modest:

> As an essay drawing fresh attention to a play extraordinarily neglected or misrepresented before that date, it does not seem to me negligible. Both its high estimate of the comedy and the particular reading it advances are things in which I still believe. But, however influential it may have been, it is now a period piece, written in a style all too redolent of a youthful passion for Walter Pater.[3]

Undoubtedly influential and far from negligible, the article not only continues to read well, for all its Paterisms, but also continues to seem an extraordinary accomplishment for an undergraduate. There is, throughout, a remarkable ability to close-read Shakespeare carefully and with sustained sensitivity, to see how the language is working on the page and how it might work in performance, though Miss Roesen had probably not yet had an opportunity to see the play on stage. If it is not quite what one might encourage one's students to write now, it is also certainly not what students were expected to write then – and I fully understand why the fine scholar

---

[1] Bobbyann Roesen, '*Love's Labour's Lost*', *Shakespeare Quarterly*, 4 (1953), 411–26.
[2] 'Contributors', *Shakespeare Quarterly*, 4 (1953), 489.
[3] Anne Barton, *Essays, Mainly Shakespearean* (Cambridge: Cambridge University Press, 1994), p. xiv.

Arthur Colby Sprague, teaching her at Bryn Mawr, encouraged this student, who could write with an authority that students rarely have the right to use, to submit the article to *Shakespeare Quarterly*. It is probably still the only article written by an undergraduate to have appeared in the journal.

Though there was not yet a trace of the interest in the piece on *Love's Labour's Lost*, characters' names were a major concern of Anne Barton's criticism. And, though I never heard her comment on it, perhaps it was a result of her own onomastic metamorphoses. Bobbyann Roesen had started as Barbara Ann or even BarbaraAnn (her birth certificate gives the former; she always claimed it was the latter), born in Scarsdale, New York on 9 May 1933, the only child of Oscar and Blanche (née Williams) Roesen. Her beloved father was a wealthy engineer whose passion was his collection of a hundred clocks, the last few of which Anne continued to cherish until her death. He was related to the painter Severin Roesen, and Anne bequeathed a splendid example of his characteristic genre of still-lifes to the British Academy. Her rather less-adored mother was, according to Anne, the daughter of someone who fought in the American Civil War, left the United States for Latin America because of his loathing of the reconstruction of the South and returned having made his fortune. He fathered Blanche at the age of 70. Certainly Anne owned a Civil War revolver that she always claimed to have been her grandfather's. If the account was true – and Anne Barton, always scrupulously accurate when reading Shakespeare, might on occasion have embellished the odd tale of her childhood – Anne must have been one of the last alive to connect back to the American Civil War in only two generations.

In spite of the link to Roesen, the family was not much concerned with literature and the arts and her parents must have found Anne's early bookishness odd. She, in return, clearly found their community's concerns with a social round of parties and dances equally bizarre. One of her favourite stories was of her experience in a different kind of academy from the one of which she later became a Fellow, the dance academy which she was forced to attend as a young girl. It was not simply that she hated dancing. What she hated was, rather, the weekly humiliation of always being the last girl to be picked as a dance-partner. So when, one week, a late-arriving boy sighed loudly when he realized who his partner would be, Anne went up to him and felled him with a single punch, to the horror of the lady who ran the academy, from which Anne was immediately expelled, causing scandal in the community, shame for her parents and unending joy for Anne.

That pugnacity, of which some were on the receiving end decades later in her brilliant and often bitingly sharp reviewing, was in part the consequence of intense vulnerability. Painfully shy, often unable to look people straight in the eye, and with an ocular tic that intensified when nervous, Anne found books not only – perhaps not even – a retreat from a society from which she at times felt alienated, but also as a space of deep intellectual pleasure. That childhood devouring of a vast range of literature and the easy way in which, throughout her life, she could memorize hundreds of poems gave her an unusual breadth of literary knowledge, even before starting at Bryn Mawr.

Bobbyann Roesen's hopes of graduate study 'at Oxford or Cambridge' were realized and, having graduated *summa cum laude* from Bryn Mawr, she arrived at Girton in 1954, supported by two fellowships, as a Bryn Mawr European Fellow and a National Woodrow Wilson Fellow, early recognition locally and nationally of her academic abilities. Now Anne Roesen, she was also no longer the ugly duckling with braces on her teeth and thick-lensed spectacles, but a strikingly attractive woman whose intellectual power impressed all. The topic of her doctoral thesis, directed by the formidable M. C. Bradbrook, had already been adumbrated in the last paragraph of the article on *Love's Labour's Lost*:

> Later, in *As You Like It* and *Hamlet* Shakespeare would begin to think of the play as the symbol, not of illusion, but of the world itself and its actuality . . . Yet he must always have kept in mind the image as it had appeared years before in the early comedy of *Love's Labour's Lost*, for returning to it at the very last, he joined that earlier idea of the play as illusion with its later meaning as a symbol of the real world, and so created the final play image of *The Tempest* in which illusion and reality have become one and the same, and there is no longer any distinction possible between them.[4]

In the six years between her arriving at Girton and the completion of the thesis in 1960, much happened. She married William Righter (1927–97) in 1957, spent a substantial period of time with him living in the South of France and a year teaching Art History at Ithaca College while he taught at Cornell. The marriage did not last long. The year teaching in the United States was marked by her failing most of the college's football team in her course and returning to England just in time to avoid the collective wrath of the College. The time in France changed her life forever. In 1960, she became Lady Carlisle Research Fellow at Girton, moving to a teaching Fellowship in 1962 and being appointed Director of Studies in English in 1963, also holding a University Lectureship in the Faculty of English.

---

[4] Roesen, '*Love's Labour's Lost*', 425–6.

The revised version of the dissertation was published as *Shakespeare and the Idea of the Play* by Chatto and Windus in 1962 and a mark of its significance was its reissue by Penguin Books in 1967 as the first volume in its new series, the Penguin Shakespeare Library. The jacket of this reprint quoted John Wain's review in the *Observer*: 'The result is one of those extremely rare critical works that change one's attitude towards the subject'. Distance has not changed the valuation by Shakespeare scholars; how we understand Shakespeare's response to the theatre may have deepened over the last half-century and the terms in which Anne Righter enunciated them may have been subtly altered, but the inflections are within the framework that she theorized and explored in that book. It is much more than a close examination of the *theatrum mundi* trope in Shakespeare's work, for, characteristically, she took the long view, starting with classical comedy, through mediaeval dramatic forms and the explorations of writers of comedy before Shakespeare. But it was the revelatory approach to Shakespeare's continually changing engagement with the topos that mattered most, an engagement that, by the end, meant that she argued that in the romances, he 'restores the dignity of the play metaphor and, at the same time, destroys it'.[5]

Carefully, accurately and stylishly she distinguishes between Shakespeare's attitude and that of a wide range of his contemporaries. This breadth, also characteristic of Bradbrook's work, was habitual for Barton. As Professor Michael Cordner, once her research student, commented,

> ... she found it natural to look, for instance to mid-Tudor plays like *Jack Juggler* and *Johan Johan* to shape a genealogy and context for Shakespeare's achievements ... Such unforced ease of reference, based on encyclopedic reading and outstanding powers of recall, is the foundation on which her richest scholarly achievements are based.[6]

This also produces a discriminating series of comparisons. Jonson, for instance, does not reject 'the theatre itself ... but only its immediate conditions, conditions which he despairs of altering', while Shakespeare's 'disillusionment is of an altogether different kind':

> It is the whole conception of the play, which seems to disgust him. The actor is a man who cheapens life by the act of dramatizing it; the shadows represented on the stage are either corrupt or totally without value, 'signifying nothing'.[7]

---

[5] Anne Righter, *Shakespeare and the Idea of the Play* (Harmondsworth: Penguin, 1967), p. 172.
[6] Michael Cordner, 'Professor Anne Barton', *The Independent*, 11 February 2014.
[7] Righter, *Shakespeare and the Idea of the Play*, p. 153.

Jonson's struggles with the theatre and with the form of the drama would preoccupy her over the next twenty years, until the publication of *Ben Jonson, Dramatist* (Cambridge: Cambridge University Press, 1984). *Shakespeare and the Idea of the Play* turns from Shakespeare at the end to look towards the closure of the theatres and 'the end of the theatre for which he wrote'.[8] Again, there is a broad sweep, moving in a few pages from the last English court masques to French explorations by Corneille and Molière, to Bernini's show in Rome in 1637 with its mirroring of one audience by a performed other and an argument between two actors as to which of the theatres was real and which fictitious. In the switch to this large view, the particularity of Shakespeare's achievements is all the more precisely manifested.

While the monograph established the basis of her reputation, it was her experience in Provence while writing it that established the basis of Anne's lifestyle. It was not her first trip to Europe; she had travelled there with her parents in her early teens and later with a school-friend, staying in Venice very grandly at the Hotel Danieli and travelling around by gondola. But this time in Provence, in a villa somewhere near both Grasse and Saint Pau de Vence, did much more than turn her into a permanent Europhile and, incidentally, someone ever less likely to want to return to the United States. She learned to enjoy, among other things, French cuisine and great gardens. Befriended by the Vicomte de Noailles, she tasted that grand style that was, for her, the hallmark of the Arcadian way of life she subsequently sought to recreate.[9] By the time she was settled as a Fellow at Girton, she refused to eat in Hall and began to entertain in her rooms with the hospitable elegance that continued to the end. Fine food, her superb cooking, good wines, setting a beautiful table, all were her essential prerequisites for the company of friends and the flow of animated conversation. If the idyll of Provence could not be sustained, then she could at least bring traces of that experience back as something that, for her, would in its new guises bring her great happiness, for I do not think I ever saw her happier than when the buzz of guests' conversation over dinner was exactly right.

Her rooms at Girton, as Alison Hennegan recalled them, 'were heady stuff for entrance candidates and young undergraduates: opulent fabrics, fine pictures, good silver, always many flowers, an unobtrusive harpsichord,

---

[8] Ibid., p. 182.
[9] Michael Reardon, 'Anne at Hillborough', address at the Memorial Service for Anne Barton, Trinity College, Cambridge, 12 July 2014.

and an open fire in winter which, during later afternoon supervisions, made the room a glowing, bejewelled place'.[10] But, while students might be slightly awed by the setting for their supervisions, they also learned Anne Barton demanded hard thinking and powerful commitment from them, delighting in their brilliance and rightly intolerant of those who thought some charm might compensate for laziness. Her fierce support of those who needed her help was invaluable. Dame Gillian Beer has recalled how she and Anne joined forces to battle the College which had wished to send down a pregnant student who told Dame Gillian later that

> one of the most valuable things for her at the time was that Anne did not treat the situation as if we had all wandered into the gloom of a Hardy novel. She saw the absurdities in the college's position as well as the pain and hopefulness in Mary's. She was determined and yet light in the support she gave.[11]

In 1968, Anne married John Barton, the brilliant theatre director whose crucial role in the formation of the Royal Shakespeare Company was in bringing a certain scholarly understanding of the Shakespeare text and transforming it into superb, thoughtful, provocative theatre, often through radical means – not least in rewriting Shakespeare. The year before their marriage, they had bought 'Haunted Hillborough', a derelict Tudor manor-house eight miles outside Stratford-upon-Avon, complete with traces of the village in the fields between the house and the Avon. Anne picked Michael Reardon, much later the architect of the Swan Theatre for the RSC, then young and comparatively inexperienced, for the restoration. His task, over the two years of the project, resulted in Anne Barton's own Arcadian home, a great house with the appropriate accompaniments: two retired racehorses in the paddock and 'a wolfhound of ferocious aspect but the sweetest possible nature, named "Bran" and known as "Brandog"'. Reardon recalled that

> The great social event of the Hillborough year was undoubtedly the 'Hillborough Christmas Party' to which the whole acting company of the Royal Shakespeare Theatre would be invited. This took place in the Great Hall of the manor, lit only by candles and firelight, where the Company would perform an entertainment such as a mummers' play – performances in which Brandog often played an enthusiastic, if unscripted, part.[12]

---

[10] Alison Hennegan, 'Barbara Anne Barton', in *The Year: The Annual Review of Girton College 2013–14*, pp. 113–5 (114).

[11] Gillian Beer, 'Anne at Girton', address at the Memorial Service for Anne Barton, Trinity College, Cambridge, 12 July 2014.

[12] Reardon, 'Anne at Hillborough'.

Hillborough Manor, in its new guise as the property of a couple of some celebrity, was the subject of articles in *Homes and Gardens*, with photographs carefully showing the owners at home. If most saw it as a house full of guests – and the Visitor's Book 'read like a Who's Who of British theatre'[13] – it was also for Anne a retreat, a place of research and writing, of calm and thought. The vast long gallery at the top of the house contained John Barton's study at one end, but its walls were lined with Anne's books, her research library as her work took on new directions.

While Brandog travelled to and fro between Hillborough and Cambridge, wedged into the back seat of the Mini Anne drove, in other respects, the two spaces were separate. The transition between the two was primarily one from home to work or from research to teaching. And her teaching was magnificent. In Michaelmas Term 1969, having just gone up to Trinity Hall, Cambridge, I went to my first lecture, the first in Dr Barton's course on Ben Jonson. I remember thinking it odd that there was a slide projector set up in the lecture room and worried that I had gone to the wrong room. The lecture opened up Jonson's work by using images from Brueghel and Bosch. It was inviting, challenging, exciting and captivating and I had never been so intellectually thrilled. I freely admit I fell under the lecturer's spell. My new college friends may have been captivated by other aspects of the experience: 'As a young lecturer at Cambridge in the 1960s ... her penchant for miniskirts and thigh-length leather boots left a lasting impression on generations of male undergraduates'.[14] But that is not what I recall and it was not what made me never miss her lectures through the rest of my undergraduate time.

The lectures were written and read. That first Jonson lecture apart, there were never any visual aids or hand-outs. Each lecture was precisely timed to fill the hour, never rushed or mismanaged. Each was shaped and structured to make its argument clear, as lucid as each sentence. Clarity of thought engaged with the complexity of the materials in order to achieve a perception of play or poem that was unfailingly fresh. Her delivery was not performative or theatrical, though her voice was smooth and strong, always precisely alert to the rhythms of the texts she quoted and the text she had written. These were as much characteristics of her published prose style as of her lecture manner and some lectures of course reappeared almost unaltered in print. But it remains for me a pity that more did not. So, for

---

[13] Hennegan, 'Barbara Anne Barton'.
[14] 'Professor Anne Barton', *The Daily Telegraph*, 19 November 2013.

instance, her 1971 article, 'Shakespeare and the Limits of Language',[15] was no more than a brief summary of a course of eight lectures on the topic. Its most substantial consideration of a single play, *King Lear*, is still only a small part of a whole lecture. Yet it contains perceptions about the ways in which Shakespeare explores language in the play that are both sharply perceptive and brilliantly articulated. Take, for instance, the comment on Edgar's reaction to the dialogue between Lear and Gloucester, 'it is / And my heart breaks at it' (*Lear*, 4.6.141–2): '"It is": to those two words, the barest possible indication of existence, much of what happens in *King Lear* must be reduced'. Or the following consideration of repeated words:

> The last two acts are filled with frenzied repetitions, some of them hammered upon as many as six times in the course of a single line: 'Kill', 'Now', 'Howl', 'Never', the monosyllable 'No'. One comes to feel that these words are being broken on the anvil in an effort to determine whether or not there is anything inside. ... If only one could crack these words: words of relationship, of basic existence, simple verbs, perhaps they would reveal a new and elemental set of terms within big enough to cope. So, Lear's five-times-repeated 'Never' in the last scene is like an assault on the irrevocable nature of death, an assault in which the word itself seems to crack and bend under the strain.[16]

No-one before had realized that the strange conversation between Marina and Leonine in *Pericles* just before he is about to try to kill her (4.1) is not really conversation at all:

> These two people may be placed, formally in the attitude of conversation. Until Leonine draws out his dagger with unmistakable intent, neither one is really listening to the other. Arbitrarily sealed off in separate worlds, they talk at but not really to each other ... They are simply not listening to any voice but the one which sounds within their own minds.[17]

The effect is, as she distinguishes, unprecedented in Shakespeare's own oeuvre and, I would argue, in all drama to that date. But if this isolation of the speakers from each other seems in some respects strikingly modern, her opening references to Beckett, Pinter, Albee and Ionesco – all so new in 1971 – show what is different between their approach to language and what Shakespeare achieves here. I have hopes that, among her papers left to Trinity College, the typescripts of the lectures might surface and the full

---

[15] Anne Barton, 'Shakespeare and the Limits of Language', *Shakespeare Survey 24* (Cambridge, 1971), 19–30.
[16] Ibid., p. 26.   [17] Ibid., p. 29.

measure of the project, of which the article is such a tantalizing fragment, might again be appreciated.

Her Cambridge lectures covered a predictable range of topics: Shakespeare, Jonson and Restoration Drama (on which last, again, too little of her writing on the topic was ever published). In other contexts, her choice of lecture topic was distinctly startling, at least to some of the audience. In 1967, she gave the British Academy's Chatterton lecture on an English Poet on John Wilmot, Earl of Rochester. When she quoted in full 'The Earl of Rochester's Conference with a Post Boy', starting 'Son of A whore, God damn you can you tell / A Peerless Peer the Readyest way to Hell?',[18] she was delighted to see some of the ladies present rise and leave in shock. Had they stayed, they would have heard an astonishing exposition of Rochester's lyrics, particularly 'Absent from thee I anguish still' with which she ended, showing how the lover's 'own fantastic mind' creates a vision of a future, asking 'leave to be faithless, knowing it will disgust him, predicting his renunciation of what he already recognizes as folly'.[19] But they had already heard her compare Rochester with Byron, moving beyond the 'biographical and critical cliché' to explore how each 'mytho-logized his life in verse'.[20] It marks, I believe, Anne Barton's first published comments on Byron whose work would form a distinct and powerful strand in her writing for the rest of her career, from an article on Byron's political plays in 1975 to one on Byron and Shakespeare in 2004, including a short book on Byron's *Don Juan* (a work of which she could quote huge swathes from memory), published in the *Landmarks of World Literature* series edited by her dear friend J. P. Stern.[21]

A few years after the Chatterton lecture, Anne was visited in Cambridge by a representative of Houghton Mifflin. Would she be interested in writing introductions to Shakespeare's comedies for the forthcoming Riverside edition of Shakespeare's works and, since they had had to sack the previously contracted scholar for this part of the project, could she do it by the end of the summer? Having already been thinking of writing on the comedies, she agreed. *The Riverside Shakespeare* appeared in 1972 and, even though all the introductions are fine, Anne Barton's thirteen pieces stood

---

[18] Anne Righter, 'John Wilmot, Earl of Rochester', *Proceedings of the British Academy* 53 (1967), 47–69 (51).

[19] Ibid., pp. 67–8.   [20] Ibid., pp. 49–50.

[21] Anne Barton, '"A Light to Lesson Ages": Byron's Political Plays', in ed. John D. Jump, *Byron: A Symposium* (London: Macmillan, 1975), pp. 138–62; 'Byron and Shakespeare', in ed. Drummond Bone, *The Cambridge Companion to Byron* (Cambridge: Cambridge University Press, 2004), pp. 224–35; *Byron: Don Juan* (Cambridge: Cambridge University Press, 1992).

out. They probably constitute her most-read work, for the edition became the standard one used in American college classrooms, selling by the thousand every year – and Anne was delighted with the annual royalty cheque. Witty and sharp, scholarly and deft, the introductions grabbed students' (and, indeed, scholars') attention and kept it through the inevitable template need to cover sources and dates, the place of the work in the canon and the play's worth. So, for instance, Barton starts out on *The Two Gentleman of Verona* with the bald announcement that it 'has the unenviable distinction of being the least loved and least regarded of Shakespeare's comedies' but can end having convincingly shown that it has 'a freshness and lyrical charm all its own', along the way having no hesitation about calling Valentine's gift of Silvia to Proteus ('All that was mine in Silvia I give thee', 5.4.83) 'Shakespeare's blunder', 'a nervous recourse to tradition' that 'occurs at the point which, in any comedy, is most difficult to handle with assurance: the resolution'.[22]

In each and every case, the play is opened up for reading without recourse to a panoply of others' critical writing. There are occasional points of connection beyond those of early modern culture. On *The Merry Wives of Windsor*, she turns finally to Verdi's *Falstaff* and its fugal conclusion, but it is less the words of Boito that matter here than, 'even more profoundly, . . . the enormous vitality and expansiveness of the music Verdi found at this point: music which flowers out of and celebrates the values of this comic society',[23] something she would expand on a decade later in her article for the *festschrift* for C. L. Barber, whose study of *Shakespeare's Festive Comedy* (Princeton, 1959) had so strongly influenced her own.[24]

Opera had been and would remain a passion of Anne's – and going to the opera with her was an experience in the grand style. But, with the introduction to *Troilus and Cressida*, there is a new note about performance sounded in her work. She begins by identifying the play as 'the discovery of the twentieth century':

> There is no record of any performance of this play before 1898. Since the Second World War it has scarcely left the stage, despite the large cast required for its performance and the considerable technical problems

---

[22] Anne Barton, '*The Two Gentlemen of Verona*', in ed. G. Blakemore Evans, *The Riverside Shakespeare* (Boston: Houghton Mifflin, 1974), pp. 143, 146, 145–6.

[23] Anne Barton, '*The Merry Wives of Windsor*', in ibid., p. 289.

[24] 'Falstaff and the Comic Community', in eds. Peter Erickson and Coppélia Kahn, *Shakespeare's 'Rough Magic'* (Newark: University of Delaware Press, 1985), pp. 131–48, reprinted in *Essays, Mainly Shakespearean*, pp. 70–90.

involved. Critics continue to disagree about the tone and meaning of *Troilus and Cressida*. The modern theatre has decided firmly, and surely rightly, that the play is a brilliant but scarifying vision of a world in pieces, all value and coherence gone.[25]

All her work had been and would continue to be strongly aware of the conditions of early modern performance, one of the compatibilities between her own interests and those of M. C. Bradbrook from their first encounters in Girton onwards. But there is nothing earlier that speaks of the conditions of current performance. The foregrounding here of theatre's discovery of the play, of the ways in which productions' engagement with the play has been decisive and accurate in taking up a position where critics are divided, is surely a consequence of the close and complex interaction between Anne and John Barton in these years. After all, the most 'brilliant but scarifying vision of a world in pieces' that the theatre had yet generated from this play was John Barton's devastating RSC production which opened in 1968.

Anne Barton's interests in seeing performance of plays by Shakespeare and his contemporaries were long-standing. Memories of particular productions, their strengths and weaknesses, filled her conversation. Her admiration of *Timon of Athens* was deeply shaped by Paul Scofield's performance of the title-role in John Schlesinger's RSC production in 1965. Her advocacy for particular long-forgotten plays led to productions by the Royal Shakespeare Company, such as Ben Jonson's *The New Inn* directed by John Caird in 1987, Thomas Southerne's *The Wives' Excuse* directed by Max Stafford-Clark in 1994 and Jonson's *Sejanus* directed by Gregory Doran in 2005, all three of which, as recoveries of a repertory too often ignored, were exactly what the RSC's Swan Theatre in Stratford-upon-Avon, designed by Michael Reardon and Tim Furby, was created for. Many of her students at Oxford and Cambridge became actors and directors; many members of the RSC were close friends. Many of her research students – myself included – wrote dissertations centrally concerned with the performance of drama in early modern and Restoration theatres. Performance inflected her approach to plays and nothing in her writing, from *Shakespeare and the Idea of the Play* onwards, allowed plays to be analysed as if their narratives could be divorced from the rhythms of performance. She was one of the finest academic theatre reviewers, always trying sympathetically to see what a production was aiming at, even when she damned its success. Especially good at reviewing plays unfamiliar to

---

[25] Barton, '*Troilus and Cressida*', in *The Riverside Shakespeare*, p. 443.

most readers, she sought to balance exposition of the play with analysis of the performance.[26] For plays she adored, a production's distrust of the text could provoke her to the sharpest critique. Peter Wood's production of Vanbrugh's *The Provoked Wife* at the National Theatre in 1980 was summed up as follows:

> Audiences all too often believe that the comedy of the seventeenth century is invariably frivolous, inhuman and glib, and that it debases women. Preconceptions of this kind will be amply reinforced by the production offered at the Lyttelton. Underneath it all there lies entombed a good and probing Vanbrugh play.[27]

She liked some aspects of Gerard Murphy's production of Marlowe's *Edward II* (RSC, Swan Theatre, 1990), such as the costumes which 'help to create a world as stark and colourless as Marlowe's uncharacteristically monochrome and pared-down verse': 'This visual reductiveness seems faithful to the spirit of *Edward II*. Less happy was the decision to strip it of its variousness and complexity'.[28]

All of this, as significant and powerful as it was as a marked and complex network of interconnections through Anne Barton between the often mutually suspicious and disengaged communities of theatre and the academy, is, though, much less radical than what emerged in the early 1970s in the exchanges – in both directions – between her critical thinking and John Barton's productions for the Royal Shakespeare Company. It was then and remained one of the closest collaborations between scholar and director and a model for many subsequent partnerings. John Barton noted, *à propos* his adaptation of the first tetralogy into *The Wars of the Roses* (RSC, 1963–4), that the director is 'engaged in an act of critical interpretation analogous to that undertaken by the literary critic in his study'[29] but, as Stanley Wells commented, 'he prefers – wisely, it seems to me – to let the interpretation emerge from the performance rather than to formulate it in critical statements'.[30] Instead, Anne Barton's programme essays for a number of John Barton's productions outlined views of the play that were tightly aligned with the production approach. In turn, the programme essays could

---

[26] See, as two examples among many, her review of the RSC's production of *The Wives' Excuse*, 'Conditions of the heart', *TLS*, 19 August 1994, p. 16, and her long and enthusiastic study of the New York staging of Tom Stoppard's *Arcadia*, 'Twice around the Grounds', *The New York Review of Books*, 8 June 1995.

[27] 'Icing on the Top', *TLS*, 7 November 1980, p. 1260.

[28] 'Managing the Minions', *TLS*, 20 July 1990, p. 777

[29] John Barton, *The Wars of the Roses* (London: British Broadcasting Corporation, 1970), p. xxv.

[30] Stanley Wells, *Royal Shakespeare* (Manchester: Manchester University Press, 1977), pp. 46–7.

become the basis for her own more substantial critical writing. So, for example, her account of *Twelfth Night* set out in the programme for his production (RSC, 1969) was expanded in her article on '*As You Like It* and *Twelfth Night*: Shakespeare's Sense of an Ending', its title showing the influence of Frank Kermode's *The Sense of an Ending* (New York, 1967).[31] As Christine Avern-Carr suggests,

> There is no doubt [her] ideas were illustrated by Barton's production, although one cannot say whether the ideas came before the production or whether they emerged from it; it is remarkable that any theatrical realization should be so closely connected to a piece of serious literary criticism, evolving in parallel to each other.[32]

John Barton's 1971 *Measure for Measure* is best remembered for the ambiguity of its ending in which, for the first time in any production, Isabella did not go off happily with the Duke towards marriage but instead remained onstage staring into the auditorium, an approach to the ending that is now almost a cliché in productions of the play. The choice was a precise parallel in the theatre to Anne Barton's approach to the ending in her *Riverside Shakespeare* introduction which viewed the marriage proposal as 'an outbreak of that pairing-off disease so prevalent in the fifth acts of Elizabethan comedy' and offered this view of Isabella's silence in response to the twice-made proposal: 'like the theatre audience, presumably, she is dumb with surprise' or, as she phrased it in the programme essay, 'It is at least possible that this silence is one of dismay'.[33]

When John Barton directed *Richard II* (RSC, 1973), his approach was heavily influenced by Ernst Kantorowicz's view of the play in his *The King's Two Bodies* (Princeton, 1957), a book which Anne Barton brought to his attention. But the distinctive comparison of the twin-bodied nature of the king with the twin-bodied nature of the actor is hers and she set it out in the programme essay: 'Like kings, actors are accustomed to perform before an audience. Like kings, they are required to submerge their own individuality within a role and, for both, the incarnation is temporary and perilous'.[34] Equally distinctive was her exploration of Richard and Bolingbroke as '[l]ike the two buckets filling one another that Richard imagines in the deposition scene, buckets which take a contrary course

---

[31] In M. Bradbury and D. J. Palmer (eds.), *Shakespearian Comedy* (London: Edward Arnold, 1972), pp. 160–80; reprinted in *Essays, Mainly Shakespearean*, pp. 91–112.

[32] Quoted in Michael L. Greenwald, *Directions by Indirections* (Newark: University of Delaware Press, 1985), p. 88.

[33] *Riverside Shakespeare*, p. 548; quoted Greenwald, *Directions by Indirections*, p. 103.

[34] Quoted in Wells, *Royal Shakespeare*, p. 75.

within the deep well of the crown': 'Both movements involve a gain and a loss. Each, in its own way, is tragic'.[35] The most remarkable aspect of the production echoed this; Richard Pascoe and Ian Richardson alternated the two roles on different nights, the choice of who would play Richard at each performance being established in an opening dumb show in which each led a file of actors before one dressed as Shakespeare who bowed to the night's Richard, only after which did the two actors put on the wigs and costumes of their character.

The most complete interrelation of Anne Barton's view of a play in print and John Barton's view in production was for his *Hamlet* (RSC, 1980). At this time, he read 'all her pieces and lectures, and I comment on them' and, at the point at which he was finally ready to direct the play, Anne was completing her introduction to the Penguin Shakespeare edition (a task taken on after the death of the editor, T. J. B. Spencer, in 1978), an essay which amplified her identification of *Hamlet* in *Shakespeare and the Idea of the Play* as 'unique in the density and pervasiveness of its theatrical self-reference', one where the discussion of the 1601 War of the Theatres can appear 'precisely because *Hamlet* as a whole is so concerned to question and cross the boundaries which normally separate dramatic representation from real life'.[36] In the rehearsal room, John frequently referred to the introduction. In performance, the production's emphasis was clear from the first view of Ralph Koltai's set, with its raked stage platform filled with 'theatre artifacts from which the RSC cast could draw to tell the story of *Hamlet*', such as the enormous chalice on the props table, prefiguring its use in the final scene, and lit by 'five naked light bulbs, suspended like theatre "ghost lights", which prompted a rehearsal hall atmosphere appropriate to the production concept'.[37] The concept made the audience hear throughout that 'stage imagery' which 'exists independently of the professional actors'.[38] Anne's introduction, of course, was not narrowly circumscribed by the play's self-conscious theatricality, nor was John's production similarly limited for, as Irving Wardle wrote in his review for *The Times*, 'a theoretical exploration of the play by a man who knows that no theory can contain it'.[39]

In 1972, Anne Barton left Cambridge for Bedford College, London, where she became Hildred Carlile Professor in English. Still under 40,

[35] Ibid., p. 75.
[36] William Shakespeare, *Hamlet*, ed. T. J. B. Spencer, introduction by Anne Barton (Harmondsworth: Penguin, 1980, reprinted 2002), p. xxv.
[37] Greenwald, *Directions by Indirections*, p. 190.   [38] *Hamlet*, introduction, p. xxv.
[39] Quoted Greenwald, *Directions by Indirections*, p. 196.

a young age to be given such a distinguished chair, Anne did not enjoy the experience of being Head of Department, nor the rhythms of a very different kind of university from Cambridge. The finest outcome of that time was her inaugural lecture on *Antony and Cleopatra*, an exploration of its 'divided catastrophe' with a memorable account of Cleopatra's 'last obstacle . . . on her way to death', the clown that here becomes 'Comedy' itself:

> . . . precisely because she has walked through the fire of ridicule . . . she has earned the right to say, 'Give me my robe, put on my crown, I have / Immortal longings in me' . . . And she does so at once. Comedy flowers into tragedy, without a break or a mediating pause.[40]

She left Bedford College in 1974 to become the first female Fellow of New College, Oxford, rather relishing the fact that one or two of the Fellows were so furious that the all-male bastion was breached that they refused ever to acknowledge her presence in their midst. Her election was later marked by a portrait commissioned by the College; characteristically, she hated the painting. After a decade in Oxford, Anne returned to Cambridge as Grace 2 Professor of English in 1984 and, after waiting out the obligatory time to avoid having to take one of the vacant professorial fellowships (she described it as being 'in purdah'),[41] she became a Fellow of Trinity College in 1986, living in rooms, exquisitely decorated as always, in Nevile's Court (first on one side and then the other) until her last illness. She loved the College and it was to be, 'however imperfectly, . . . [an] embodiment' of an ideal, the last of the perfect places, like Hillborough, that she tried to find again and again.[42] She also used her considerable 'intellectual and personal authority [to help] pave the way for a significant increase in the number of women Fellows'.[43] If she could, at times, be ungenerous to young academic women, she could also dedicate her energy to aiding some of them in achieving what they richly deserved.

While at New College, she encountered the person she identified as the most brilliant undergraduate she ever taught, John Kerrigan, now Professor at Cambridge and FBA. Anne was the first to realize his exceptional talents and she directed his doctoral work on revenge drama. Kerrigan helped her enormously with her own work, both the study of

---

[40] '"Nature's Piece 'gainst Fancy": The Divided Catastrophe in *Antony and Cleopatra*' in *Essays, Mainly Shakespearean*, p. 132.
[41] Adrian Poole, 'Anne at Trinity', address at the Memorial Service for Anne Barton, Trinity College, Cambridge, 12 July 2014.
[42] Ibid.   [43] Ibid.

Ben Jonson (published in 1984) and her investigation of names in comedy (1990), enabling her to 'talk out my ideas, ... pinpoint[ing] muddles ... while forcing me continually to re-write and re-think'.[44] Her approach to Jonson had been set out in articles which would be revised into *Ben Jonson, Dramatist* (Cambridge, 1984), especially her demand for a complex and subtle revaluation of Jonson's late plays, not least as deliberately part of a nostalgic reformulation of Elizabethan drama.[45] But the eventuating book was conceived on the grand scale as a detailed and revisionary account of Jonson's dramatic *oeuvre* in relation to his predecessors and contemporaries, not least Shakespeare. On plays that have long been highly praised, her views are always incisive and revelatory; on plays that have been largely ignored, the revaluation was powerfully transformative. *The New Inn* stood out in bold relief as Jonson's masterly negotiation with 'the premises of Shakespearean comedy, to explore its attitudes and, up to a point, make them his own' in a play whose plot of the reuniting of sisters parted since childhood is 'wholly alien to the Jacobean Jonson, however familiar from *The Comedy of Errors, Twelfth Night, Cymbeline* or *The Winter's Tale*'.[46] And *A Tale of a Tub*, treated by Herford and Simpson in their great edition of Jonson as Jonson's earliest surviving work, was persuasively redefined as Jonson looking back at the very end of his life to a much earlier kind of drama, writing 'an immensely sophisticated attempt to re-create the atmosphere of early Elizabethan drama, and exploit some of its resonances'.[47] An eloquent consideration of Jonson's last, unfinished play, *The Sad Shepherd*, ends the book, but starts Anne Barton's investigation of the drama of woods and forests about which she was writing in her own final monograph.[48]

Barton is alert to the centrality of the urban environment for Jonson so that *Every Man in His Humour*, the earliest play Jonson included in the great folio of his *Works*, stands out, in its revised form that shifted the location from Florence to London and 'thickened the dialogue with topographical reference and contemporary allusion', as a drama whose unity of time, a single day, 'evok[es], in detail, the life of a great, mercantile Renaissance city as it moves through a typical day ... The city is the true

---

[44] Anne Barton, *Ben Jonson, Dramatist* (Cambridge: Cambridge University Press, 1984), p. xii.
[45] See '*The New Inn* and the Problem of Jonson's Late Style', *English Literary Renaissance* 9 (1979), 395–418 and 'Harking Back to Elizabeth: Ben Jonson and Caroline Nostalgia', *ELH* 48 (1981), 706–31.
[46] *Ben Jonson, Dramatist*, p. 259.   [47] Ibid., p. 322.
[48] In addition, she provided the introduction to *The Sad Shepherd*, in eds. Martin Butler et al., *The Cambridge Edition of the Works of Ben Jonson*, 7 vols. (Cambridge, 2012), vol. VII, pp. 419–23.

centre of the comedy and, to a large extent, its main character'.[49] Throughout the book, it is the investigation of location and how it could be reconciled with innovative dramatic forms that concerns her and which she triumphantly explores as Jonson's greatest achievement. Her own achievement lies in the placing of Jonson in a historical context and finding his 'greatness as a writer of comedy' visible 'only when his output is considered as a whole',[50] as someone 'tirelessly experimental',[51] always restlessly and anxiously exploring; not for nothing was 'tanquam explorator' Jonson's motto.

At the midpoint of *Ben Jonson, Dramatist*, Anne Barton allowed herself a respite from the chronological, play-by-play structure to write a 'chapter interloping' on Jonson's names for his characters from his earliest plays to *Bartholomew Fair*, a chance to see a continuity that she is well aware might be more difficult to see elsewhere in the monograph.[52] The fascination with names led to her topic for the Alexander Memorial lectures at the University of Toronto, 'Comedy and the Naming of Parts', given in 1983. The four lectures were expanded into a book-length study, *The Names of Comedy* (Toronto, 1990), a work of great erudition as it considered the very different conditions of naming that comedy sets up. As Antiphanes argued, as soon as a character called Oedipus appears, 'the audience knows all about him even before he says a word' but 'a character in comedy ... must be named and built up from scratch'.[53]

It is especially appropriate that the book opens with an analysis of T. S. Eliot's poem 'The Naming of Cats', for Anne carefully named her succession of beloved cats after characters in Elizabethan literature or actors in Shakespeare's theatres, such as Thaisa and Elissa, Damon and Pythias, Tarleton, Armin and Burbage. But the Introduction explores the potency of names from children's nicknames to a letter from Mozart, from Elizabeth I to Lévi-Strauss' account of the Nambikwara Indians and Derrida's rejection of the anthropologist's account. Inevitably, Barton soon reaches her core text, Plato's *Cratylus*, and its opposition between cratylic names and Hermogenes' argument for the arbitrary quality of language. The dispute becomes crucial for comedy precisely because of the frequency of cratylic naming practices that are almost unknown in tragedy. The puns in the name 'Oedipus' are an exception, but so too is 'Desdemona', for in Cinthio's tale that was Shakespeare's source, she is the only character named, as Disdemona, and the listeners blame her father for

---

[49] *Ben Jonson, Dramatist*, p. 46.   [50] Ibid., p. xi.   [51] Ibid., p. x.   [52] Ibid., pp. 170–93.
[53] *The Names of Comedy*, p. 17.

giving her an unlucky name. When Barton reaches *Othello*, she becomes intrigued by the words buried in the names Shakespeare gives his characters: *hell* in Othello, *ass* in Cassio, *demon* in Desdemona, even the *ill* in Emilia.

The book's scope takes us from the cratylic names of Old Comedy to the bland ones of New Comedy as a tension in the practice of onomastics that will inform comedy thereafter. But Barton is equally interested in the moments when the names are released into a play's dialogue, for example the holding back of Viola's name until the last scene. For play after play, both the distinctiveness of its naming practices and the relation of those names to the long tradition of comedy is incisively revealed until, at the end, the namelessness of Samuel Beckett's characters in his late plays links back to 'A' and 'B' in Medwall's *Fulgens and Lucres* (1497) and the 'extraordinary' way in which Beckett is '(in effect) reinventing, from a position of extreme sophistication, the primitive name taboo'.[54]

Anne Barton was elected a Fellow of the British Academy in 1991 and gave the British Academy Shakespeare lecture in the same year under the title 'Parks and Ardens', continuing her frequent explorations of the city,[55] but here concerned with the park scenes of Restoration drama and the ways in which the cultivated and controlled landscape of London's parks needs to be set against Shakespeare's interest in the different world of parks as rural, not urban spaces, enclosures reserved for hunting. The lecture was dazzling in its scope, from the landscape of Warwickshire and the transformation of Shakespeare's precision in adaptations of, for example, *Love's Labour's Lost* and *The Merry Wives of Windsor* in the eighteenth century, through to the fleeting appearance of the park in Pinter's *Old Times* or the dystopic vision of it as a landscape of urban decay and danger in Botho Strauss' *Der Park* (1983), a remarkable rethinking of *A Midsummer Night's Dream*. It also marked her first foray into her last topic for research, the world of the forest. In 1994, Cambridge University Press published a collection of essays in her honour, edited by John Kerrigan, Michael Cordner and myself, taking as its topic *English Comedy* as 'a reflection on and tribute to her work on comedy',[56] considering a wide range of drama, poetry and novels and even philosophy from the pedigree of Crab in *The Two Gentlemen of Verona* to Wittgenstein and Noël Coward as

---

[54] *The Names of Comedy*, p. 186.

[55] See, for instance, 'London Comedy and the Ethos of the City', *The London Journal*, 4 (1979), 158–80 and 'Comic London' (1990), both in *Essays, Mainly Shakespearean*, pp. 302–28, 329–51.

[56] Michael Cordner, Peter Holland and John Kerrigan (eds.), *English Comedy* (Cambridge: Cambridge University Press, 1994), p. 3.

a way of representing the breadth of her sustained interests in the forms comedy has taken.

English Comedy appeared in the same year as her carefully constructed collection of sixteen of her own articles, *Essays, Mainly Shakespearean*. The most recent piece in the volume, 'Wrying but a little', starting from and ending with *Cymbeline*, considers marriage, law and sexuality, delving into the technicalities of handfasting and marriage contracts in the early modern period to make sense of the particularity of Shakespeare's analysis of how people behave or, as she phrases it in her introduction, exemplifying her interest in 'law and social structure, in patterns of human interaction on and off stage on Renaissance England'.[57] The volume as a whole shows shifts in her concerns, primarily, as she notes, towards 'an increasing emphasis on historical and social contexts' and 'an increasing need for footnotes, the product (in part) of a tendency . . . to situate texts within a complexly understood moment of time'.[58] But there is, too, a recurrent and unaltered fascination 'with what language can and cannot do, both for the characters who must rely upon it and, in more specifically theatrical terms, for the dramatist'.[59] The second section of the book centres on 'the active interrelations between Shakespeare and his contemporaries' and does so, not least, by enjoying writing about a 'considerable number of obscure and minor works' not only to set the great plays in relief but also because these, such as 'Heywood's delightfully preposterous *The Foure Prentises of London* . . . [,] can richly repay attention when allowed to speak for themselves', and, quoting Bacon's belief that critics 'are the brushers of noblemen's clothes', she allows that many of the plays she rescues 'are very minor gentry indeed, but I have liked presenting them to other readers looking well turned-out'.[60] There is, throughout, that same clear-sighted concentration on language in performance that she had made so central to her writing, noting traditions such as the 'disguised king' line that Shakespeare drew on for *Henry V*,[61] and enabling us to understand the potency of dramatic forms.[62] Above all, there is, as she herself found when she read back over the articles, 'a long-term insistence upon literature as a source of pleasure and . . . by my habitual use of it to complicate and extend my own understanding', as with Montaigne whom she quotes lovingly: 'if I studie, I onely endeavor to find out the knowledge that teacheth or handleth the knowledge of my selfe'.[63]

---

[57] *Essays, Mainly Shakespearean*, p. xiv.   [58] Ibid., p. xvii.   [59] Ibid., p. xiv.   [60] Ibid., p. xv.
[61] 'The King Disguised', in ibid., pp. 207–33.
[62] As, for instance, in 'Oxymoron and the Structure of Ford's *The Broken Heart*', in ibid., pp. 261–81.
[63] Ibid., p. xvii.

Anne Barton retired from her Cambridge chair in 2000, but continued to supervise a few lucky undergraduates until her final illness. As always throughout her career, she deeply loved working with undergraduates who were excited by the materials they were discovering and she was just as irritated by those others who thought that native wit would be a sufficient cover for indolence and ignorance. She equally enjoyed supervising doctoral students and many, such as Germaine Greer, have spoken of how much they owed to her willingness to work with them when their topics had taken them outside the concerns of most faculty. She continued to the end to entertain an international circle of friends, cherish her cats and, increasingly infrequently, write long review articles for the *New York Review of Books*, where she had started publishing in 1981 and for which she covered, especially, books on Shakespeare and Byron. Some of her reviews were brutal, as, for instance, her devastating exposition of Stephen Greenblatt's 'tendency to handle historical circumstances approximately' in his book *Learning to Curse*.[64] Bad scholarship offended her and she was not prepared to excuse it.

Anne inspired and offered intense loyalty from and to those closest to her, but her pugnacity could upset others. Cruelly, macular degeneration radically diminished her omnivorous taste in reading and she came to rely on her undimmed memory. In her last months, exiled from her beloved rooms in Trinity and her even more beloved cats, she lay in her hospital bed, relieving the tedium and astonishing nursing staff and patients alike by reciting Shakespeare sonnets by the dozen.

But I want to end with a different moment of her powers of recall. It was June 2013, shortly before the fall that led to her last illness, and my wife and I were, as so often, sitting in Anne's rooms over a glass of wine together in the early evening along with other friends. The name of Richmond Lattimore came up, for he had taught Anne at Bryn Mawr. We all of course knew him for his translations of Greek tragedy, but my wife wondered if he wrote poetry as well as translating. 'Yes, he did', said Anne, 'and I remember some. Do you want to hear one?' We did. She looked down at the carpet for a few seconds and I am ashamed to admit that I felt a mounting anxiety in case, for once, she would not remember. And then she started to speak. After 30 lines or so, she stopped. 'There's plenty more but that's probably enough'. It was not just that she spoke but rather how she spoke that transfixed us. If she had rehearsed the poem that day she could not have spoken it better – every line perfectly marked,

---

[64] *New York Review of Books*, 28 March 1991.

every cadence in place, the metre always exact, the effect overwhelming. It was not an act of memory, not an act of respect for a loved teacher, not a demonstration of how to speak a poem. It was more than that: a deeply felt explanation of precisely why we read poetry, why Anne had committed hundreds of poems to memory, why literature mattered to her and to us, what her lifetime of learning and discovering and writing and enjoying others' writing was for. This was the profound pleasure in engaging with poetry made manifest. That moment, movingly and passionately, through the calm and caring speaking of Lattimore's poem, explained to me, better than anyone else could do, why we do what we do as academics and why I have spent more than forty years inadequately imitating Anne's example. We often talk of modelling for our students, exemplifying what they might achieve. It can be done modestly or extremely arrogantly. This was the modest practice that perfected the lesson of the values of the academic life. It was the sign of a great humanist scholar whose writings were devoted to revealing the power of imaginative language precisely as a sign of our humanity.

Further Reading

by Hester Lees-Jeffries

This bibliographical essay gives an overview, and in many cases a detailed account, of recent work (mostly at the level of the monograph and edited collection, with some key essays and articles) in the various areas explored by *The Shakespearean Forest*, taking in publications which have appeared since Anne Barton's delivery of the Clark lectures (2003) and in some cases a little earlier. This is a field which has both flourished and changed since Barton began her work, with the rise of eco-criticism and the new nature writing in particular. It cannot claim to be exhaustive, but rather aims to be useful particularly for those working in the field of early modern literature, allowing readers to set *The Shakespearean Forest* in a larger critical context as well as providing suggestions for further reading. Its assessments are the editor's, rather than making any attempt to channel what Barton might have said (although those who knew her might on occasion take some pleasure in imagining just that). The essay begins with detailed accounts of recent major monographs on early modern literature, especially drama, and the environment, especially forests. This is followed by sections on 'Eco-criticism', 'Forest History', 'Nature Writing', 'Hunting', 'Robin Hood and Outlaws', 'Folklore' and 'Theatre and Performance'. These categories overlap, and many of the works here could have been included in multiple categories.

Two recent monographs explore similar, but far from identical, territory to *The Shakespearean Forest*: Jeffrey Theis, *Writing the Forest in Early Modern England: A Sylvan Pastoral Nation* (2009), and Vin Nardizzi, *Wooden Os: Shakespeare's Theatres and England's Trees* (2013). They are discussed here in some depth, with substantial quotation; other works are surveyed more briefly.

Jeffrey Theis begins his *Writing the Forest in Early Modern England: A Sylvan Pastoral Nation* (Duquesne University Press, 2009) with the observation that 'A tree is not just a tree and a forest is not merely a forest – especially in early modern England' (xi). 'Sylvan pastoral' is his own category, which he defines as follows:

> Perhaps the simplest definition of 'sylvan pastoral' is pastoral or pastoral
> moments set in the wood. But it is a danger to apply the transformation of
> the pastoral open plain or solitary tree to the forest in a concrete, literal way
> that overemphasizes historical land-use practices. Sheep may graze in early
> modern English forests, but historically one would expect to find a prosaic
> pig grazing on acorns – not necessarily a lively subject for 'high art' – but
> pigs are scarce in the English pastoral wood. Sylvan pastoralists, then,
> engage forest-related issues, but they often do so with a light touch where
> literary form and tradition intermix with early modern forest history (p. 5),

also suggesting that

> Shakespeare's theatrical forest – where, like the stage itself, characters
> consciously try on different roles – complicates the assumption that culture
> comes from the city; instead, culture is formed out of one's interaction with
> the land and the social roles that are possible in the wood . . . Like the stage
> itself, the forest is always a multiple place that means different things to
> different characters. But unlike a blank stage, the geography of the green
> plot often disrupts or qualifies each character's forest definition and the
> personal identity that character hopes the forest will support. In the process
> of equating forest and stage, Shakespeare also engages and then recasts early
> modern practices like forest migration and hunting to explore ways in which
> definitions of nature are implicated in gender, class, and political roles
> (pp. xiii, 35).

Theis' approach is emphatically ecocritical, but one which moves beyond 'a
spoliation versus preservation binary' (p. 26); he discusses Shakespeare and
Civil War literature, but very few non-Shakespearean texts (although he
notes *The Spanish Tragedy*, Drayton's *Poly-Olbion* and Sidney's *Arcadia*
and *Lady of May* in passing). The three chapters of the book's first part,
'Sylvan pastoral, Shakespeare, and 1590s England', focus on *As You Like It*,
A Midsummer Night's Dream and *The Merry Wives of Windsor*. The
discussion of *As You Like It* is the most interested in staging, although
Theis also states in his introduction that 'Staging the forest scenes on the
early modern stage emphasizes the reliance on language to construct sylvan
space' (p. 37). There is also some consideration of migration patterns and
enclosure. Surveying practices and discourses are explored, among other
things, as context for *Midsummer Night's Dream*. The discussion of *Merry
Wives* explores forest law and ideas of property, together with a lengthy
discussion of poaching and goes into considerable detail concerning the
Little Park at Windsor, although only briefly mentioning Herne.

In the book's second part, 'Forest Knowledge/Forest Power: Sylvan
Pastoral in Mid-seventeenth Century England', Theis suggests that

> If Shakespeare's forest comedies demonstrate the ability to radicalize wooded spaces, life in woodlands during the middle of the seventeenth century put into everyday practice this particular definition of sylvan space. Forest life for the poor and middling sorts created a culture that was open to radical and anti-authoritarian attitudes (p. 169).

He goes on to give a fascinating and detailed account of the breakdown of forest order in the 1630s and 1640s, attempts to reassert monarchical power, and mismanagement by Charles I, exploring texts by, among others, Andrew Marvell, James Howell (*Dendrologia*) and John Evelyn (*Sylva*), describing 'Civil War sylvan pastorals' as 'nationalizing texts immersed in literary and environmental tensions between intelligibility and instability. For these writers, it is neither the city nor the field that resonates as the symbolic and imaginative catalyst of or balm for revolution; rather, it is the forest' (p. 241).

Vin Nardizzi's *Wooden Os: Shakespeare's Theatres and England's Trees* (University of Toronto Press, 2013) is largely focused on drama and performance, as its title suggests, with each chapter discussing a particular play in a specific theatre. Noting that 'these venues were fashioned almost entirely from wood products', he describes the pre-fabricated construction of the theatres as an 'eco-material tie', and notes that 'In an era of perceived and real shortage, theatres represent a massive investment in wood' (pp. 4, 5). Central to his argument throughout the book is that 'Unlike other structures in "wooden" London, theatres called frequent (but not invariable) attention to themselves as woodlands in performance' (p. 20), that is, that the theatre buildings remained intelligible to playwrights, actors and audiences, as re-erected and revived forest structures. Chapter 1 discusses the tree prop in Greene's *Friar Bacon and Friar Bungay*, linking the vanishing of the tree to environmental concerns and anti-theatricalism; Nardizzi also suggests a link to the legend that, had the Spanish Armada succeeded, the Spanish had intended to destroy the Forest of Dean. Chapter 2, on *Merry Wives*, explores the play in relation to Manwood, forest law, and saw-pits, arguing that Falstaff becomes a tree as much as a stag. Chapter 3 takes as its starting point the centrality of the bower in *The Spanish Tragedy*, which it reads in terms of deforestation as well as the 'family tree' and the tree of polity, and suggesting that the play 'marks the disappearance of (English) woodlands as an unfortunate eco-political loss' (p. 87). In the fourth and final chapter, as in the other chapters, Nardizzi discusses forestry in Virginia, here specifically in relation to *The Tempest*. Although he notes that '*The Tempest* does not call prolonged attention to a single and noteworthy onstage tree', he argues that Caliban's logs, and the woods from which they have presumably been derived, 'are the vital matter of *The Tempest*'s eco-fantasies of colonial extraction and theatrical production' (p. 112), and that 'wood is the material substrate of the spectacles that Prospero mounts on the island' (p. 127).

Four further recent monographs write more generally about the natural world in relation to early modern literature, especially drama. Julie Sanders' *The Cultural Geography of Early Modern Drama: 1620–1650* (Cambridge University Press, 2011) engages with theories of the cultural production of space, utilizing geographical discourses as well as literary critical approaches, and 'seek[ing] constantly to connect so-called province with metropolis, domestic with public space, and homeland with colony, as well as imaginative geography with material site' (p. 12). Sanders begins Chapter 2, 'Into the Woods: Spatial and Social Geographies in the Forest' by pointing out that 'the early modern stage proves perfectly able to hold simultaneously literary and material understandings of a site' (p. 65). She gives a succinct account of the legal and political status of forests under Charles I, going on to explore the Robin Hood story in relation to Jonson's *The Sad Shepherd*, Massinger's *The Guardian*, Brome's *A Jovial Crew* and Shirley's *The Sisters*, as well as the masques *Britannia Triumphans* and Milton's *Comus*; the latter is discussed particularly in relation to unrest in the Forest of Dean in the 1630s. The chapter's final section focuses on Jonson's *Sad Shepherd* in relation to forest law, hunting, and ideas of hospitality, the practical details of forest life in the Midlands, and engaging extensively with the edition, by Anne Barton and Eugene Giddens, in the *CWBJ*, especially as regards questions of staging. Sanders describes all these plays as 'limn[ing] for us the cultural geography of individual seventeenth-century woodland pastoral communities ... in ways that afford us considerable insight into topical concerns centring on land use, royal prerogative, social mobility, resources, and food security', and she suggests that forests emerge from them, 'as well as within wider Caroline culture', as 'dynamic political arenas' (p. 99); 'what remains key, however, to the ways in which these spaces operate on the stage is the subtle way in which early modern drama invites its audience to retain simultaneously a sense of the literary and the material semiotics of woodland space' (p. 100).

Todd Borlik's *Ecocriticism and Early Modern English Literature: Green Pastures* (Routledge, 2011) notes at its outset that 'people in the sixteenth century thought about a number of issues that continue to vex and galvanize the environmental movement four hundred years later' (p. 2), going on to cite rapid population increase, deforestation, and pollution (including air pollution), as well as the growth of consumerism, 'which engendered unease about materialism as both a spiritual hazard and a contributing factor to the scarcity of the land's biomass resources', suggesting that 'Elizabethan attitudes toward the natural world were . . . far more multi-faceted, and even at times conservation-oriented, than has generally been recognized' (p. 3). It is in this context that he situates early modern pastoral, arguing that its nostalgia 'reflects more than a puerile longing for a mythical Golden Age the post's lost childhood, or a state of epistemological innocence; it is often stirred by real environmental trauma' (p. 4). His second chapter focuses on Sidney's *Old Arcadia* (in which he particularly discusses the tree catalogue, pp. 77ff., and 'the first tree-hugging in English literature', p. 80) and Drayton's *Poly-Olbion*, which he describes as 'the lament of a society without an Environmental Protection Agency or properly staffed Forest Service' (p. 104). Chapter 3 is concerned with *Midsummer Night's Dream* and *Merry Wives*, especially in the context of Rogation processions and rituals, and Chapter 4 considers pastoral as an ethical form, particularly in relation to the Mammon episode in Book II of Spenser's *Faerie Queene*, Milton's *Comus*, and coal-mining. Part of the fifth and final chapter is on 'Hunting and Enclosure in the Forest of Arden'; Borlik notes unease about hunting, poaching and enclosure in *Titus Andronicus*, *The Rape of Lucrece*, *Love's Labour's Lost*, *Merry Wives* and especially *As You Like It* (pp. 179ff.). In this chapter, as elsewhere, he is not concerned with issues of staging or performance. His conclusion suggests that ecocriticism can be 'a version of the pastoral'.

Charlotte Scott's *Shakespeare's Nature: From Cultivation to Culture* (Oxford University Press, 2014) is focused on husbandry and the cultivated landscape. Her introduction suggests that 'husbandry was fundamental to Elizabethan life: a practical method of production, a social record of community values and welfare, and a moral discourse of righteousness' (p. 27). In Chapter 4, 'Darkness Visible: *Macbeth* and the Poetics of the Unnatural', Scott discusses 'the emerging distinction between nature and culture' (p. 121), and suggests that, in *Macbeth*, 'the natural world manifests as a border country through which the human must travel in order to assert his or her self-possession' (pp. 121–2). Scott's short conclusion canvasses sources including Standish's *The Commons Complaint* (1611).

Tom MacFaul's *Shakespeare and the Natural World* (Cambridge University Press, 2015) begins by noting that, in Shakespeare's time, 'the sense of order in the natural world was becoming increasingly provisional', but that 'recognizing the compromised and compromising quality of the natural world enables Shakespeare's characters to be happy in this world, and possibly points towards the more permanent happiness of the afterlife' (p. 1); a 'central subject' of the book is '[the] sense of excess, of the irreducible untidiness and slipperiness of the natural world' (p. 2). Macfaul's interests are more philosophical and theological than many other critics writing on the natural world; he is interested in nature as a category and its relationship to the human rather than the environment, as the latter is explored by ecocritics in particular, although he does situate his work in relation to ecocritical approaches (p. 10). Chapter 1, 'Country Matters', explores the ways in which early modern literature, especially drama, imagined and represented the rural, especially in relation to the urban, interpreting these categories broadly and allusively and focusing in particular on movements between them; it discusses *Paradise Lost*, as well as many of Shakespeare's plays, including *As You Like It*, *The Two Gentlemen of Verona*, *Hamlet*, *Cymbeline* and *King Lear*; Macfaul concludes that 'place is fundamentally human ... while the rural world is a place of translations, it is never simply so, because people bring the weight of their own histories and identities to it' (p. 89).

Ecocriticism

One of the first explicitly ecocritical studies of Shakespeare was Gabriel Egan's *Green Shakespeare: From Ecopolitics to Ecocriticism* (Routledge, 2006). It is avowedly political, writing in the context of climate change and the crisis in Green politics, and in particular taking issue with the apolitical slant of much earlier ecocritical writing, especially about Romantic literature, and 'the blind alley of treating of ecocriticism as the study of nature writing' (p. 45). The introductory chapter concludes that

> Shakespeare's plays show an abiding interest in what we now identify as positive- and negative-feedback loops, cellular structures, the uses and abuses of analogies between natural and social order, and in the available models for community. Characters in Shakespeare display an interest in aspects of this natural world that are relevant for us, and if we take that interest seriously we find that there is nothing childlike or naïve about their concerns (p. 50).

Egan's second chapter explores models of social structure, community and order in relation to *Coriolanus*, *Henry V* and *Macbeth*; Chapter 3, on *As You Like It*, *Antony and Cleopatra*, *Pericles*, *Cymbeline* and *The Winter's Tale*, suggests that 'We tend to think of the green-world plays such as *As You Like It* in terms of plant and landscape imagery but in fact our relations with animals are its central subject' (p. 102), a subject which Egan explores here particularly in relation to food, as well as family trees and incest in the late plays. The final chapter, on *The Tempest* and *King Lear*, argues that 'Prospero's main activity since his arrival on the island has been its deforestation' (p. 155), which Egan explicitly links to colonization: 'Shakespeare's play proleptically links colonization, deforestation, and extreme weather in ways that can now be seen as prescient' (p. 171).

At the beginning of *Back to Nature: The Green and the Real in the Late Renaissance* (University of Pennsylvania Press, 2006), Robert N. Watson announces his project as 'the offspring of two seemingly incompatible parents: one a desire to bring ecological advocacy into the realm of Renaissance literature (where it has usually been deemed irrelevant at best), the other a desire to articulate the intricate philosophical ironies of Shakespeare's *As You Like It*, Marvell's "Mower" poems, and seventeenth-century Dutch painting' (p. 4), positing that 'the familiar efforts to recover simple experience out in the fields or the wilderness, to re-immerse oneself in the natural order, were partly fueled by a craving for unmediated knowledge in any form' (p. 4). He sets it squarely, and at times sceptically, within the ecocritical movement. In exploring 'artistic responses to the nostalgia for unmediated contact with the world of nature' (p. 5), Watson links such early modern impulses to a larger epistemological crisis, played out politically and theologically as well as in literature, philosophy and art. Chapter 3 ('As you liken it: simile in the forest') is the most Shakespeare-centric, although there are references to many other plays and poems throughout; here, the focus is on the similes, but there is also considerable discussion of the forest, as Watson investigates 'the chronic nostalgia for nature as a sentimental manifestation of Pyrrhonist anxieties, the suspicion that we can know things only as we liken them, never in or as themselves' (p. 77). There are extended discussions of Jaques and the deer, Orlando's poems, the myth of Actaeon and hunting more generally. Other chapters discuss *The Merchant of Venice*, Marvell's garden and mower poems, Metaphysical and Cavalier poetry, Dutch painting and the works of Thomas Traherne.

That ecocritical approaches to Shakespeare in particular are now entirely mainstream is attested by recent volumes in two major critical series, *Shakespeare and Ecocritical Theory* (Bloomsbury Arden Shakespeare, 2015) by Gabriel Egan (Arden Shakespeare and Theory) and *Shakespeare and Ecology* (2015) by Randall Martin (Oxford Shakespeare Topics). Egan's introduction, 'Done and Undone', considers Shakespeare's own use of 'anticipated retrospection' (p. 6), suggesting that 'in his use of this *done/*

undone phrasing, Shakespeare shows his sense of what we now call entropy'
(p. 9), and his approach is avowedly presentist and polemical. His four
subsequent chapters consider 'The rise of ecocriticism' (which includes
a survey of major monographs and collections published since 2006),
'Shakespeare and the meaning of "life" in the twenty-first century'
(which focuses in particular on the late romances and questions of genetic
inheritance), 'Animals in Shakespearian ecocriticism', and 'Crowds and
social networks in Shakespeare'.

Randall Martin's *Shakespeare and Ecology* (Oxford University Press,
2015) begins with an overview of 'Ecological modernity in Shakespeare',
suggesting that 'Informed by new information about the natural world on
global as well as local and regional levels, Shakespeare's work contributed
to the formation of this new ecological world view', whereby 'early modern
men and women came to recognize that England's natural bounty of
woodland, rivers, and arable soil, hitherto assumed to be unlimited,
could no longer be taken for granted' (p. 5). His overview continues with
accounts of climate change and extreme weather, demographic pressures,
over-consumption and environmental exploitation, conservation, biodiversity and evolution, as they can be discerned in a variety of Shakespeare's
plays, set in their historical contexts. Subsequent chapters explore
'Localism, deforestation, and environmental activism in *The Merry Wives
of Windsor*' (which also discusses *The Tempest* and other plays, more
briefly); 'Land-uses and convertible husbandry in *As You Like It*',
'Gunpowder, militarization, and threshold ecologies in *Henry IV Part II*
and *Macbeth*' and 'Biospheric ecologies in *Cymbeline*'. The final chapter is
'"I wish you joy of the worm": evolutionary ecology in *Hamlet* and *Antony
and Cleopatra*', which does indeed focus on worms in an exploration of
transience and change, and the interconnectedness of food and species
chains. A brief epilogue considers 'Shakespeare and ecology in performance', specifically Rupert Goold's production of *The Tempest* for the
Royal Shakespeare Company (2006), with Patrick Stewart, set in an Arctic
wasteland.

Simon Estok's *Ecocriticism and Shakespeare: Reading Ecophobia*
(Palgrave Macmillan, 2011) is interested in the ecocritical project per se
and in the need for 'confluent theorizing . . . permeable borders' in ecocriticism (p. 2); he is interested in 'ecophobia [as] . . . an irrational or
groundless fear or hatred of the natural world' (p. 4), by analogy with
racism, homophobia and other forms of prejudice; he sees it as playing out
in all attempts to control or manipulate the natural environment. Estok
also notes that 'doing ecocritical Shakespeare is a difficult business . . .

a balancing act between valid Shakespearean scholarship on the one hand and real ecological advocacy on the other' (p. 8); he particularly sets his project and approach in opposition to those of Gabriel Egan and Robert Watson. Estok is avowedly activist in his approach.

As Egan's *Green Shakespeare* attested, much ecocritical writing informs and is informed by presentist criticism. *Shakespeare and the Urgency of Now: Criticism and Theory in the 21st Century* (Palgrave Macmillan, 2013), ed. Cary DiPietro and Hugh Grady, includes essays by Cary DiPietro ('Performing place in *The Tempest*'), suggesting that 'the performance of the ecology of the island might ... be used in the context of a global environmentalism to motivate an ethic of responsibility' (p. 86), Charles Whitney ('Green economics and the English Renaissance: from capital to the commons'), which explores *As You Like It* in relation to new economic theory and globalization and Lynne Bruckner ('"Consuming Means, Soon Preys upon Itself": Political Expedience and Environmental Degradation in *Richard II*'), a play which she describes as 'a thoughtful meditation on land use and rule ... underscore[ing] how political leadership encourages and perhaps requires the misuse and exploitation of the natural world' (p. 126).

In *Environmental Degradation in Jacobean Drama* (Cambridge University Press, 2013), Bruce Boehrer announces his objective as being to understand the phenomenon of the Shakespearean stage 'from the standpoint of ecological change, to consider how that change imprints itself upon the theater's history and practices, and to offer some account of the theater's response to ecological pressures' (p. 4). He considers population growth, pollution, the depletion of resources, disease and the ways in which these affected society and culture, with his introduction offering a succinct summary of the environmental state of England, and specifically London, in the period. Boehrer suggests that 'the works of Middleton and Jonson display a morbid fascination with the dysfunctional aspects of early modern England's relationship to the natural world ... inventory[ing] a range of social abuses which leave their mark upon the land, water, and air of the city itself', whereas 'Shakespeare and Fletcher revive the conventions of pastoral and festive drama for purposes that are largely escapist in character' and Dekker and Heywood 'celebrat[e] a notion of Englishness grounded in robust, proletarian urban experience ... a panegyric to the working people of London' (p. 26). He devotes a chapter to each of these six playwrights. 'Shakespeare's Dirt' considers *As You Like It* at length, as well as *The Tempest, Coriolanus* and others, in relation to enclosure and other issues. 'Dekker's walks and orchards' concludes that 'the spirit of

Stow looms large in Dekker's work ... manifest[ed] as a longing for endangered green space, as a yearning for a London that has already ceased to exist' (pp. 140–1); in 'Heywood and the spectacle of the hunt', focusing on the *Age* plays and *A Woman Killed with Kindness*, Boehrer explores changing attitudes to hunting. He suggests, in his conclusion, that 'although the writers of the Jacobean stage can in no way be characterized as environmentalists *avant la lettre*, they do develop certain recurring narrative devices to make sense of the ecological changes besetting them and their culture' (p. 168).

The Shakespearean International Yearbook 2015, ed. Tom Bishop, Alexa Huang and Tiffany Jo Werth, is a special issue on 'Shakespeare and the Human'. It includes an essay by Todd A. Borlik ('Plants: Shakespeare's Mulberry: Eco-materialism and "Living On"'), which considers silk, arboriculture and the relationship between tree-planting and posterity, as well as the brief, playful collaboration 'Birds: Shakespeare's Tweets: A Choir', by Tom Bishop, Jean E. Howard, Gordon McMullan and Vin Nardizzi.

Almost half of the essays in *Ecological Approaches to Early Modern English Texts: A Field Guide to Reading and Teaching* (Ashgate, 2015), ed. Jennifer Munroe, Edward J. Geisweidt and Lynne Bruckner, focus on Shakespeare; the volume seeks, in part, to be 'a snapshot of the field' (p. 9). There is a usefully brief account of ways of reading forest and timber history by Ken Hiltner ('Reading the Present in Our Environmental Past'). Jennifer Munroe's essay, 'Is it Really Ecocritical if it Isn't Feminist? The Dangers of "Speaking For" in Ecological Studies and Shakespeare's *Titus Andronicus*', takes an ecofeminist approach to the play, which she describes as 'trumpet[ing] the dangers of reducing the nonhuman to human conception ... and the inadequacy of words to convey the complexity of human and nonhuman interconnectedness' (p. 40). She discusses Lavinia as deer, and the forest setting. Lynne Bruckner, with Dan Brayton, also edits *Ecocritical Shakespeare* (Ashgate, 2011). This ranges widely in the ecocritical sphere (including animal studies), and particularly engages with presentism. There are essays by Robert Watson ('The Ecology of Self in *Midsummer Night's Dream*') and Vin Nardizzi ('Felling Falstaff in Windsor Park').

One of the first contributions to the now-flourishing field of ecofeminist studies of early modern literature was Jeanne Addison Roberts, *The Shakespearean Wild: Geography, Genus, and Gender* (University of Nebraska Press, 1991). It explores women, 'barbarians' and animals in terms of the opposition between 'culture' and 'the wild', and Roberts suggests that 'the female Wild [is] often associated with the malign and benign forces of the green world' (p. 5). Her discussion ranges widely through Shakespeare's plays, with Chapter 1, 'The Wild Landscape', particularly focused on forest settings. *Ecofeminist Approaches to Early Modernity* (Palgrave Macmillan, 2011), edited by Jennifer Munroe and Rebecca Laroche, is mostly concerned with poetry (especially Milton), prose (Wroth) and non-fictional texts such as recipes (there are no essays exclusively on drama); the editors suggest in their introduction that the way which much ecocritical writing on early modern texts thus far have tended to privilege Shakespeare has limited the development of a specifically feminist ecocriticism (p. 5). In their essay on 'The Secrets of Grafting in Wroth's *Urania*', Vin Nardizzi and Miriam Jacobson discuss carving names into trees in Sidney's *Arcadia* and *As You Like It*, as well as in the *Urania*.

There is a little discussion of Shakespeare and other early modern material in the essay by Terry Gifford, 'Pastoral, Anti-pastoral, and Post-pastoral' in *The Cambridge Companion to Literature and the Environment* (Cambridge University Press, 2013), ed. Louise Westling. *The Cambridge Introduction to Literature and the Environment* (Cambridge University Press, 2011), ed. Timothy Clark, does not include any substantial discussion of early modern material, but is a comprehensive introduction to ecocriticism more generally. *The Oxford Handbook of Ecocriticism* (Oxford University Press, 2014), ed. Greg Garrard, includes Robert N. Watson's essay 'Shadows of the Renaissance', which ranges widely in early modern literature and visual art, and includes some detailed readings of passages from Shakespeare's plays; Gillian Rudd's essay 'Being Green in Late Medieval English Literature' discusses *Sir Gawain and the Green Knight*, as well as several of the *Canterbury Tales*.

Forest history

From the 1970s onwards, the leading historian and ecologist of British woods and the countryside more generally was Oliver Rackham, who died in 2015. He was a prolific writer and his works have often gone through many revisions and editions. Two in particular are useful in this context: *Woodlands* (Collins, 2006) has already been reissued many times, most recently in 2015, and its foreword sets out its case in terms which, in their theatrical conceit, are nicely apt here:

> This is not a book about the Environment. It does not pretend that trees are merely part of the theatre of landscape in which human history is played out,

or the passive recipients of whatever destiny humanity foists on them. This is a book about Ecology. It deals with trees as actors in the play ... (p. 9)

It is almost impossible to point to especially 'relevant' sections in such a rich and comprehensive work, but Chapter 3 offers an 'Outline of Woodland History', Chapter 4 is about 'Wildwood' and Chapter 5 'Wildwood into Woodland'; all are essential reading in the long history of forests. Chapter 6, 'Of Wood-pasture and Savanna', is heavily early modern in its focus, as is Chapter 11, 'Uses of Wood and Timber: Reconstructing the Woods from Buildings, Hurdles and Ships', with many detailed examples from surviving buildings. There are many maps, tables and photographs. Rackham's *Trees and Woodland in the British Landscape: The Complete History of Britain's Trees, Woods and Hedgerows* was first published by Dent in 1976, with revised editions in 1990 and 2001. Much shorter than *Woodlands*, but overlapping with it somewhat in terms of its scope and approach, it includes a chapter specifically on parks (Chapter 8: 'Parks: Private Wood-pasture') and on royal forests (Chapter 9: 'Wooded Forests: The King's Wood-pasture'), as well as earlier chapters on the history of forest management.

John Evelyn's *Elysium Britannicum, or The Royal Gardens*, has been edited by John E. Ingram (University of Pennsylvania Press, 2001), and the proceedings of a 1993 Dumbarton Oaks colloquium on the *Elysium* and its influence appeared in 1998: *John Evelyn's Elysium Britannicum and European Gardening*, edited by Therese O'Malley and Joachim Wolschke-Bulmahn (Dumbarton Oaks Research Library and Collection, 1998). There is also a full-length biography of John Evelyn by Gillian Darley, *John Evelyn: Living for Ingenuity* (Yale University Press, 2006); another full, accessible, and lavishly illustrated introduction to the life and work of John Evelyn is *A Passion for Trees: The Legacy of John Evelyn* (Eden Project, 2006), by Maggie Campbell-Culver. She also edits John Evelyn, *Directions for the Gardiner and Other Horticultural Advice* (Oxford University Press, 2009).

John F. Richards' *The Unending Frontier: An Environmental History of the Early Modern World* (University of California Press, 2003) aims 'to identify, describe, and reflect on the processes by which human beings intervened in the natural environment during the early modern period' (p. 1). Two introductory chapters on 'The global context' establish broad historical and environmental outlines; thereafter, case-studies are grouped geographically. Chapter 6 is 'Landscape Change and Energy Transformation in the British Isles'; it narrates with great clarity the environmental condition of Britain in the period: the pressures of population growth, the shift from wood to coal as the main fuel source (which it concludes was 'remarkable', p. 241), bad harvests and years of famine in the late sixteenth century and, eventually, changing agricultural practices; it also discusses the draining of the fens and increasing deforestation (pp. 221ff.), and concludes that 'the lands of the British Isles were among the most intensively managed of any society during the early modern period' (p. 240). Other chapters offer case-studies of land-use and settlement in Taiwan, China, Japan, Russia and South Africa; of sugar plantations, ranching and mining in the Caribbean, Mexico and Brazil; and hunting, fishing and whaling in Siberia and North America.

Much of the micro history of forests has historically, and continues to be, written by amateur local historians. Historical and archaeological society publications tend to be more scholarly; see, for example, the exemplary volumes of the New Forest Record Series published by the New Forest Ninth Centenary Trust. Volume I, *Use and Abuse of a Forest Resource: New Forest Documents 1632–1700* (New Forest Ninth Centenary Trust, 2006) ed. R. P. Reeves, includes more than two hundred pages of letters, accounts and other documents, in modernized form, indexed by name, place, and subject and including a glossary as well as extensive introductory material; Volume III, *Preservation and Decay: New Forest Documents 1565–1624* (New Forest Ninth Centenary Trust, 2007), also edited by R. P. Reeves, is similar, beginning with the 'Survey of Woods' of 1565. See also Andrew Watkins, *Small Towns in the Forest of Arden in the Fifteenth Century* (Dugdale Society, 1998), Beryl Schumer, ed., *Oxfordshire Forests 1246–1609* (Oxfordshire Record Society, 2004), and *Forests and Chases of England and Wales, c.1500 to c.1850: Towards a Survey and Analysis* (St John's College Research Centre, 2005) and *Forests and Chases of Medieval England and Wales, c.1000 to c.1500* (St John's College Research Centre, 2010), both edited by John Langton and Graham Jones. Other recent publications (or republications) of this kind include many on the Forest of Dean: *Civil War in Dean: The History and Archaeology of the English Civil Wars in the Forest of Dean and West Gloucestershire* (Dean Archaeological Group, 2001), *Later Medieval Dean: The Forest of Dean and West Gloucestershire, 1272–1485AD* (Dean Archaeological Group, 2002), and *Tudor Dean: The Forest of Dean and West Gloucestershire, 1485–1642AD* (Dean Archaeological Group, 2002), all edited by Alf Webb; Nicholas Herbert, ed., *The Forest of Dean Eyre of 1634* (Bristol and Gloucestershire Archaeological Society, 2012); Cyril Hart's *The Forest of Dean: New History 1550–1818* (Sutton, 1995) and *The Free Miners of the*

Royal Forest of Dean and Hundred of St. Briavels (Lightmoor Press, 2002) and, most recently, Christine Martyn, *The Forest of Dean Revisited: A Modern History* (Holborn House, 2015).

Nature writing

Roger Deakin's *Wildwood: A Journey Through Trees*, published posthumously in 2007 (Hamish Hamilton), has become a classic of the 'new nature writing'. Deakin's introduction describes his book's genesis in its predecessor, *Waterlog*, an account of wild swimming; wood, he states, borrowing from the poet Edward Thomas, is 'the fifth element' (p. ix). He goes on to cite Shakespeare's greenworlds, Hardy's Woodlanders, and to draw on his own long experience of planting and managing a wood in Suffolk; '*Wildwood*', he concludes, 'is a quest for the residual magic of trees and wood that still touches most of us not far beneath the surface of our daily lives' (pp. xii–xiii). Deakin writes of wood, and trees, as landscape, environment and building material, as he enumerates the posts and beams of his house and calculates that, in the sixteenth century, 'some 300 trees were felled to build this house' (p. 7). He travels in both time and space, part memoir, part chorography; he visits bluebell woods, the New Forest, the Forest of Dean, the French and Spanish Pyrenees, Greek islands and the Carpathians, outback Australia; he traces the origin of the cultivated apple to Kazakhstan and visits the walnut forests of Kyrgyzstan.

Sara Maitland's *Gossip from the Forest: The Tangled Roots of Our Forests and Fairytales* (Granta, 2012) is structured, month by month, as paired sections of forests and tales, the forest parts a mixture of natural and cultural history, memoir and manifesto, and an account of its own writing, the tales retellings chiming with the experiences and concerns of their accompanying forests. Oliver Rackham is one of its presiding geniuses, and Maitland's son Adam supplies one of the book's controlling metaphors, the mycorrhiza, the symbiotic relation between tree and fungi: 'The fairy stories teach us how to see the forests, and how to love them too . . . [they are] partners necessary to one another and at risk if *either* fails or cannot find and connect with the other' (p. 21). The book is a meditation on myth-making and on ecologies of many kinds; it includes a particularly fascinating account of the 'Free Miners' still at work in the Forest of Dean. Its final tale is Sleeping Beauty, dreaming a forest into being for a hundred years.

Richard Mabey's *The Ash and the Beech: The Drama of Woodland Change* (Vintage, 2013) revises and builds on his earlier *Beechcombings* (Chatto and Windus, 2007). In his foreword, Mabey describes his book as 'a brief history of the narratives we've constructed about trees over the past thousand years, to make them accessible, useful, comprehensible, and obedient to us' (p. xiii). Taking the beech and the ash as his focus, although not exclusively, he writes in the context of the threat of ash die-back caused by the *Chalara* fungus, and in the medium-term aftermath of the Great Storm of October 1987, offering 'a series of discursive essays around some key episodes in the history of trees in Europe' (p. xv). Chapter 3 in particular, 'Wooden Walls', explores forestry in early modern England, juxtaposed (as in the rest of the book) with more contemporary and personal meditation. Richard Fortey's *The Wood for the Trees: A Long View of Nature from a Small Wood* (William Collins, 2016) is similarly grounded in an ancient beech (and bluebell) wood, in this case, Grim's Dyke Wood in the Chilterns. Fortey, an eminent geologist and science writer, explores the interconnectedness of all the various flora and fauna of his woodland (with a particular interest in fungi), in a study of biodiversity that is both lyrical and rigorous, and which sets that biodiversity in its human, historical and cultural contexts.

The Botanical series from Reaktion Books so far includes *Apple* (Marcia Reiss, 2015), *Bamboo, Cannabis, Geranium, Grasses, Lily, Oak, Pine* (Laura Mason, 2013), *Snowdrop, Weeds, Willow* (Alison Syme, 2014) and *Yew* (Fred Hageneder, 2013). Lavishly and thoughtfully illustrated, the series, aimed at a general (and connoisseur) readership 'integrat[es] horticultural and botanical writing with a broader account of the cultural and social impact of trees, plants and flowers'. Peter Young's *Oak* (2013) includes discussion of building in oak and of ship-building, as well as a chapter on 'Symbols and Superstitions'. Another beautifully illustrated volume is Frances Carey's *The Tree: Meaning and Myth* (British Museum, 2012); it is international in its range and devotes its second half to an 'arboretum', depicting trees in art (and in objects) species by species.

Hunting

Edward C. Berry's *Shakespeare and the Hunt: A Cultural and Social Study* (Cambridge University Press, 2001) organizes its six substantive chapters around particular texts: 'Huntresses in *Venus and Adonis* and *Love's Labor's Lost*' (also particularly interested in the ritual of 'blooding', and masculinity); '"Solemn" Hunting in *Titus Andronicus* and *Julius Caesar*' (further ideas about ritual, and about savagery); 'The "Manning" of Katherine: Falconry in *The Taming of the Shrew'* (here Berry makes fascinating use of the Berkeley papers, discussed above, pp. 133–4); 'The "Rascal" Falstaff in Windsor' (making illuminating connections with the *Henry IV* plays, and discussing poaching), 'Pastoral Hunting in *As You Like It*' (the boundaries between the animal and the human, with a little discussion of Robin Hood, and the historical Forest of Arden) and 'Political Hunting: Prospero and James I', bringing together anxieties about tyranny and violence through an evolving mythology of the hunt. An introductory chapter surveys the theory and practice of hunting, giving a useful account of hunting manuals and terminology and including many illustrations, and the book ends with a brief overview, which surveys other texts (notably *A Midsummer Night's Dream*) and concludes that Shakespeare 'forc[es] us to consider, even in the flash of a metaphor, what it is to be a hunter and what to be a hunter's prey' (p. 225). Daniel C. Beaver's *Hunting and the Politics of Violence before the English Civil War* (Cambridge University Press, 2008) is a comprehensive account of 'the political economy of venison' (p. ix) in early modern England, with a particular focus on 'the series of attacks on parks, chases, and forests in southern England during the late spring and summer of 1642' (p. 1). Chapter 1, 'Blood, Sacrifice, and Order: Meanings of the Forest and Hunt in Culture, Politics, and Society' sets out the rituals and ceremonies of the hunt, and interprets them in terms of the social and cultural codes of gentility and honour, as well as forest law. The four chapters following each take a particular forest as their focus, as well as specific thematic concerns: 'Honor, Property, and the Symbolism of the Hunt in Stowe, 1590–1642'; 'Ancient Liberties and the Politics of the Commonweal in Waltham Forest, 1608–1642'; 'Royal Honor, Great Parks, and the Commonweal in Windsor Forest, 1603–1642' and 'Venison and the Politics of Honor in Corse Lawn Chase, 1620–1642'. Beaver briefly discusses *The Merry Wives of Windsor*, and draws on a wide range of contemporary sources. Catherine Bates' *Masculinity and the Hunt: Wyatt to Spenser* (Oxford University Press, 2013) is largely focused on poetry and prose fiction; Chapter 3 discusses George Gascoigne's translation of *The Noble Arte of Venerie* and Chapter 4 George Turberville's *Booke of Falconrie* (and especially the poems which form part of both volumes). Other chapters are devoted to Sidney, Spenser, Greville and Wyatt. Bates' introduction explores the long history of the association between hunting and heroic masculinity, with particular reference to the *Odyssey*, the *Aeneid* and *Sir Gawain and the Green Knight*.

Robin Hood and outlaws

Thomas Hahn, ed., *Robin Hood in Popular Culture: Violence, Transgression, and Justice* (D. S. Brewer, 2000) is – unsurprisingly – more concerned with the popular culture angle, although it does include essays on the 'Gest' (by Thomas H. Ohlgren) and on 'Lords of the Wildwood: The Wild Man, the Green Man, and Robin Hood (by Lorraine Kochanske Stock). Stephen Knight, ed., *Robin Hood: An Anthology of Scholarship and Criticism* (D. S. Brewer, 1999) is more literary-historical in its focus and organization; there are essays on 'The Earl of Huntingdon: The Renaissance Plays' (by M. A. Nelson) and a number on the ballads; Peter Stallybrass' essay '"Drunk with the Cup of Liberty": Robin Hood, the Carnivalesque, and the Rhetoric of Violence in Early Modern England' is also reprinted here. *Images of Robin Hood: Medieval to Modern*, ed. Lois Potter and Joshua Calhoun (University of Delaware Press, 2008), is more literary still in its scope; it includes essays on ballads, on '"Merry" and "Greenwood": A History of Some Meanings', by Helen Phillips, and on 'Picturing Robin Hood in Early Print and Performance, 1500–1590', by John Marshall, and includes many illustrations of Robin Hood in both mediaeval and 'post-mediaeval' versions. Stephen Knight is also the editor of *Robin Hood in Greenwood Stood: Alterity and Context in the English Outlaw Tradition* (Brepols, 2011). Many of its essays discuss forests. Stephen Knight's own most recent work, *Reading Robin Hood: Content, Form and Reception in the Outlaw Myth* (Manchester University Press, 2015) is in part a history of Robin Hood scholarship itself; it builds on and consolidates recent scholarship, exploring the ballad tradition and other sources but also 'the Romantic reception and re-formation of Robin Hood' (p. 8), 'Rabbie Hood: The Development of the English Outlaw Myth in Scotland', and concluding with two chapters which consider the tradition's multiplicity, particularly in relation to the character of Maid Marian. It argues for 'the concept of rhizomatic structure as the way of understanding this tradition ... With Robin Hood you have the forest, not the mere trees' (p. 9). The book includes two appendices listing, first, 'Robin Hood Broadside Ballads in Collections' and 'Robin Hood Broadside Ballads by Date'. Knight's *Robin Hood: A Mythic Biography* (Cornell University Press, 2003) brings together many sources and traditions in a readable survey, more accessible to the general reader than some of his edited collections, exploring the 'biography', and tradition, of Robin Hood from the middle ages to the present. Chapter 2, 'Robert, Earl of Huntingdon', includes some discussion of early modern Robin Hood plays. Lisa Hopkins discusses Robin Hood plays in the context of the royal succession in Chapter 3 of her *Drama and the Succession to the Crown, 1561–1633* (Ashgate, 2011); she considers (among others) Peele's *Edward I*, Munday's *The Downfall* and *The Death of Robert Earl of Huntington* and, briefly, *The Sad Shepherd*. In an earlier chapter on 'Romans and Fairies' she also discusses, briefly, *The Scottish History of James IV*. Tom Lockwood's *Ben Jonson in the Romantic Age* (Oxford University Press, 2005) structures its discussion around Francis Godolphin Waldron's edition and continuation of Jonson's *The Sad Shepherd* (1783), specifically considering the play in Chapter 1 and Chapter 5. There is a more polemical and theorized discussion of Jonson's play in Tom Hayes' *The Birth of Popular Culture: Ben Jonson, Maid Marian and Robin Hood* (Duquesne University Press, 1992). In *Myth and National Identity in Nineteenth-century Britain: The Legends of King Arthur and Robin Hood* (Oxford University Press, 2000), Stephanie L. Barczewski surveys a wide range of retellings of the Robin Hood story, dramatic and non-dramatic, including Thomas Love Peacock's *Maid Marian* (1822) (pp. 191–3) and Tennyson's *The Foresters* (1892) (pp. 196, 209); she also discusses Sherwood Forest and the growth of tourism (pp. 208ff.). More popular accounts of the Robin Hood 'legend' appear regularly; one of the more recent, which includes summaries of many of the sources, a useful chronology, and which makes some use of recent scholarship, is Nigel Cawthorne, *A Brief History of Robin Hood: The True Story Behind the Legend* (2010). Robin Hood also appears in the *Oxford Dictionary of National Biography*.

A revised edition of Maurice Keen, *The Outlaws of Medieval Legend* (first published 1961, with revised editions in 1977 and 1987), was published in 2000 (Routledge). *British Outlaws of Literature and History: Essays on Medieval and Early Modern Figures from Robin Hood to Twm Shon Catty* (McFarland and Co., 2011), edited by Alexander L. Kaufman, includes essays on 'Portraits of Outlaws, Felons, and Rebels in Late Medieval England' (Barbara A. Hanawalt), 'Fouke le Fitz Waryn and King John: Rebellion and Reconciliation' (Catherine A. Rock), 'Fouke le Fitz Waryn: Outlaw or Chivalric Hero?' (Kathryn Bedford), 'Robin Hood: Outlaw or Exile?' (Antha Cotton-Spreckelmeyer) and Kaufman's own 'Histories of Contexts: Form, Argument, and Ideology in *A Gest of Robyn Hode*', as well as other essays on the ballad tradition. Gillian Spraggs' *Outlaws and Highwaymen: The Cult of the Robber in England from the Middle Ages to the Nineteenth Century* (Pimlico, 2001) includes extensive discussion of Robin Hood and the wider outlaw tradition in both history and literature. 'Outlaws in Arcadia', in particular, briefly considers *As You Like It*, Lodge's

Rosalynde and *The Two Gentlemen of Verona*, as well as other early modern literary texts; Spraggs also includes a chronology of key texts and events in the history of English outlawry. Jane Kingsley-Smith's *Shakespeare's Drama of Exile* (Palgrave Macmillan, 2003) includes discussion of outlaws (including Robin Hood), particularly in the central chapters 'Historical-pastoral Exile in *Henry IV* Parts One and Two' and '"Hereafter in a Better World than This": the End of Exile in *As You Like It* and *King Lear*'. *Bandit Territories: British Outlaw Traditions* (University of Wales Press, 2008), edited by Helen Phillips, overlaps in its coverage and contributors with a number of other recent works on Robin Hood; its texts and topics extend into the twentieth century.

Folklore

Carolyne Larrington's *The Land of the Green Man: A Journey through the Supernatural Landscapes of the British Isles* (I. B. Tauris, 2015) is focused on supernatural beings, with the landscapes in which they are to be found of secondary, although still significant interest. The second chapter, 'Lust and Love', particularly focuses on romances with forest settings, encounters with fairies, and the idea of fairyland; the third, 'Death and Loss', includes some discussion of Herne the Hunter. The final chapter, 'Continuity and Change', draws to its conclusion with 'The wild man and the green man', discussing wodewoses in mediaeval romance and in the Chester pageant for Prince Henry in 1610, and what it terms the 'invention' of the green man, in an article in *Folklore* in 1939 by Julia Raglan, as 'a representation of some ancient vegetation god, the spirit of spring regrowth and natural fertility ... for a world which was beginning to need him, a world in which people were gradually realising how industrialisation was stealthily degrading our planet' (pp. 226, 227). Larrington suggests that the green man 'has become a representative of all that the modern world under-values, excludes or lacks. He doesn't *do* anything; he has no story, no legend, except those invented for him by modern writers, but his appearance, as a hybrid of man and plant, insists that humans are inextricably part of that natural world which we in the West are so keen to subjugate' (p. 232). *Uprooted: On the Trail of the Green Man* (Faber and Faber, 2016) by Nina Lyon is similarly written for a general readership. Mostly in memoir form, it explores folklore, shamanism, and neo-paganism in a way that combines nature writing and ecological and metaphysical spec-ulation and meditation; there are good accounts of green men in parish churches, especially in Herefordshire.

'Wild Man: "The Naked Fellow": Performing Feral Reversion in *King Lear*' in Julián Jiménez Heffernan's *Shakespeare's Extremes: Wild Man, Monster, Beast* (Palgrave Macmillan, 2015) is, like the rest of the book, highly theoretical; there is a useful discussion of the wild man episode in *Cardenio* (and *Don Quixote*), set in the larger context of the wild man tradition in mediaeval and Renaissance literature, especially romance. *Merlin: A Casebook* (Routledge, 2003), edited by Peter H. Goodrich and Raymond H. Thompson, includes 'Master and Mediator of the Natural World', by Jean Markale, mostly in relation to Celtic mythology. *The Birth of Merlin* is noted in passing by several contributors, and there is a brief discussion of Merlin Silvester and the Galfridian tradition in the essay by A. O. H. Jarman, 'The Merlin Legend and the Welsh Tradition of Prophecy', as well as by several other contributors. Anne Lawrence-Mather's *The True History of Merlin the Magician* (Yale University Press, 2012) concentrates largely on mediaeval sources, which it explores in detail; it does not discuss *The Birth of Merlin*, but does consider the Merlin Silvester tradition.

Theatre and performance

Mary Ellen Lamb and Valerie Wayne introduce their collection *Staging Early Modern Romance: Prose Fiction, Dramatic Romance, and Shakespeare* (Routledge, 2009) with an essay entitled 'Into the Forest', noting that 'a forest of romance is an apt metaphor in a variety of senses ... The metaphor catches the chaotic proliferation of early modern romances, in prose as well as drama, growing together at the same time and in the same space ... What romance may have meant to early moderns extended well beyond any single kind of text, for here, to return to the forest metaphor, there were many kinds of trees' (p. 2), going on to cite Franco Moretti's evolutionary model of genre, the 'culture-tree' (p. 3); their introduction concludes by noting the way in which the forest metaphor 'collides' with that of the 'sea of stories' (p. 14). Erika Lin briefly considers trees on the early modern stage in the context of staging concealment in 'Staging Sight: Visual Paradigms and Perceptual Strategies in *Love's Labor's Lost*', the second chapter in her *Shakespeare and the Materiality of Performance* (Palgrave Macmillan, 2012).

Jean-Pierre Bordier begins his essay 'Planter le décor: arbres de théâtre' with Beckett's initial stage direction for *Waiting for Godot*: 'Route à la campagne, avec arbre' (a country road with a tree), and the observation 'Sur une scène de theatre, un arbre, cela intrigue. Sous cet arbre, près cet arbre, dans cet arbre, il se passera quelque chose' (on a stage set, a tree intrigues. Under this tree, near this tree, in this tree, something will happen) (p. 139). Considering trees in mediaeval drama, he notes their association with paradise in plays such as the *Jeu d'Adam*, but also the difficulty of staging trees, citing examples of real trees being used on stage as well as the making of artificial trees, for example an orange tree and a fig tree for a garden of Eden in Châteaudun in 1510 (pp. 140–1). Mostly concerned with religious drama, he discusses the *Moralité a cincq person-nages*, which presents the discussion between an old and a young shepherd, Counsel, Justice and (the mythological) Paris (chosen both for his name and for his association with scenes of discernment) about the necessity of cutting down an églantier (eglantine rose), which chokes a fountain and overshadows the land: it is an allegorical representation of the English presence in France. Asking 'Arbre peint sur une toile, arbre naturel, arbre artificiel?' (Tree painted on canvas, a real tree, artificial tree?), Bordier speculates that

> la solution la plus compatible avec le texte est un arbre en trois dimensions, un arbre naturel que les bergers abattent facilement, puisqu'il a été coupé et fixé sur la scène. Un églantier se déracine et se transporte plus facilement qu'un sycomore ou qu'un palmier. Si on a joué la pièce en janvier ou février, les fleurs pouvaient être en papier ou en tissu (the solution most compatible with the text is a three-dimensional tree, a real tree which the shepherds could easily destroy, since it has been cut down and fastened to the stage. An eglantine can be uprooted and transported more easily than a sycamore or a palm tree. If the play was performed in January or February, the flowers could have been made out of paper or fabric) (p. 147).

In *La Sottie a VIII personnages*, performed in Toulouse in 1507, by contrast, Bordier suggests that the trees required by the action were probably represented by painted cloths at the back of the stage (p. 149). As he began, Bordier concludes that 'Sur le théâtre, un arbre est un objet à la fois banal et surprenant' (in the theatre, a tree is something that is simultaneously banal and surprising) (p. 150), but also that it would be unwise to draw any general conclusions about trees on the mediaeval stage from so few examples. His essay is in *L'arbre au Moyen Âge* (Presses de l'Université Paris-Sorbonne, 2010), ed. Valérie Fasseur, Danièle James-Raoul, Jean-René Valette; other chapters focus on trees in romance and in spiritual and magical writing.

As well as providing a detailed overview of Tudor court revels, their function and their administration by the various offices of court, W. R. Streitberger's *Court Revels 1485–1559* (University of Toronto Press,

1994, 2016) includes, as appendices, a list of all sources (with modern editions, where possible) and a calendar of all documents, including payments and other aspects of organization as well as performances, with sources. There are useful accounts of Tudor entertainments, in both preparation and performance, in Glenn Richardson, *The Field of Cloth of Gold* (Yale University Press, 2013), drawing on Hall's *Chronicle* and other sources. Sandra Logan's *Text/Events in Early Modern England: Poetics of History* (Ashgate, 2007) includes a chapter on the Kenilworth entertainments for Queen Elizabeth, 'Inscribing Performance: Art and Artlessness at Kenilworth, 1575'. She discusses Kenilworth both historically and theoretically, and spends some time considering the 'savage man'. In *Writing and Reading Royal Entertainments: From George Gascoigne to Ben Jonson* (Oxford University Press, 2010) Gabriel Heaton explores, in detail, a range of entertainments, with a particular focus on manuscript sources (including presentation manuscripts). His first chapter discusses 'The Queen and the Hermit: *The Tale of Hemetes* (1575)', devised by George Gascoigne and performed at Woodstock; in the second, 'Armed Address: The Elizabethan Tournament' he considers, among other texts and events, 'Love and Self-love', featuring a hermit, which was devised (at least partly by Francis Bacon) for the earl of Essex at the Accession Day Tilts in 1595. A later chapter on the 1607 *Entertainment at Theobalds* notes that when King James and his brother-in-law Christian IV of Denmark were welcomed to Theobalds in 1606, an artificial oak with leaves of green taffeta at the gate showered the kings with its leaves as they entered, each leaf having 'Welcome' written on it in gold (p. 169).

In Chapter 3, '"Whatsoever We Present": Lyly's Elusive Theatre (1583–c.1590)', of *John Lyly and Early Modern Authorship* (Manchester University Press, 2014), Andy Kesson speculates thoughtfully on Lyly's staging, drawing in particular on printed prologues and epilogues as well as printed stage directions, and exploring the role of the audience; he considers some of Lyly's trees (pp. 118–20), and concludes that 'with his emphasis upon the "vehement thought" of his audience members, Lyly aimed to create onstage worlds that were allusive and playful, requiring active and imaginative participation' (p. 134). *Writing Robert Greene: Essays on England's First Notorious Professional Writer* (Ashgate, 2008), edited by Kirk Melnikoff and Edward Gieskes, includes Alan C. Dessen's discussion of 'Robert Greene and the Theatrical Vocabulary of the Early 1590s', which considers the emblematic or allegorical staging traditions on which Greene drew, and Greene's 'awareness of the potential in the pre-1585 drama for putting ideas and images in action onstage' (p. 37). Kirk Melnikoff's '"That

Will I See, Lead and Ile Follow Thee": Robert Greene and the Authority of Performance' includes some discussion of the character of Bohan, the Timon-like figure in *James IV*; Edward Gieske's 'Staging Professionalism in Greene's *James IV*' considers Bohan at greater length. The editors include a bibliography of 'Recent Studies in Robert Greene (1989–2006)' and a list of editions. The volume on Robert Greene in the Ashgate series *The University Wits*, edited by Kirk Melnikoff (2011) includes A. R. Braunmuller's 1973 essay 'The Serious Comedy of Greene's *James IV*' (*English Literary Renaissance* 3), as well as Ian McAdam, 'Masculinity and Magic in *Friar Bacon and Friar Bungay*' (*Research Opportunities in Medieval and Renaissance Drama* 37 [1998]) and Kent Cartwright, 'Robert Greene's *Friar Bacon and Friar Bungay*: The Commonwealth of the Present Moment' (from *Theatre and Humanism: English Drama in the Sixteenth Century* [1999]). Cartwright's essay pays some attention to the material conditions of performance, although not the tree. In *The Aesthetics of Spectacle in Early Modern Drama and Modern Cinema: Robert Greene's Theatre of Attractions* (Palgrave Macmillan, 2013), Jenny Sager explores Greene's spectacular aesthetic in parallel with modern cinema, stating that 'the principal objective of this book is to advocate the rejection of a purely text-based interpretation of drama and to emphasise the powerful visual dimension of the early modern stage' (p. 3), drawing on film and film theory. Her discussion of *Friar Bacon and Friar Bungay* does note the tree (pp. 91–2) but doesn't comment on its staging, mostly focusing on the brazen head.

The Merry Wives of Windsor: New Critical Essays (Routledge, 2015), ed. Evelyn Gajowski and Phyllis Rackin, includes a section entitled 'Nature'. Rebecca Ann Bach's essay, 'Falstaff Becomes the (Hu)man at the Expense of *The Merry Wives of Windsor*', discusses Falstaff's animality and the way in which his 'devotion to his body was a marker of his bestiality when he was created' (p. 173), rather than a sign of his quintessential humanity; in so doing, she argues against the influential readings of Harold Bloom and others. In '"Cabbage and Roots" and the Difference of *Merry Wives*', Rebecca Laroche notes that 'From its beginning to its end, *The Merry Wives of Windsor* names five different garden vegetables – cabbage, pumpkin, carrots, turnips, and potatoes – more than any other play in Shakespeare's oeuvre (the next highest number being two)' (p. 184), and she goes on to discuss the relationship between vegetables and the body, and between plants and genre: 'vegetables degrade any high-minded romantic or tragic theme' (p. 184). In addition, Jean E. Howard considers the play's small-town setting, with some discussion of Windsor Forest, in

'Sharp-tongued Women and Small-town Social Relations in Porter's *Two Angry Women of Abington* and Shakespeare's *The Merry Wives of Windsor*', and Wendy Wall writes on animality and appetite in 'Finding Desire in Windsor: Gender, Consumption, and Animality in *Merry Wives*'.

Index

CPSIA information can be obtained
at www.ICGtesting.com
Printed in the USA
LVHW03*0412150818
586961LV00010B/289/P

9 780521 573443